Keeping Care Pastoral

The Heart of Gospel-Shaped Pastoral Care

Dr Paul B. Coulter

PESIOD
Eager & Earnest

Keeping Care Pastoral
Copyright © 2022 by Paul Brian Coulter
Published by   PESIOD
                     Lisburn
                     Northern Ireland

Copyeditor: D.M. Davidson

Cover design: Jess Coles

First published 2022

ISBN: 9798366236218

DEDICATION

To Gar-Ling, whose dedication to her caring profession reminds me of
our Lord and inspires me to care more.

CONTENTS

ACKNOWLEDGMENTS

I am grateful to my copyeditor, D.M. Davidson, for her diligent attention to this manuscript prior to publication. Any remaining errors are entirely my own! Words cannot express my gratitude to the wonderful Jess Coles for her work designing the cover and graphic.

In anything of value that I might say on pastoral care, I am indebted to my friend and former colleague Dr Jill Harshaw. Several years co-teaching pastoral care with her in Bible College and online have undoubtedly shaped my thinking more than I realise.

Finally, I could not have produced this book without the many conversations I have had with people I have trained in pastoral care and practical theology over many years as well as pastors I continue to support in their ministry. All truth is God's truth and any book is a distillation of wisdom from multiple sources. Thank you for being my teachers.

PREFACE: WHY THIS BOOK?

One year into his first role as minister in a church, Sam was struggling with provision of pastoral care. He was the church's sole staff member and he needed someone to share the load, especially in caring for women and older people. His wife, Beth, was too busy with her work as a solicitor to do more than she already did. She helped him lead a home group meeting in their house, but now she was three months pregnant, so they might soon need to rethink that. Sam had heard rumours of grumblings about Beth's limited involvement in ministry. People's expectations that the pastor's wife would be 'part of the package' were just one of several things he wished he had clarified when he interviewed for the position!

Sam had been thinking of asking Jude, a committed member of the congregation, to take on a voluntary role as a pastoral worker. Last night, he finally composed an email asking her to consider it, saving it as a draft (he had learnt by experience not to hit send late at night!). As he sipped his first morning coffee, Sam re-opened the draft on his phone and scanned over it. He had no concerns about Jude's character or ability. She already cared for others informally, and he felt certain she would grow into this new role. The committee would support his recommendation. They always did in ministry matters. Sometimes he wished they would ask more questions! He felt isolated in decisions like this. Sam's thumb hovered over the 'Send' button. His hesitation came from conflicted emotions. He feared Jude might say 'no', leaving him at a loss. At the same time, he worried she might say 'yes' and he would be unable to give her the clarity about the role and the support to do it well that she might expect. He prayed once more for wisdom and strength. With his 'Amen', he tapped.

PREFACE: WHY THIS BOOK?

This book emerges from my experiences receiving and providing pastoral care and training people like Sam and Jude. It is written for 'Judes' and 'Sams'. It is for the many willing people like Jude who care about others and want to help them but feel inadequate to be involved in pastoral care. It is also for spiritual leaders in churches like Sam (ministers, pastors or elders). They too care about people and feel a responsibility to shepherd people in their needs, but they often feel overstretched by pastoral need on top of leadership and preaching responsibilities. In my experience, many in both groups are confused about what exactly pastoral care is. In a therapeutic culture in which many varied sources of 'help' are available, what is the role of the church? What makes 'care' truly pastoral? How does pastoral care fit with the urgent mission of the church?

I am convinced that pastoral care is vital in a Church that understands that it exists for God's mission but also recognises that it needs deep foundations if it is to be faithful to God's purposes. That is why I have written this book. I want to help 'Judes' utilise their God-given gifts for the health of the Church and to encourage 'Sams' in their God-given responsibility as shepherds of his flock. This is a book seeking a vision and skills for pastoral care that is thoroughly and consistently shaped by the gospel.

Pastoral care in the Church faces two major challenges in our age. The first challenge is lack of confidence in what distinguishes Christian pastoral care from the predominant ideas of 'care' in the surrounding culture. Historically, it was the Church that coordinated provision for the educational, social, physical, and mental health needs of people in European countries and their colonies. Now, those needs are met, in theory, by State or private healthcare. Yet economic challenges and ageing populations expose gaping holes in welfare provision, while the values of State and business seem to have diverged from Christian beliefs. Biblical values no longer predominate in Western cultures. People no longer instinctively interpret their problems in biblical categories like sin and judgement or grace and the hope of glory. Alternative helpers of varied kinds – therapists, counsellors, self-help theorists and mindfulness gurus – seem at least as qualified as any pastor. Their approaches seem to have the backing of science or sociology. Their advice somehow seems more relevant and tangible than traditional Christian spirituality. The term 'pastoral care', having originated in the Church, is now used in schools and workplaces, but with different connotations than it historically had. What contribution can Christian pastoral caregivers make in this complex landscape?

The second great challenge is how to provide pastoral care within the limited resources of churches under strain. The emergence of a 'post-Christian society' has led many Christian leaders to a fresh sense of urgency in missional engagement with the many people who are outside the church. Against this need, pastoral care can seem like an indulgence or even a distraction. It seems less pressing than church planting and less visibly fruitful than church growth strategies. Classic strategies for pastoral care were developed in a time when populations were settled with strong family networks and work was at home or close to it. Most people respected the Church and looked to its clergy as a vital source of help in times of need. The landscape has changed dramatically over the past two centuries. Industrialisation and urbanisation uprooted populations. Families are smaller and people more individualistic. Religious belief is no longer monolithic and organised Christianity has declined in numbers and influence. In this challenging context, should the church be a lifeboat station training strong people who venture out on stormy seas to save the lost or a hospital bringing in weak people to be cared for by professionals?

This is, of course, a false dichotomy. A church committed to making disciples must both reach the unreached and nurture those who already believe. Pastoral care is vital to both reaching needy unchurched people and retaining needy church members. Christ's love in action through his people often opens ears to the gospel and lack of love for one another within the Church hinders its mission and harms its members. Pastoral care is vital, but there is a problem. Who will provide it? The harvest seems plentiful, but the workers seem so few. Some denominations face shortages of clergy, forcing them to reconsider traditional patterns of universal provision of 'services' to people in a geographic 'parish'. Many pastors are chronically over-worked and under-encouraged, leaving them uncertain about what to prioritise. They often struggle to mobilise enough people to serve in the varied programmes of the church. Wanting to mobilise every member, many churches have recruited pastoral workers, introduced pastoral care teams, or asked small group leaders to be the frontline of pastoral care, but many of these people lack training. At the same time, ministry has become more specialised. Larger churches often employ multiple staff in specific areas, while 'senior pastors' function as staff team leaders or CEOs of the organisation. Some people whose job title includes the word 'pastor' may not play a role in pastoral care at all and, if they are honest, may not be entirely clear about what it is.

What, then, is the future of pastoral care? I am convinced that we need deeper roots and a clearer vision for pastoral care in our time. Deeper roots in the biblical gospel and a clearer vision of what exactly pastoral care is. I hope this book can go some way to providing both. Its basic aim is to captivate the hearts of readers with a vision for pastoral care that is truly shaped by the biblical gospel. This book is structured around the following definition of 'gospel-shaped pastoral care':

Gospel-shaped people responding to gospel-shaped needs with gospel-shaped help

Section 1 explains this definition, laying the foundations for our understanding of gospel-shaped pastoral care. Chapter 1 explains the central concepts behind the definition: what the gospel is and why it is so important that it shapes pastoral care. Chapter 2 then outlines four ministries that comprise pastoral care. The remaining three sections of the book explore each of the three components of the definition: people, needs and help.

Section 2 explores what it means for providers of pastoral care to be gospel-shaped people. Chapter 3 explores the call of the triune God to join him in his work in people's lives so that our motivations, methods and means of pastoral care are rooted in the gospel of God. In Chapter 4, this work is set in its proper context – the community that is formed by the gospel, which we commonly call the Church. I propose five levels of pastoral care and identify three groups of people who should be involved before considering how pastoral care provision can be structured in the church to work at all five levels through all three groups. Then, Chapter 5 discusses the immensely important subject of boundaries that must surround pastoral care if it is to be faithful to God and worthy of the gospel.

Section 3 aims to shape our understanding of the needs of people around the gospel by considering needs in three dimensions: in relationship to God, in personal health, and in relationships with others. Chapter 6, presents a gospel perspective on human nature, contrasting it with ideas prevalent in our culture and focusing on our deepest need for restored relationship with God. Next, Chapter 7, explores the problem of suffering, the nature of health and questions about healing. Chapter 8 then expands from this individual focus to relationships between people and the pastoral needs that arise when they go wrong.

Finally, **Section 4** explores two vital skills necessary for providing gospel-shaped help: pastoral listening (Chapter 9) and pastoral speaking (Chapter 10).

This book is designed to be used in various ways. You may be reading it as an individual or a couple, as a pastoral care team or a pastor, or even as recommended reading in a course about pastoral care. With these varied audiences in mind, I have included several additional elements around the main text.

Each chapter opens with an episode in the lives of Jude or Sam or both, so their stories unfold throughout the book. I hope every reader will identify with some of their experiences. I should emphasise that these characters are entirely fictional, although details in their stories reflect real-life experiences I have had or observed. I hope these stories help to prepare you for the content of each chapter and aid you in personal reflection.

A second feature is the inclusion of a box entitled 'REFLECTION' at the end of each section of each chapter. These boxes contain questions intended to help you reflect personally on what you have read, on your own experience and on what you may be learning. I encourage you to take time to engage with them prayerfully for a few minutes each time, making notes as you do. That will help you not only gain theoretical knowledge but also to apply it. I know it is a big ask to suggest you take time to reflect as you read. I confess I have ignored similar instructions from other authors! I am convinced, though, that reflection will enrich your learning and help you towards this book's most important goal: your growth in Christ as a pastoral caregiver.

Thirdly, at the end of each chapter you will find a summary of its main ideas, to reinforce what you are reading and help you refer back to the book later, followed by a box entitled 'DISCUSSION QUESTIONS'. These questions are included for couples, groups or teams working through the book together. I encourage you to use them to help you understand my content, to evaluate it against Scripture, and to apply it appropriately to your own context.

As we begin our journey into the heart of gospel-shaped pastoral care, my prayer for you is that this book will help you develop confidence in caring for others and a coherence in understanding your part alongside others. Above all, I pray you will be inspired to introduce those you care for to the Chief Shepherd of their souls, the Lord Jesus Christ, who said: "Come to me, all you who are weary and burdened, and I will give you rest".[1]

---

[1] Matthew 11:28

SECTION 1

WHAT?

DEFINING PASTORAL CARE

1. GOSPEL-SHAPED PASTORAL CARE

Sam's email came as a shock. Jude had never considered herself a pastoral caregiver. In her work as a classroom assistant in a primary school, children and staff alike warmed to her, often seeking her out with grazed knees or bruised feelings. But that was not 'pastoral care', was it? The vice principal's job description included 'pastoral care' for pupils, while the principal had overall responsibility for 'pastoral care' of staff. They were qualified professionals, and those responsibilities were way above her pay grade! In church, too, Jude instinctively looked out for people in need, but she never thought of that as 'pastoral care'. After all, she was not a pastor, and she did not aspire to be one! All she could do was listen and pray. It took people like Sam to pastor people. Yet here was Sam's email, expressing his confidence in what she could offer. She could not just dismiss it. She would have to give him a proper reason if she was going to say no, so she decided to pray and sleep on the invitation.

In his most honest moments, Sam was also more than a little confused about what constitutes pastoral care. He loved to preach. A desire to show people Jesus from the Scriptures was what led him into ministry. He was passionate about the gospel, enthused by the person of Christ, confident in the authority of Scripture and committed to evangelism and disciple-making. At seminary, biblical studies and preaching classes had inspired and stimulated him. Pastoral studies, on the other hand, were a disappointment. The lecturer quoted psychologists and sociologists more often than theologians or pastors. The methodology seemed muddled, and he could not see a connection with the gospel. Their idea of pastoral care just sounded like social work. He realised he would need to get a lot clearer in his understanding if Jude accepted the role and expected him to enlighten her! Sam picked a book off his shelf that he had inherited from his granddad. It was a reprint of a book from the 1500s called 'Concerning the True Care of Souls'. That sounded like a good place to start.

The Challenge of Definitions

Definitions are tricky. They can exclude people. Sometimes that is deliberate and appropriate – you really want 'doctor' to mean a properly qualified person – but, at other times, it is unintentional and unhelpful. Jude believed she was not involved in pastoral care because she was excluded by the definition she carried in her mind. She knew 'pastoral care' was not in her job description in work and had no aspiration to be a 'pastor'. So long as she thought of herself as unqualified, her gifts, which were evident to Sam, could not be fully developed. She would never gain knowledge and skills to make her more effective in caring for others. Definitions had barred the way for her growth. Yet, definitions can be helpful. They bring clarity and focus on what is most important. The activities Jude's school labelled 'pastoral care' were not what happened through the church under the same name. In schools and workplaces, 'pastoral care' has come to denote the goal of creating a nurturing environment in which pupils or workers are supported through personal challenges. That is good, but it falls short of biblical soul care and cure. We need a clearer definition of pastoral care!

Contemporary approaches to care often assume that the caregiver's role is simply to facilitate individuals in finding their way through troubles to a place of stability and functioning. Coping is, of course, important, but it hardly describes the fullness of Christian life described in the New Testament. More worryingly, the idea that caregivers help others on a journey of self-help assumes that people can find the resources they need inside themselves. If people are affirmed in this belief, they may be left unaware of their need for God. Authentically Christian pastoral care embodies different values and has a greater goal than the survival of individuals, or even their 'flourishing'. In Chapter 1, I said we need deeper roots and a clearer vision for pastoral care in the twenty-first century. I laid the foundations in that chapter and said there are four ministries that comprise pastoral care. Now I must clarify our vision of those ministries.

What is the 'gospel'?

This book is about 'gospel-shaped pastoral care'. Its intent is to help people who care for others do so in a way that is completely consistent with the gospel. Sam's training failed to connect the rich biblical truth he learned from (mainly dead) theologians with what he was expected to do with real, living people. He had the gospel but could not see how it shaped pastoral care. Jude, meanwhile, was held back from thinking of herself as a pastoral caregiver because her understanding of pastoral care was shaped by her experiences rather than a biblical vision. People like Sam and Jude need a truly gospel-shaped understanding of pastoral care. To develop that, we need first to understand what the gospel is.

A word worth keeping

The word 'gospel' sounds old-school. It has the ring of 'Christianese jargon' that should be jettisoned in the interests of clarity. Some people try to demystify it by replacing it with the phrase 'good news'. That is understandable since it is a literal translation of the New Testament Greek word *euangelion* that is traditionally translated 'gospel'.[2] In principle, it is best to use plain English whenever possible when communicating biblical truth, so why is this book not about 'good-news-shaped pastoral care'? The reason is not simply that it does not sound as catchy, but because the phrase 'good news' is open to even greater misunderstandings than the word 'gospel'. In common speech, 'good news' is likely to mean a favourable headline in the papers or a well-liked post on social media. It does not normally mean something life-changing or of universal significance. Indeed, one person's 'good news' might be another's 'bad news', especially if the headline is about a sports result! In the Bible, *euangelion* means an announcement of something that will have unavoidable, profound life-changing consequences. So, this book works on the basis that it is better to explain the unfamiliar word 'gospel', than to clarify the

---

[2] The English words 'evangelism' (sharing the gospel), 'evangelist' (someone who communicates the gospel) and 'evangelical' (people who believe the gospel) all derive from *euangelion*.

familiar phrase 'good news'.

The word 'gospel' has certainly been used in unhelpful ways. It has been reduced to shorthand for a list of propositional statements or a formula for salvation. Sometimes it has been thought of as a message for the unsaved that is 'old hat' for Christians. When I was growing up, a 'gospel meeting' or 'gospel mission' was an evangelistic event. The biblical usage of the word 'gospel' cannot be confined in these ways. The *euangelion* contains truths that can be stated a propositions and it is the power of God for salvation, but it is more than a list or formula, and no matter how long a person has been a Christian they can never be over-familiar with it or out-grow its usefulness. The gospel is a message. In its fullness, it embraces the whole story of Scripture from Genesis to Revelation, from God's creation of the world until God's revelation of the new creation. As such, the gospel is about everything and everyone. It contains every true proposition that was ever stated. It is the greatest story ever told – the true story of human life in relationship to God.

The gospel is expansive and massive. It impacts every issue a human mind has ever considered. Yet, the gospel is also remarkably simple. Its essence can be expressed in just a few words, as, for example, in one of the most famous Bible verses, John 3 verse 16, which has often been called 'the gospel in a nutshell'. The gospel has a clear centre in Jesus. At its heart are the truths of his identity as Israel's Messiah (Christ), his death for sins and his resurrection from the dead as the foretaste of the resurrection awaiting all who believe in him. These are the truths 'of first importance'.[3] The person and work of the Lord Jesus are the climax of the gospel narrative, the turning point of history's story, the pinnacle of all wisdom, the ultimate answer to every question.

The gospel is *good news* for people, but it is good because it is true, not because it is always convenient. When we think of 'good news', we usually mean we like what we are hearing. Our candidate was elected, or our asking price was met, or our team won. We decide what is 'good'. The gospel is news that is important whether we think it is good or not. It is good not because we think it so, but because God declares it so. In the Roman world

---

[3] 1 Corinthians 15:3

11

and in the Greek translation of the Old Testament that predated Jesus,[4] the word *euangelion* was used to refer to important messages, for example about the death of a king, the birth of a new king, or a military victory. Events like these signalled a coming transfer of power. The news would seem 'good' to you if you were loyal to the new king. Hearing a herald announce in the marketplace, you could breathe a sigh of relief and rejoice, even though it might take some time before his reign became effective in your region. To enemies of the new ruler, however, the news would not seem 'good'. They would be faced with the choice either of changing their allegiance or continuing in rebellion, hoping the new ruler might be overthrown. Or they could simply dismiss it as 'fake news' and the herald as false.

The writers of the New Testament, carried along by the Holy Spirit,[5] took the word *euangelion*, along with many other words in circulation around them, and invested it with greater significance by centring it on Jesus Christ. Mark began his Gospel account of Jesus' life with the announcement, 'The beginning of the *euangelion* of Jesus Christ, the Son of God'.[6] The Christian *euangelion* is the news that Jesus of Nazareth, a man who lived, died and rose again, was Israel's long-promised Messiah and God's Son and has become Saviour for all through his death on a Roman cross for our sins and has been declared Lord over all through his resurrection from the dead. This gospel is a true message about things that really happened in history, but it is also a message of cosmic significance. There is a new king, not just for Israel, but for people of all nations. We can either embrace this truth and live accordingly or we can continue in rebellion, but our response does not determine the facts of the matter. The gospel calls us to acknowledge Jesus' rule. Reduced to its simplest, shortest form, the gospel is that 'Jesus Christ is Lord', but we will need a bit more detail than that if we are to see how the gospel shapes pastoral care.[7]

------

[4] This Greek translation of the Old Testament is often called the Septuagint, because Jewish tradition says it was produced by seventy scholars.

[5] 2 Peter 1:21

[6] Mark 1:1

[7] The title 'Lord' has a rich meaning. Against the background of the Old Testament it identifies Jesus as Yahweh, the God of Israel, while, in the context of the Roman world, it declares Him, not Caesar, to be the one rightful ruler.

God's kingdom, king and power

In the Gospels of Matthew, Mark and Luke, *euangelion* refers to the message Jesus preached about the kingdom of God, which called people to repent.[8] Towards the end of Matthew and Mark, Jesus says the "gospel [*euangelion*] of the kingdom will be proclaimed throughout the whole world".[9] Recognising this, some people mistakenly think the gospel we are to believe and proclaim is simply an ethical message about loving others and relieving suffering. Jesus certainly commanded those things of his followers, but his gospel was more than this. He did not only call people to live like him and in obedience to his commands; he called people to trust in him, to follow him, and to lay down their lives to do so.[10] He declared that God's kingdom had arrived with his coming and people needed to enter it through childlike faith and spiritual rebirth.[11]

Jesus also pointed to an end point of history when God would intervene to restore all things and called people to enter the kingdom in preparation for the future day of judgement that would precede that good ending to this world's story.[12] In this judgement, some would enter into eternal life and blessing, while others would face eternal loss. The determinative factor on that day will be whether people trust in Jesus, confess him before people, and live in obedience to his teachings.[13] The new king demands our allegiance.

The kingdom has a king. His name is Jesus, and the 'gospel of the kingdom' points people to him. Furthermore, the Gospels are not simply a record of Jesus' teachings and healing miracles. They move inexorably towards a climax in the crucifixion and resurrection of Jesus. Jesus described his death as a ransom that sets many people free from sin.[14] His resurrection showed that the freedom Jesus offered was not only from sin

---

[8] Matthew 4:23; 9:35; Mark 1:14-15; Luke 9:6; 20:1

[9] Matthew 24:14. See also Matthew 26:13; Mark 13:10; 14:9; and also Mark 16:15, which is part of the 'long ending' of Mark's Gospel.

[10] Matthew 16:24-26

[11] Matthew 18:3; John 3:5

[12] See the parables of Matthew 13:24-50

[13] Matthew 7:15-27; 10:32-33; John 11:25-26

[14] Mark 10:45

in this life but from death for eternal life. It affirmed everything he had claimed about his unique relationship with God and his pivotal role in God's plan of salvation. Without the empty cross and the empty tomb, Jesus' teaching about the kingdom makes no sense.

Acts records how the apostles preached the *euangelion* about God's kingdom as Jesus had commissioned them to do.[15] Paul's epistles and 1 Peter use *euangelion* to refer to the message the apostles proclaimed. Theirs was not a different message from Jesus' 'gospel of the kingdom', but a development of it. They explained the significance of Jesus' life, death and resurrection in light of the Old Testament Scriptures and called people to repent and acknowledge him as Lord.[16] They taught the same principles for obedient life in God's kingdom as Jesus had, but insisted, as Jesus did, that it is only through faith in Jesus that people can be made right with God and by the power of the Holy Spirit that they can live as God desires.

The gospel was received by the apostles Jesus appointed as his authorised representatives. They had authority from Jesus to speak on his behalf and they recorded their teachings faithfully in the New Testament, so that we have them clearly presented to us. In doing this, the apostles entrusted the gospel to the whole Church to be passed on faithfully to others across the generations.[17] There can be no separation, then, between the Lord Jesus and his apostles or the Scriptures that testify to him. To be gospel-shaped is to be Christ-shaped and Bible-shaped.

The gospel is more than just truth to be acknowledged. It calls people to repent and believe the message, to reorient their lives in line with reality. It is the gospel of salvation and peace and it is 'the power of God for salvation'.[18] That is not to say that the words of the gospel are a magical incantation but that God the Holy Spirit works in people as they hear and

---

[15] See Matthew 24:14; Mark 13:10; Acts 8:25, 40; 14:7, 21; 15:7; 16:10; 20:24

[16] The words most commonly connected with *euangelion* in the New Testament are 'Jesus' and 'Christ' (e.g., 2 Corinthians 4:4).

[17] See Ephesians 3:1-7 and Jude verse 3, where 'the faith' is another way of describing the gospel. See also the insistence in Galatians 1:6-10 that the apostolic gospel must never be distorted.

[18] Ephesians 1:13; 6:15; Romans 1:16

believe gospel truth with the power that raised Jesus from the dead.[19] The Spirit assures those who believe of God's love, sets them free from the law of sin and death, leads them to kill off their sinful deeds and to walk in right ways, enables them to call God Father, helps them in their weakness by interceding for them, and causes them to overflow with hope.[20] The gospel, proclaimed by people, is God's way of calling us into relationship with God the Father, Son and Holy Spirit. This is true when a person is born again into God's family, but it is also true as people continue to trust in gospel truth. The truth of the gospel is how the Spirit continues to change us.

A story in five acts

We have already seen that the gospel is the whole story of God's purposes for humankind from creation to new creation. This story centres on Jesus, who fulfils those purposes and is the turning point in the story from sin and death to life and obedience. Jesus Christ crucified and risen is central to New Testament summaries of the gospel.[21] We must never lose sight of him as we learn more about God's truth. The risk is not so much of being unable to 'see the wood for the trees' but losing sight of *the* tree (the cross) within the wood (the big story). Jesus is the centre not only of our salvation from sins, but of everything. The gospel needs to shape everything because nothing has meaning without Jesus illuminating it.

The gospel story, like most great stories, has a series of five scenes or movements, from the setting of the scene to the conclusion. The whole story presents the wisdom and glory of the person(s) who are its main character: God the Father, Son and Spirit. The story has what we can call a trinitarian pattern: it begins with God the Father, turns on God the Son and is completed by God the Spirit. The five movements of the gospel can be described using five words beginning with 'r':[22]

---

[19] Romans 11:23; 15:19; Titus 3:5; James 1:21; 1 Peter 1:23,25
[20] Romans 5:5; 8:2, 4-16, 27; 15:13
[21] John 3:16; Romans 1:1-6; 1 Corinthians 15:1-11; Philippians 2:5-11; Colossians 1:15-20; 1 Timothy 3:16; 2 Timothy 2:8; 1 Peter 3:18-22
[22] A similar approach is taken, although reaching conclusions that differ

1. **God rules** – the story starts with God, the Creator, who is the powerful and good sovereign over everything and cares for his creation like a good Father. Without God, the gospel would not exist.

2. **We rebelled** – human beings are loved by God and made to live with him but rejected his rule and so stand under his wrath and judgement, resulting in death. Without sin, the gospel would be unnecessary.

3. **God rescues** – beginning with the call of Abraham God worked through the nation of Israel to bring salvation through Israel's Messiah, God's Son, Jesus. Without Jesus, the gospel could not save us.

4. **We respond** – we can reject Jesus and face judgement or humble ourselves, confess our sin and acknowledge him as Lord and so be saved. Without faith, the gospel does not save us.

5. **God restores** – the Holy Spirit forms believers into a community in which he begins a work of changing them that he will complete when Christ returns. Without the Spirit, the gospel would be powerless.

Each of these points could be expanded until we would have the whole Bible, but until a person understands these five scenes in the gospel as they experience it, they will be missing something. The people we care for need to know who God is, what sin is, how Jesus is Saviour and Lord, what faith looks like and what the Spirit is doing in their lives. I will use these five headings throughout this book as a framework through which to understand different aspects of pastoral care. They can also guide us in helping care-seekers work through issues (see Chapter 10) and provide answers to the big questions of life (see the Appendix).

REFLECTION

- Take time to thank God for the wonder of the gospel and your salvation through Christ. The gospel is intended to be enjoyed by us as we appreciate Jesus and the wonder of God's grace to us in him.

---

somewhat from mine, by David Lyall (2001). My approach is not dependent on Lyall's, having been developed before I read his book.

- Rehearse the five 'movements' of the gospel in your mind (using one digit on one hand for each point may help you do this) and ensure you have a clear grasp of it to shape your pastoral practice.

What is pastoral care?

Having explained what the gospel is, we must consider the meaning of 'pastoral care'. This is important in our time, because the phrase is used in schools and workplaces (and sometimes in churches) in ways that do not reflect the roots of the term. To appreciate what 'pastoral care' is, we need to think about each of the two words: 'pastoral', which has foundations in the Bible, and 'care', which derives from a medieval Latin phrase.

Pastoral: the biblical idea of shepherding

'Pastor' is a direct transliteration into English of the Latin word meaning 'shepherd'. Something 'pastoral', then relates to shepherds and their work. Those of us who live in urban settings in the modern world may know very little about shepherding, but the Bible has a lot to say about shepherds and sheep. Many leaders of God's people, from Jacob to Moses to king David, were literally shepherds. That is no coincidence, as the role of the shepherd illustrates the priorities of leaders of God's people. God chose people who knew how to shepherd sheep to shepherd his people. God describes himself as Israel's shepherd and holds the nation's leaders accountable to shepherd his people in the way he does.[23] This image flows into the New Testament. Jesus described himself as the Good Shepherd and commissioned Peter and the other apostles to tend his sheep.[24] The apostles Peter and Paul describe those who give spiritual leadership to the church shepherds and command them to shepherd the flock.[25] In doing so, they are to remember they are accountable to Jesus, the Chief Shepherd, who will return one day for his flock.[26] So, the idea of shepherding people starts

[23] Psalm 23; 78:52; 80:1; Ezekiel 34
[24] John 10; 21
[25] Acts 20:28; Ephesians 4:11; 1 Peter 5:2
[26] 1 Peter 2:25; 5:4; Revelation 7:17

with God. Any work that is 'pastoral' entails joining God in his work and learning from him how to do it.

Three biblical passages are especially helpful in building a picture of the role of the shepherd: Psalm 23, Ezekiel 34 and John 10. In Psalm 23, David the shepherd king describes God as his personal shepherd. Ezekiel 34 powerfully describes God's care for his sheep and his anger at the bad shepherds who had neglected and abused them. In John 10, Jesus describes himself as the Good Shepherd who lays down his life for the sheep in contrast to hirelings and thieves who abandon or destroy them. Four aspects of shepherding are found in all three passages (see Table 1):

- ensuring the sheep are well fed and watered;
- restoring the sheep to health by tending wounds;
- protecting the sheep from harm; and
- guiding the sheep to a secure destination.

In short, shepherds feed, restore, protect and guide.

A potential limitation of the shepherding image is that in the New Testament it relates particularly to the work of the recognised shepherds of the church who are called 'pastors' in many of our church traditions. Pastors like Sam do have a particular role in pastoral care, as I will explain in Chapter 3, but every believer has a part to play under their oversight. There is a role for people like Jude. The New Testament does not describe every believer as a pastor, but it does expect every believer to use whatever gifts God has given them for the health of the whole church. Pastoral care includes dimensions that can and should be fulfilled by every believer.[27] These dimensions should, however, have the same priorities and approaches that characterise the task of pastors. To be worthy of the name 'pastoral', our work must aim to feed, restore, protect and guide people

---

[27] Another way to think about this is as the 'priesthood of all believers', which was a key principle re-emphasised in the Protestant Reformation. The ministries of pastoral care could be thought of in terms of priestly roles: presenting God to people (provision, presence and instruction) and people to God (intercession).

Table 1   *Four aspects of the shepherd's work*

	Psalm 23	**Ezekiel 34**	**John 10**
Feeding	He makes me lie down in green pastures. He leads me beside still waters. (verse 2)	I will feed them on the mountains of Israel […] I will feed them with good pasture (verses 13-14)	If anyone enters by me, he will be saved and will go in and out and find pasture (verse 9)
Restoring	He restores my soul. (verse 3)	I will seek the lost, and I will bring back the strayed, and I will bind up the injured, and I will strengthen the weak, and the fat and the strong I will destroy. I will feed them in justice. (verse 16)	I lay down my life for the sheep (verse 15)
Protecting	your rod and your staff, they comfort me. (verse 4)	I am against the [bad] shepherds, and I will require my sheep at their hand and put a stop to their feeding the sheep. (verse 10)	I am the door. If anyone enters by me, he will be saved (verse 9)
Guiding	He leads me in paths of righteousness for his name's sake. (verse 3)	I will bring them out from the peoples and gather them from the countries, and will bring them into their own land. (verse 13)	he goes before them, and the sheep follow him, for they know his voice. (verse 4)

Care: the historical idea of *cura animarum*

A second foundation, this time from church history, can help us understand what 'care' means in the phrase 'pastoral care'. The word 'care' comes into 'pastoral care' from the medieval Latin phrase, *cura animarum*. *Animarum* means 'of souls' and this phrase has sometimes been expressed in English as 'soul care'. That translation is helpful, but it loses some of the richness of the Latin phrase. *Cura*, as you might guess, gave us the English word 'cure' as well as the word 'care'. So, *cura animarum* could also be translated 'soul cure'.

The concept of *cura animarum* as it developed in the history of the church clearly had the cure sense in mind. Fourth century bishop of Constantinople Gregory of Nazianzus described a pastor as a 'physician of souls'.[28] In his classic *Book of Pastoral Rule*, Gregory the Great, who was pope from 590 to 604, similarly described the heart of pastoral ministry as healing 'the sores of the thoughts of men' and called priests 'physicians of the heart'.[29] There is an unmistakable dimension of curing here, which fits with the fact that shepherding is not only concerned with feeding and protecting the sheep, but also with restoring and guiding them.

Realising the emphasis on healing in early accounts of *cura animarum*, we may be tempted to speak of 'pastoral cure' instead of 'pastoral care', although that would risk missing the equally important supportive aspects of pastoral care. We must be careful, though, when we think of pastoral care. We must think not only of *supportive* care, but also *transformative* cure. Pastoral care includes supporting people by being present with them and providing for their practical needs as well as curing people's soul sicknesses by interceding for them and sharing instruction from God's Word.

One risk inherent in the phrase *cura animarum* is that its reference to the soul as what is cared for could lead to a unidimensional understanding of people and their needs. Care and cure *of souls* should not mean that physical needs are unimportant or should be neglected. It may be argued that they were neglected at times in church history, especially as negative ideas about the body that came from the theories of Greek philosopher Plato influenced Christians. The Bible does not regard the body as negative and presents people as embodied souls, calling us to care for people in their whole beings. It is fair to say, though, that the primary focus of pastoral care is on the health of the soul. The soul is the inner person, comprising emotions, thoughts and will. Pastoral care aims for soul health.

Recognising that soul health is the goal of pastoral care can also help us recognise how important it is that pastoral care does not merely support

---

[28] Gregory of Nazianzus, undated, p.16-17
[29] Gregory the Great, undated, Chapter 1

people through challenges. Rather, it must challenge them to grow in faith and godliness. This is clear in the classic texts of Protestant pastoral care. The book Sam found on his shelf, Martin Bucer's 1538 *Concerning the True Care of Souls*, was based on Ezekiel 34.[30] It challenged pastors to commit to the spiritual formation of their parishioners by applying the truths of Scripture to their specific needs. The same emphasis is found in the seventeenth century books *The Country Parson* by George Herbert and *The Reformed Pastor* by Richard Baxter.[31]

In the twentieth century there was a dramatic shift in the understanding of pastoral care due to influences from the developing field of psychology.[32] People like Carl Rogers advocated 'person-centred counselling' in which 'unconditional positive regard' creates a safe space in which they could examine themselves. Theologians like Seward Hiltner applied these ideas to pastoral care. Hiltner questioned the notion that the Church should discipline its members according to an external standard and reframed the pastor as a supportive friend helping individuals along a personal journey of unearthing insights within themselves. Traditional emphases on repentance from sin and growth in a community of discipline gave way to 'personal wholeness and well-being'.[33] The strengths of these approaches in creating a safe space for people to share about their needs are clear, but the non-directive approach left pastors with care without cure. This way of thinking of 'pastoral care' predominates in the use of the phrase in schools and workplaces and still has immense influence in churches too.

In the mid to late twentieth century, there was a backlash against this non-directive idea of pastoral care.[34] Psychological theories that assumed people to possess inherent goodness that could be drawn out through 'positive thinking', seemed inadequate to explain brutal totalitarianism and the industrialised carnage of two World Wars. Sin was back on the agenda. Some therapists, meanwhile, noted that their clients made little progress

---

[30] Bucer, 2009

[31] Herbert, 1632; Baxter, 1656

[32] Bunting, 2000; Crossley, 1992

[33] Graham, 2006, p.857

[34] Ian Bunting (2000, p.389-390) provides a helpful summary of the reasons for this development on which I have drawn.

until they took responsibility for their actions. It seemed like they needed a challenge rather than just a listening ear. Theologians like Dietrich Bonhoeffer and Thomas Oden argued that psychology was displacing the gospel and called for a return to the classic understanding of soul care.[35]

The idea of 'gospel-shaped pastoral care' advanced in this book stands in the great tradition of soul care. Both supportive care and directive cure are important. Cure without care would be cold and domineering. Care without cure might feel nice but leaves people in their sins. Pastoral caregivers must love people enough to care for them even if they do not want a cure, but to share truth with them when it is clear they need one.

REFLECTION

- How do these biblical and historical foundations enhance your understanding of pastoral care and your role in it?

- How can you ensure that care and cure are integrated in pastoral care in your context?

How can pastoral care be gospel-shaped?

Having gained some sense of what the gospel and pastoral care are, it remains to consider how one can shape the other. That is the question the rest of this book aims to answer, but this section will explain why it is so important that our thoughts about care are shaped by the values of the gospel.

Care needs values

Caregivers are motivated and guided by convictions. These underlying

---

[35] Bonhoeffer, 1985; Oden, 1984

beliefs can be assumed and implicit or reasoned and explicit, but they are always there. The idea of 'value free care' is a myth. When a caregiver's values are not explicit, care can become paternalistic – not allowing care-seekers to make their own judgements. To force our convictions on another would be unworthy of the gospel, but we must know what we believe if we want to honour God, the Shepherd, and we must be transparent about it if we want to honour other people, his sheep. Beliefs about three things influence the way we care for others: need, health and help. We would not be motivated to care if we did not believe people have problems (need) and that we can do something (help) which might help them to a better place (health). Let us think a little more about each of these aspects.

Firstly, care depends on convictions about need. It is a response to needs we perceive in others. Some needs are obvious, either because we see them, or the person expresses them. Others are not, either because we do not look for them or because the other person does not recognise them, hides them or finds them difficult to express. Care, therefore, is inevitably judgemental. Do not misunderstand. Care never condemns people and it works hard not to prejudge or to jump to conclusions, but it does eventually make judgements about their needs. When people express felt needs, the caregiver makes a judgement about the true nature and extent of their problems. The caregiver decides which needs are greatest or most urgent and tries to discern the unexpressed or unrecognised needs underlying the issues they describe. Not to do so would be neglectful. We must ensure that our values about needs are true.

Secondly, care depends on convictions about people. Only by knowing what a fulfilled human life is can we recognise when someone has a need. We distinguish between variations on normal in people's bodies, thoughts and emotions, and harmful deviations from the norm. We must ensure that our values about people are true.

Thirdly, care depends on convictions about help. What can be done to help this person with their needs? What is the best thing for us to do and what would be inappropriate even if it might have some benefit? Our motivations for care and the methods and means we employ depend on our convictions about ourselves and about God and how he can help people through us. We must ensure that our values about help are true.

Values from the gospel

Where else can we find a true perspective on what people truly need and how we can help them? We can, of course, learn much from psychology and science about human nature and needs, but these sources cannot provide values. Values derive from our worldview, meaning our beliefs about ultimate reality. Gospel-shaped pastoral care seeks to base and develop our understanding of people, needs and help based on the gospel. It aims to follow the priorities God has revealed to us in the Bible and its story of God's rescue plan for human beings. If we are not consistent about applying the gospel to every aspect of pastoral care, we will end up following some other set of values without even realising we are doing so.

The definition of gospel-shaped pastoral care already presented in the Preface bears repeating at this stage:

Gospel-shaped people responding to gospel-shaped needs with gospel-shaped help

This definition says that all three key elements in pastoral care should be shaped by the gospel. The gospel should shape the people we are as we engage in pastoral care as well as our understanding of what the people we care for are. We need to know that we are God's people, belonging to Him, living in community gathered to Him, and serving in a way worthy of Him. We also need to understand the needs of people in light of the gospel, appreciating that people are made for God, for relationships and for wholeness. As we seek to respond to these needs, the gospel guides us in the help we bring. These three concepts – people, needs and help – are the focus in turn of each of the three sections of the rest of this book.

REFLECTION

- What convictions do you hold about the nature of people, need and help? How do these shape your pastoral care practice for good or ill?

- As you begin on the journey of learning about gospel-shaped pastoral care, what are you interested to know more about and what concerns do you have? Why is that so? Pray about these feelings.

CHAPTER SUMMARY

The gospel provides a framework for understanding health, need and help. It is the message that our Creator God has acted to save us from our sins through His Son, Jesus, Israel's Messiah, which calls us to respond in repentance and faith and so to participate in the new creation through present forgiveness of sins and the hope of complete restoration when Christ returns in glory. We can frame our understanding of various aspects of pastoral care by working through five acts in the gospel story, commencing with God's reign in creation, centring on God's rescue in Christ, and concluding with God's restoration by the Spirit. Pastoral caregivers should be shaped by the gospel to respond to needs understood in light of the gospel with forms of help consistent with the gospel. Their goal is to see people fed, restored, protected and guided and their focus is on the health of the soul. This task of pastoral care has a role for pastors, who shepherd the flock, and all believers using their gifts for the health of the flock.

CHAPTER 1 - DISCUSSION QUESTIONS

1. Take time in a group to study the following passages, which summarise the gospel. What common themes run across them and why is each element important?

   - Romans 1:1-6;
   - 1 Corinthians 15:1-11;
   - Philippians 2:5-11;
   - Colossians 1:15-20;
   - 1 Timothy 3:16;
   - 2 Timothy 2:8;
   - 1 Peter 3:18-22.

2. In what ways should the gospel shape our approach to pastoral care? Think about the following aspects:

   - Our motivations and attitudes;
   - Our expectations and hopes for care-seekers;
   - Our priorities in what we do.

3. What do you find illuminating, helpful, confusing or unhelpful in the idea of shepherding? How do you think the people identified as pastors and those who are not can work together in pastoral care?

4. What negative impact would it have if we reduced pastoral care to either the *cure* or *care* dimension of *cura animarum* alone?

2. FOUR MINISTRIES OF PASTORAL CARE

Sam's reading of the classic book on pastoral care, a revisit to the limited notes he had on the subject from seminary and an internet trawl had helped him get some sense of what pastoral care entails. There was a lot about being with people. The classics talked about visiting them in their homes. Some online articles majored on the idea of being a representative of God, although Sam was not sure he agreed entirely with their theology. He had stumbled on a helpful flow chart about what to do in pastoral emergencies, although it was mainly about contacting emergency services and charitable organisations that could help with practical needs. It said very little about a spiritual dimension to care.

Sam tried to visualise what pastoral care entails. He tried using a tool he encountered back in the days when he was revising for exams – the mind map. On the whiteboard on his study wall he wrote pastoral care in a 'bubble' in the middle and then began writing related words around it, drawing lines from the central bubble. Words like 'support', 'companionship', 'listening' and 'compassion' came first. Then he thought about a different set of words: 'counsel', 'advice', 'prayer' and rebuke. He realise the first set of words did not entail the caregiver speaking, while the second set were all to do with words. As he added further words – 'help', 'friendship', 'crisis' and many others – the whiteboard became increasingly crowded but his mind was not getting any clearer. It seemed like there were so many aspects of pastoral care and he was unsure how to group these various ideas into something manageable. Then he remembered something he had heard at a pastors' conference: "Pastoral ministry is relational". Could that work as a way of understanding pastoral care? Was it not all about relationship with people in which we help them grow in relationship with god? He rubbed the whiteboard clean and began again, this time with 'Pastoral relationships' in the central bubble.

Forging Pastoral Relationships

Sam's insight that pastoral cate is fundamentally relational is absolutely true. In Chapter 1, we saw that the shepherding image as expressed in Psalm 23, Ezekiel 34 and John 10 expects shepherds to feed, restore, protect and guide the sheep. Another vital emphasis comes through in each passage: the shepherd does these four things in committed relationship with the sheep. The psalmist David can say to God his Shepherd, 'you are with me'.[36] To the false shepherds who had ravaged Israel, God their true Shepherd says, 'I myself will be the shepherd of my sheep, and I myself will make them lie down'.[37] Jesus says that the Good Shepherd, 'calls his own sheep by name and leads them out'.[38] A shepherd in ancient Israel was close to the sheep, committed to them and cared for them. Closeness, commitment and care are also vital in pastoral relationships.

Paul Tripp warns us against non-relational approaches to pastoral work. Using powerful images inspired by 1 Corinthians 13, he writes that, 'We would prefer to lob grenades of truth into people's lives rather than lay down our lives for them. [...] we are resounding-gong people in cymbal-clanging relationships. There is a whole lot of noise but not much real change'.[39] Gospel-shaped pastoral care proceeds through loving relationships because the gospel calls people into relationship with God. Through his under-shepherds, the Good Shepherd, calls his sheep to himself. We cannot be 'pastoral' if we do not draw alongside people and commit to them.

Building pastoral relationships entails four steps, which Jesus exemplified in his interactions with people. These four steps relate to four ministries that together comprise pastoral care:

---

[36] Psalm 23:4
[37] Ezekiel 34:15
[38] John 10:3
[39] Tripp, 2002, p.118-119

1. GOING to the person. Jesus, like the shepherd in his parable of the lost sheep,[40] came to people where they were and valued each individual. The incarnation was his coming into our world of suffering and the Gospels show how he travelled to be with people and often paused in his journey to give an individual his attention. We meet people in their natural context on their terms, associating with them in their experience, prepared to spend unhurried time with the person through the ministry of **presence**.

2. SHOWING the person love. Jesus looked at people with compassion as sheep without a shepherd and treated each person with dignity.[41] In words and actions, he demonstrated God's love for people whether they accepted him or not. He showed his disciples love to the full extent of washing their feet and then going to the cross for them.[42] We accept people as we find them, opening ourselves to the betrayals and denials Jesus experienced, and demonstrating sacrificial and selfless love in the ministry of **provision**.

3. KNOWING the person. Jesus knew the hearts of people without them speaking.[43] Even so, he took time patiently to listen to people, like Nicodemus or the Samaritan woman at the well,[44] engaging with their questions. We do not have Christ's perfect knowledge of other's thoughts and feelings, but as we listen attentively to their stories, we turn to God for insight and help in the ministry of **intercession**.

4. GROWING with the person. One of the most astounding truths concerning the incarnation was that Jesus had to grow not only physically

---

[40] Luke 15:1-7
[41] Matthew 9:36; Mark 6:34
[42] John 13:1
[43] Matthew 9:4; Luke 9:47; John 2:24-25
[44] John 3 and 4

but also in wisdom and in favour with God and people.[45] It was not that he lacked God's favour in anything he did, but that every step in his human development through childhood led to increasing favour with his Father. In his interactions with people, he helped them to grow in wisdom and in favour with God too. We share Christ's goal for people of faith in His Father but, unlike him, we commit to grow with those we care for as we humbly engage in the ministry of **instruction**.

Figure 1   *Four steps in building pastoral relationships and four ministries of pastoral care*

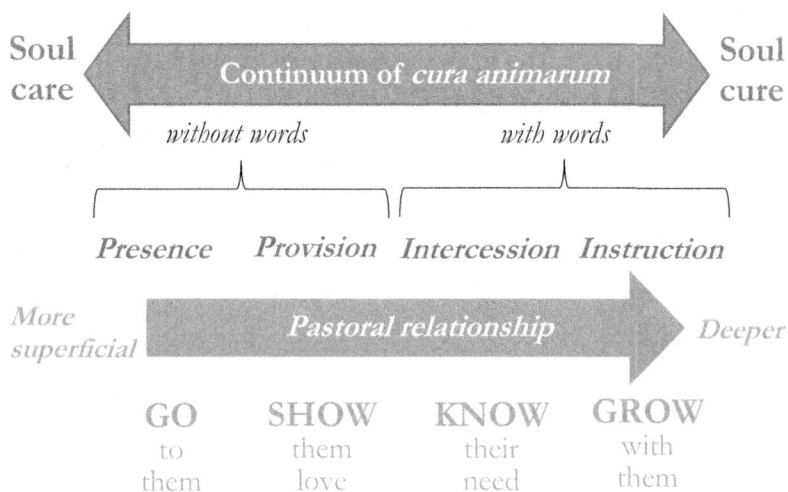

The relationship between the four steps in building a pastoral relationship and the four ministries of pastoral care is illustrated in Figure 1. This diagram also suggests that the ministries sit on a continuum of *cura animarum* between care and cure of souls. Each of the four ministries contributes to both care and cure of souls, but care is expressed primarily without words through provision and presence, while cure happens principally with words through intercession and instruction.

The order of these steps is important. They lead us progressively from a

---

[45] Luke 2:52

more superficial relationship to a deeper one. 'Knowing' and 'growing' come after 'showing' and 'going'. Our work of understanding people's inner struggles and challenging them with God's truth is grounded in committed love. If we have already demonstrated concern, people will be more likely to share deeply with us and to receive truth from us. 'Going' and 'showing' can convince wounded people that we are interested in their good when we talk of 'knowing' and 'growing', although we do not go to them and show them love just with this agenda, but because the love of Christ compels us.

Putting actions before words shows people that our care is not conditional upon their response. Over time, as a pastoral relationship develops, we can expect to progress from care for the person's soul to soul cure, moving through the ministries in order. In practice, of course, the ministries will often happen in parallel rather than sequentially, but it is helpful to ask which point individual care-seekers are at and how to move them along towards the goal of growth in Christ-likeness.

The four ministries also come logically in this order. We establish presence with the person and listen well to identify their needs. If there is an urgent need for practical provision, we respond immediately. As we do so, we intercede for the person, seeking divine wisdom and power. In the context of a growing, trusting relationship, we begin to instruct the person in God's truth. Pastoral care in its totality must entail provision, presence, intercession and instruction. Only when all four are at play can a person be fed, restored, protected and guided in relationship to Christ. Some pastoral caregivers may focus on one or other of these ministries, but all are vital. In the remainder of this chapter, we will outline the nature of each of these four ministries.

The Ministry of Presence

The ministry of presence means being with others in their need. Perhaps the greatest reason why pastoral care in churches can be deficient is busyness. Time is our most valuable commodity. Without investing in it, we cannot genuinely care for others. There is no substitute for presence through times of trouble. Echoing a famous line from Psalm 23, Eugene Peterson warns that ,'Writing cheerful graffiti on the rocks in the valley of deep shadows is no substitute for companionship with the person who must walk in the darkness'.[46] Henri Nouwen, similarly writes, 'The emptiness of the past and future can never be filled with words but only the presence of a man'.[47] Simply being present, without saying anything, is often enough in a pastoral crisis, especially when distress, anger or pain is so deep that words cannot be heard. Doing so, however, is costly since, 'no one can help anyone without becoming involved, without entering with his whole person into the painful situation, without taking the risk of becoming hurt, wounded or even destroyed in the process'.[48] Pastoral presence follows in the sacrificial 'self-emptying' way of Christ, laying aside one's own needs and desires.[49]

Effective pastoral presence requires three qualities:[50]

- Firstly, **awareness of oneself.** Caregivers must be and aware of their own feelings and reactions. This is essential if they are to avoid being overwhelmed and to ensure they do not misinterpret situations by seeing them only through their own lenses (i.e., how they would feel or what they would do).

- Secondly, **awareness of the other.** Caregivers must experience, as far as possible, the thoughts and emotions of unique person you are with. Pastoral listening is a key skill for doing so (see Chapter 9).

- Thirdly, **awareness of God.** The sense that God is distant or absent is often an acutely painful aspect of suffering. Caregivers represent God in the literal sense of the word – presenting God afresh to people in need. In pastoral presence, the caregiver becomes, 'a living reminder of Jesus Christ',[51] 'a physical sign of the gracious presence of the triune God',[52] and a 'living doxology'.[53]

---

[46] Peterson, 1980, p.114
[47] Nouwen, 2014, p.68
[48] Nouwen, 2014, p.75
[49] See Anderson, 2005, p.207
[50] See also Patton, 2005, p.22ff.
[51] Nouwen, 1977, p.1
[52] Bonhoeffer, 1954, p.20
[53] Dawn, 2000, p.41

Representing God does not mean taking his place. Realising this helps us in two ways: to cope with our inadequacy – we need not be perfectly like God to remind people of him – and to avoid dependency – we point past ourselves to Christ as the only eternally dependable one. A tension can arise for caregivers between the feeling they must represent God by being a solid example of faith and the reality of their life of faith with its inevitable weaknesses and failings.

Caregivers should not fall into the trap of presenting themselves as perfect, 'sorted' people. To do so would not help to model what faith looks like to the people we care for and it would make pastoral relationships inauthentic. Appropriate self-disclosure is, therefore, important. At the right time, and to the right degree, we can share about our own struggles. This is generally best done about past failures or about ongoing struggles in which we have learnt enough to pass on helpful advice. Where we have not reached that point, we are best to seek pastoral care ourselves or to keep our sharing with spiritual friends who are themselves mature and stable enough to cope with it.

Appropriate sharing about oneself should not be seen as a barrier to helping others. Indeed, often it can be the very thing that helps them see how they too can make progress. Henri Nouwen, reminds us, 'What matters most, what transforms, is the influence of a humble, vulnerable witness to the truth'.[54] Our goal in pastoral presence is twofold. First, as Kenneth Boyd writes, we 'remind the sufferer that we are more than our suffering, that we have had other experiences than those which now threaten to overwhelm us, that we have other goals than simply recovering'.[55] Second, in Nouwen's words, we 'help people find a friendly distance from their own lives so that what they are experiencing can be brought into the light in the form of a question to be lived'.[56] We might add that we may help provide answers to some of these questions through the ministry of instruction.

When speaking of presence, we should recognise that absence can also

---

[54] Nouwen, 2006, p.10
[55] Boyd, 2000, p.85,
[56] Nouwen, 2006, p.7.

be important. At times, withdrawing our presence is necessary for the care-seeker to make progress in faith. As Jesus prepared his disciples for his death, he made a remarkable statement: 'it is to your advantage that I go away'.[57] This must have sounded outrageous to the disciple. How could it possibly be better not to have the person they had come to trust in with them in person? Jesus explained with two reasons. First, only when he left could the Holy Spirit come to comfort them. Not only would the Spirit continue to do what Jesus had done for them – feeding, restoring, protecting and guiding them – but through the Spirit living in them, Jesus' presence could extend across the world. We can have confidence to be absent from people in need because the Spirit continues to be with them when we are not.

Secondly, Jesus said that the Spirit would enable the disciples to learn new truths they could not learn while he was with them.[58] Similarly, pastoral absence creates space for people to encounter the Holy Spirit and learn what we cannot teach. Sometimes this will happen by reflection on words we have shared with the person. Sometimes it will not, but that should not matter if our goal is simply to see the person grow. This means that it may be purposeful at times to reduce the frequency or intensity of pastoral contact or pass a care-seeker on to a different caregiver who can help towards the next step. We need sensitivity to the Spirit's leading to know when to step aside and get out of his way. This is one of the key reasons why we need to set boundaries in pastoral care (see Chapter 5). If we do not, we risk transgressing the proper limits of our part in people's healing and trying to do what only the Spirit can do. We also risk creating unhealthy dependency on us rather than life-giving trust in God.

REFLECTION

- When have you been helped or helped someone else through a simple supportive presence? Give thanks to God for that experience and reflect on how you can fulfil this ministry even more faithfully.

---

[57] John 16:7
[58] John 16:13

The Ministry of Provision

There is little point speaking of soul care and cure if we do not consider the physical needs of people. Christ modelled the ministry of provision when he fed the crowds and healed the sick. The New Testament churches practised it, both spontaneously [59] and by design in their organised responses to the needs of widows.[60] It is expected in Jesus' parables,[61] and commanded in the epistles as a natural outworking of love.[62] In theory, many material needs are met by the State in modern Western countries. In reality, there are many gaps in welfare provision.

Pastoral caregivers can mobilise practical help from the church, such as food donations, babysitting, transport, gardening, home cleaning or repairs, washing and ironing. They can also connect people with help from charities and statutory bodies. In doing this, however, pastoral caregivers should not lose sight of the priority of soul care and cure. Material provision should be one part of a pastoral care approach that includes presence, intercession and, where possible, instruction. It is important, however, not to make such provision dependent on the care-seeker's interest in the gospel. In the pattern of Christ, it should be given freely.

Material provision is always important in crises. As the situation stabilises, our commitment to the growth of care-seekers means we should work to develop their capacity to provide for their own material needs and even to contribute to the needs of others as far as they can. Provision should, therefore, include education and training in skills as well as donations. Whilst we should have this aim, there will inevitably be some people who, due to poor mental or physical health or social factors, require long-term practical support from the church community.

---

[59] See Acts 2 and 4
[60] Acts 6; 1 Timothy 5:3-15
[61] Matthew 25:31ff.
[62] 1 John 3:17

REFLECTION

- How is material provision coordinated in your church and how could it be improved?

The Ministry of Intercession

Prayer is central to gospel-shaped pastoral care because our confidence is in God's work in people's lives. Dietrich Bonhoeffer writes that 'spiritual love will speak to Christ about a brother more than to a brother about Christ'.[63] We pray for two reasons. Firstly, prayer changes us. It shifts us from dependence on self to dependence on our Father and replaces our anxieties with peace and thankfulness.[64] Secondly, prayer changes things. Scripture assures us that, 'The prayer of a righteous person has great power as it is working'.[65] This principle is easily misunderstood. We cannot claim that something happened because we prayed for it that could not have happened if we did not. God works out his eternal purpose and does not need us to do so. At the same time, we must not say that our prayers are unimportant or ineffective. God chooses to use our prayers to accomplish things and we have the privilege through prayer of becoming part of God's work. As Blaise Pascal wrote, prayer gives us the 'dignity of causality'.[66] If this seems odd, C.S. Lewis reminds us that it 'is not really [...] less strange [...] than that my other actions should do so'.[67] In our prayers as in our presence and provision, God uses us as instruments of his will.

Since prayer is joining in God's work, its priorities are not for us to decide. They are set in Scripture. New Testament prayers, including the 'Lord's Prayer' and the apostle Paul's prayers for the churches, teach us how to pray for others.[68] In line with these examples, we should:

---

[63] Bonhoeffer, 1954, p.36
[64] Matthew 6:5-8; Philippians 4:6-7
[65] James 5:16b
[66] Pascal, 1958, para. 513
[67] Lewis, 2018, p.10-11
[68] See Matthew 6:5-13; Ephesians 3:14-2; Philippians 1:9-11; 4:6-7; Colossians

- acknowledge God as our Sovereign Lord, loving Father and wise Shepherd;

- recognise our place in God's purposes and our unity with all God's people;

- request wisdom to discern the best path, strength to endure, provision for needs, protection from the evil one and the world's opposition, and power from the Spirit to serve God and resist temptation;

- seek forgiveness and grace to forgive others and transformation into Christlikeness through life's experiences.

These are always legitimate things to pray both for oneself and for others. Prayers from Scripture can also help suffering people, who may struggle to formulate their own words, to begin to voice their prayers.

The heart of true prayer is surrender to God's will. This principle is clear at three pivotal moments in Luke's Gospel: Mary accepting Gabriel's words; the prayer the Lord taught his disciples; and Jesus' prayer in Gethsemane before the cross.[69] The prayer of faith trusts that God knows best even when we cannot understand. We pray sincerely for what we think is best but acknowledge God's infinite wisdom, power and goodness. This fact should cause us to understand that the phrase 'God answered our prayers' is true not only when we got what we asked for. Our Father knows what we need and will not give us something bad.[70] So, we can accept his wisdom in answering 'no', confident in his promised grace to sustain us through any situation.[71]

We do not pray primarily to get what we want, but to deepen our faith in God and increase our obedience. Prayer should, therefore, surround everything we do in pastoral care. In personal prayer before pastoral meetings, we acknowledge our limitations and offer our availability. In

---

1:9-14; Philippians; James 5:13-18

[69] See Luke 1:38; 11:2; 22:42
[70] Matthew 6:5-8; 7:7-11
[71] 1 Corinthians 10:13; 2 Corinthians 12:9

prayers with care-seekers, we model trust in God and surrender to him. In prayers for care-seekers in their absence, we pray for God to work in their need and to guide us in how we can be his instruments. As we engage in pastoral care, we seek prayerful support from others in the church community and encourage care-seekers to pray as well.

So far, I have discussed prayer generally, but the specific kind of prayer that is a ministry within pastoral care is 'intercession'. To intercede for others means to bring them before God to seek his power and grace in their needs. This kind of prayer is modelled several times in the Old Testament: Abraham interceded for Sodom on behalf of Lot;[72] innocent Moses interceded for idolatrous Israel after their worship of the golden calf;[73] Daniel and Ezra interceded for the remnant of Israel, confessing sins of which they were not personally guilty.[74] The prime biblical example is, however, Jesus' prayer for those who would believe in him recorded in John 17. He prayed for:

- our protection in the Father's care from the evil one (verses 11 and 15);
- our sanctification by God's truth (verse 17);
- our unification in God's love (verse 21);
- our testimony to the world (verses 21-23); and
- our ultimate glorification in his Father's presence (verse 24).

Hebrews tells us that the risen and ascended Jesus continues to intercede for his people.[75] Jesus is constantly praying these priorities for us! The apostle Paul also referred to the Holy Spirit helping us when 'we do not know what to pray for' by interceding 'for us with groanings too deep for words'.[76]

Our ministry of intercession is grounded in the intercessory work of the

---

[72] Genesis 18:22ff.
[73] Exodus 32
[74] Daniel 9; Ezra 9
[75] Hebrews 7:25
[76] Romans 8:26-27

Son and the Spirit. Jesus is continually asking the Father to protect, sanctify and unify his people. The Spirit is always translating our wordless groans and clumsy prayers into the Father's purpose of making us like Christ. When we intercede for others, we join this fellowship of the triune God, coming 'near to the throne of grace, that we [and others] may receive mercy and find grace to help in time of need'.[77] We are bold not because we have a right on our own merits to come into God's throne room, but because Jesus, our great High Priest who knows our weakness, opened a new and living way for us.[78] We can ask that care-seekers will be confident in God's love and promises. We can plead for their sanctification and preservation. We can seek their transformation into Christlikeness and reconciliation for their broken relationships. We can ask specifically for their needs in detail and for insights to connect God's truth with them.

REFLECTION

- Do you have any doubts about the importance and effectiveness of intercessory prayer? If so, how can you overcome them or commit to this vital ministry despite them?

The Ministry of Instruction

The fourth ministry of pastoral care is instruction. Specifically, we are considering the private instruction of care-seekers, which entails application of God's Word to their specific needs, rather than public instruction through preaching, in which applications will be more general. Pastoral instruction is the ministry of working with care-seekers to discover and apply God's truth from the Scriptures to their needs with the aim of biblical faithfulness. Through it, we should expect the Spirit to bring lasting change in the lives of people.

---

[77] Hebrews 4:16
[78] Hebrews 4:14-15; 10:20

It is important to be clear about what is meant by the word 'instruction'. It does not mean a one-way process, with the caregiver dictating to or directing the care-seeker. Rather, the caregiver and the care-seeker come together to receive instruction from the Word of God. An alternative name for this ministry might be 'pastoral guidance'. Still, the word 'instruction' is useful because it reminds us that there is God-given truth, found in the Scriptures, which we need to be taught, and that God uses other believers to teach us. Instruction may range from a few comments in the context of a much longer conversation to more intensive, systematic and intentional engagement with Scripture.

This ministry most obviously sets gospel-shaped pastoral care apart from other caring approaches. As explained in Chapter 1, direction in pastoral care fell from favour in the early twentieth century. Despite an increased recognition of its importance among some, pastoral care often continues to neglect instruction even in churches that believe in the biblical gospel.

The gospel should shape the way we instruct others. Through the gospel, God calls us to obey him without forcing us. Pastoral caregivers must do the same when instructing others. English pastoral theologian Stephen Pattison warns against direction in pastoral care becoming coercive.[79] He argues that correction, or discipline, must not be punitive but part of a positive journey of discipleship and entered willingly by the person receiving it. Instruction must never over-ride a person's conscience. It does not dictate or manipulate but seeks to persuade and convince people about biblical truth.

We may think that instruction is unhelpful for people who have experienced suffering and loss. We must certainly be careful to recognise the limited capacity of people in crisis to receive instruction. In our approach to them, we must follow the example of Jesus who applied Isaiah's prophecy to Himself: 'a bruised reed he will not break, and a smouldering wick he will not quench'.[80] Truthful words, even of encouragement, carry weight that can crush. In moments of acute pain and

---

[79] Pattison, 2000, p.69
[80] Matthew 12:20

confusion, it is often best to say little and simply be present. Nevertheless, our conviction that only the Spirit and Word of God bring lasting change should motivate us to work towards instruction over time. People wounded by physical or mental illness need help to encounter God's truth in their situation.

The aim of the ministry of instruction is to move with the care-seeker towards greater trust in God and alignment of emotions, thoughts and actions with what truth God has revealed in Scripture. Pastoral instruction involves three steps, which Pierre and Reju describe as:

(1) listening to the problem;

(2) considering heart responses; and

(3) speaking the truth in love.[81]

These steps can be related to the three body parts that are engaged: ear, brain and mouth. We listen with our ears, process what we hear with our brains, and speak with our mouths. Problems arise when we jump straight to speaking without listening well or evaluating what we have heard.

The ministry of instruction is of such importance in gospel-centred pastoral care, and so often misunderstood, that it requires further exploration. I will return to it in the final section of this book. Chapter 9 will consider pastoral listening and Chapter 10 will explore pastoral speaking.

REFLECTION

- How much do you expect instruction to be part of your pastoral work? How can you be better prepared to do it?

---

[81] Pierre and Reju, 2015, p.49

CHAPTER SUMMARY

Pastoral care is always relational and pastoral relationships deepen as we go to people, show them love, get to know God's heart for them and grow with them in faith. The care and cure of souls, which happens within such relationships, involves four ministries: provision, presence, intercession, and instruction. Presence is a reminder of the God who is ever-present to comfort and heal. Provision is an expression of love that ensures that material needs are met. Intercession brings others before God's throne of grace. Instruction journeys with them through growth in Christ in response to biblical truth.

CHAPTER 2 - DISCUSSION QUESTIONS

1. What mechanisms for provision of material needs do you have in your church or organisation? How can these be improved or streamlined? Is there capacity for these to change over time if needs change?

2. Share about a time when you were helped, or helped someone, by a simple pastoral presence. What made it helpful and what was challenging about it?

3. In pairs, take time to intercede for one another. Afterwards, discuss how this experience impacted you and how you understand the reasons why we should pray.

4. When have you seen instruction done well or badly? Why do we find this ministry so challenging in the church today?

SECTION 2

WHO?

GOSPEL-SHAPED PEOPLE

3. PEOPLE OF GOD

It was the day after Sam's email arrived and Jude did not know how to reply. She was tempted to ask, 'Is that not your job?' or 'Is there not someone better qualified?' She felt flattered that Sam would ask her, but she also felt out of her depth. A small voice was saying 'If not you, who do you think will do it?', but she could not discern for sure if that was the Holy Spirit or her unholy ego. She had never thought of herself occupying any formal position in the church. The thought of seeing her name on the website and in weekly bulletins both excited and frightened her. She did not know if she was more afraid of saying no to something God wanted or saying yes for selfish reasons. She bowed her head and prayed words buried deep in her heart, 'not my will but yours be done!'

Sam was also wrestling with his thoughts. Had he done the right thing asking Jude to take this role? His uncertainty was fed by a celebrity pastor's tweet: 'Pastors who don't labor in pastoral care are only hirelings'. Was he failing in his duties? He never felt confident in pastoral visits, but he did his best to do a couple every week. As a lone pastor he could not see how he could do more. A small voice was saying, 'If you do not get help somewhere, you will crumble under the pressure', but he was unsure if that was the Spirit of God or his chronically low self-esteem. Either way, he hoped God would guide Jude to the right response. He bowed his head and prayed words from a poster on his wall, 'Your will be done on earth as it is in heaven'.

The Challenge of Motivation

If the internal struggles Jude and Sam experienced with their conflicting motives is familiar in your own experience, please do not give up on the idea of involvement in pastoral care. Keep reading! It is vital to think about motivation for pastoral care. Good motives are often assumed in Christian ministry. We know that Scripture warns against people doing ministry for the wrong reasons, but we might dismiss those warnings as irrelevant to pastoral care. Those warnings seem to major on the motivation of financial gain,[82] and it is hard to imagine anyone getting rich through pastoral care. A more careful reading of these warning verses, however, reveals that what they warn against is 'dishonest gain'. While that certainly includes greed for money as a motivation, it is not limited to it.

Pastoral caregivers can be greedy for forms of dishonest gain other than money. Illegitimate personal rewards can include praise, approval and, above all power. There is power in pastoral care. Even a person who normally feels weak, when entering the lives of vulnerable people, will be the strong one. Mixing this power imbalance with the low self-esteem many caring Christians like Sam struggle with creates a toxic cocktail.

Recognising the risk of temptation to dishonest gain, pastoral caregivers must do two things. They must put in place boundaries to protect those they care for and keep themselves from undue temptation. That is the subject of Chapter 4. They must also test their motives. Mixed motivations are inevitable for fallen-yet-redeemed human beings, but pastoral care is more than a human endeavour. It is, ultimately, the work of the one true Shepherd whose motives are never mixed. As Chapter 1 explained, when we engage in it, we are offering ourselves to the triune God as his servants and instruments. We need an understanding of pastoral care that begins not with ourselves but with the God of the gospel.

---

[82] Acts 20:33; 1 Timothy 3:3,8; Titus 1:7; 1 Peter 5:2

REFLECTION

- Do you struggle with mixed motivations? If so, how can you handle them so that they do not paralyse you and you do not give in to the wrong motives?

God in Gospel Perspective

In Chapter 1, we saw that the gospel is not an impersonal saving force or set of truths. It is the powerful word of God through which he calls people into trusting relationship with himself. Gospel-shaped pastoral care, then, begins with a gospel vision of God. We can begin to build a picture of who God is by thinking of the five acts of the gospel story.

God rules – the sovereign Father

'In the beginning God'. Like the Bible, the gospel begins with the eternally pre-existent person of God who created and sustains the cosmos by his word.[83] God is sovereign over everything, but his sovereignty is not only worked out in his big-scale governance of the universe. The dramatic landscape painting of God's power over creation in Genesis 1 is beautifully balanced in Genesis 2 by a domestic portrait of tender care for the people he crafted by hand and placed in a designer garden home. God attends perfectly to the 'big story' of human history *and* to the little details of human stories. This same truth is demonstrated in the book of Daniel, where we read of God's sovereign power at work in both the rise and fall of empires and in the protection of his beloved servants.

Perhaps a richer word than sovereignty to describe God's rule is providence. It refers to God's caring provision for the needs of each person as he works out his purposes. This providential knowledge and concern is expressed beautifully in Psalm 139.[84] As we engage in pastoral care, we do so with confidence that God is intimately concerned with individuals in the

---

[83] Genesis 1:1,3; Hebrews 1:3
[84] See especially verses 1-6 and 16-17 of Psalm 139.

details of their lives. He is not distant and uninvolved, but near and active. Whatever chaos we encounter in the news headlines or in our noisy headspaces, God is not out of control. His limitless power is guided by his boundless wisdom.[85]

God's word is not merely upholding of the universe. It is addressed to us. He spoke the so-called 'creation mandate' to our first parents: 'Be fruitful and multiply and fill the earth and subdue it and have dominion over […] every living thing'.[86] This is a vision of great liberty. Within this freedom, God made the man and the woman morally accountable by issuing one prohibition, against eating the fruit of the tree of the knowledge of good and evil.[87] This limitation was for their good. It is not to our advantage to experience both good and evil. They had to trust God's word that the consequence of disobedience would be death and that meant trusting that his motivation was only good and pure.

Even here, God gave them freedom. He did not bar them from accessing the tree. They could either obey or reject his words. Life was, thus, to be lived by faith and faith is a response to words. To trust God's words is to trust him.[88] That is how relationships work. Words create understanding, invite trust and assure of intentions. We have God's words recorded in Scripture. Through them, he brings himself into our understanding, invites us to trust him and assures us of his good intentions. The gospel calls us to confidence in God and his word.

We rebelled – false gods

An anomaly appeared in God's good creation: a talking serpent who questioned God's words.[89] Revelation tells us he was none other than Satan.[90] His questions were not innocent. They were an invitation to join

---

[85] Romans 11:33.

[86] Genesis 1:28

[87] Genesis 2:16-17

[88] See, for example, Psalm 56:10-11, which equates trust in God's word with trust in Him.

[89] Genesis 3:1

[90] Revelation 12:9; 20:2

his rebellion against God. With his words, the devil brings his thoughts into our understanding, invites us to trust our own judgement and assures us of good consequences if we do so. In a reversal of the dominion God had granted them over the animals, Eve and Adam followed the serpent's lead. God had warned them. They disobeyed. This is the essence of sin: distrusting God, rejecting him, rebelling against him. From this root a plethora of different sins grows.

God's response to Adam and Eve reveals his character. There was no immediate act of judgement. Rather, he sought them out, spoke to them and served them by giving them skins to cover their shame.[91] He promised that the serpent would not always have his way. There would be a battle to the death between him and Eve's descendants, raising the hope that a human being would one day triumph over temptation and destroy Satan's power.[92] Even exclusion from the Garden was a sign of God's grace. It was not to prevent them from returning to him, but to stop them from living forever in rebellion against him.[93] Death was the consequence of sin, yes, but it was also an opportunity to return to Eden for those who would return to God and trust in him once more. The possibility of return is left open, but it is somehow tied up with the serpent-crushing descendant of the woman.

Sin has not rendered us totally incapable of knowing truth about God. By observing creation, we may still perceive, 'His invisible attributes, namely, his eternal power and divine nature'.[94] Yet, people continue to reject their Creator, instead creating gods for themselves.[95] The essence of sin is rejecting God, but when we do that, we end up exchanging God for lesser things. It is vital that we realise, though, that our problem is not simply ignorance or weakness, but a wilful preference to devote ourselves to things we think we can comprehend or control. The ancients did this by personifying powers of nature in a pantheon of gods they could placate and flatter. Moderns, instead, make idols of humanity. Their devotion is to the

---

[91] Genesis 3:9,11, 21
[92] Genesis 3:15
[93] Genesis 3:22
[94] Romans 1:20
[95] Romans 1:21-23

pursuit of other's opinions or simply to themselves. They may not have statues of household gods on a shelf or in a cupboard, but they have idols in every recess of their hearts. False gods they thought they could control or manipulate for personal gain, but which repay them with nothing but death. Sometimes the idolatry looks like fun and freedom. Sometimes it is patently slavery and misery. In the long run it is always deadly.

Tragically, false gods initially seem like something we can control, but they end up controlling us. We become trapped in addictions and compulsions. We are ensnared in the destructive consequences of our own selfish choices. Behind every idol is the deception of the devil, who has been lying ever since the beginning, telling us that this idol can give us something we want or need and that the path that seems right to us is good. If 'God' appears in the equation at all, it is a god of our own imagining, like some cuddly grandfather who would never chastise us. The God of the Bible is painted as a controlling abuser imagined by less enlightened minds. He is portrayed not as a God of providence but as a cosmic spoilsport. As idolators and rebels, we stand before a holy God against whom sin is a personal offence. We are without excuse, subject to death and to God's wrath.[96]

God rescues – the incarnate Son

God's rescue plan for human beings began with Abraham, through whose descendants he promised to bless all nations.[97] In the fourth generation of his dysfunctional family, the embryonic nation of Israel went into Egypt for protection from a famine, eventually becoming enslaved there. Roll on Moses, who led Israel, now a great people as God had told Abraham they would be, out of Egypt towards the promised land and received in the Law God's standards of right and sacrifices for the people's wrong. After Moses' death the nation entered the land God had promised Abraham and for generations they struggled against the peoples who already lived there and newcomers like the Philistines. This struggle to

---

[96] Romans 1:18.
[97] Genesis 12:1-3; 20:15-18

possess the land was, however, a symptom of a deeper struggle against God's rule, which persisted despite his repeated raising of judges to deliver them. The people thought the answer was a strong king, so God let them taste what that was like through the messed-up man called Saul, before giving them king David, who was told that his descendant would rule over an eternal kingdom.[98]

The shape of God's relationship with Israel was a covenant, meaning a set of binding promises accompanied by a sign (in this case circumcision). The covenant began with Abraham and to its promises were added the law under Moses and the eternal kingship under David. We should not take for granted how amazing it is that God the sovereign Creator should bind himself to people in a covenant. This is the providence of God in working out salvation. The God who wants to live with his people and for them to know him but who is separated from them by their sin.

God was faithful but Israel was unfaithful. The nation followed Adam's example in rebellion and idolatry. Many of them abandoned sacrifices to God altogether in favour of worshipping other gods. For many of those who kept sacrificing to God, their sacrifices, rather than being expressions of repentance and faith, became empty rituals or declarations of self-righteousness. God judged them through exile, but he also promised through prophets a coming king in David's line under whose reign the Spirit would transform God's people. The last of those prophets, a wild man named John, was sent to prepare the way for this deliverer. When Jesus, who he recognised as the promised one, came to be baptised by him, John received an insight that would transform our understanding of God. A voice from heaven called Jesus his Son, while the Holy Spirit descended on Jesus in the form of a dove.[99] Israel's God revealed to be three in one: Father, Son and Spirit.

A gospel understanding of God centres on Jesus who brought the attributes of the invisible God into visible space and time. He was the embodiment of God's powerful Word and liberating truth.[100] The God who

---

[98] 2 Samuel 7:8-16
[99] Matthew 3:13-17
[100] John 1:1,14; 8:31-38.

reached out in words now reaching out hands of flesh and bone. From Jesus shone the grace and truth God had shown to Israel magnified to the next level.[101] Obedient to the law, loving outcasts, submitting to His Father's will, Jesus taught his followers that they too could know God as Father and receive new and eternal life through the Spirit's power.[102] His mighty miracles and powerful teaching displayed the power of God's sovereign word. His compassion to the broken and marginalised revealed God's tender justice. His death as our substitute and sin-bearer upheld both love and justice. Sinners could be declared right with God without ignoring their sin.[103] Jesus' resurrection affirmed the unquenchable power of God's love and the indestructibility of the life God offers to those who return to him.

We respond – the true God

If sin rejects God's rule, faith returns to acknowledge it. The gospel calls us to admit our rebellion, lay down our arms and submit again to God, acknowledging that he is right in his judgement and trusting in his promise of salvation. God accepts those who come to him through Jesus. When we came to faith in Jesus as Saviour and Lord, we 'turned to God from idols to serve the living and true God'.[104] We must turn from idols. This is what we can call repentance. It means admitting that our idols are false and that our actions in following them have brought death to us and offended God, then saying no to them and to the lies of Satan that lie behind them. We must turn to God. This is what we call faith. It means admitting that God is true and that his commands bring life to us and pleasure to him, then saying yes to him, trusting in Jesus for forgiveness for our sins and entrusting our lives to him as Lord.

For modern people, the central issue in turning *from* idols is dethroning the self. I need to remove myself from the throne of my life to make way for its true king, Jesus. This means not only giving up my sense of my right

---

[101] John 1:14
[102] See John 3:5-8
[103] Romans 3:26
[104] 1 Thessalonians 1:9

to choose for myself, but also rejecting self-satisfaction or self-protection as the goal of life. As Jesus put it, that means recognising that I cannot keep my own life, but if I lose it for his sake and the gospel then I gain eternally.[105] When we realise the power and majesty of the true God, we see our inadequacy. When we recognise the goodness and grace of the living God, we surrender our independence. We humble ourselves before him, casting ourselves on his mercy and grace.

God restores – the indwelling Spirit

The gospel story begins with God in creation, centres on God in Christ in redemption, and climaxes with God in believers by the Spirit. Jesus promised his disciples that after his departure the Holy Spirit would come to lead them into fuller knowledge of God and empower them to make him known to others.[106] The Spirit works a new creation in the lives of those who trust in Christ as they believe the gospel.[107] He leads us to do God's will and changes us to become more like Jesus.[108] The Spirit is a deposit guaranteeing that God will complete this transformative work in us when Christ returns in the glory of the fullness of the new creation.[109]

The work of the Spirit is not only in the individual believer. He also unites us in Christ with others in the Church, the new humankind.[110] This reality is now imperfectly expressed in the counter-cultural communities we call churches. Involvement in a church fellowship expresses our interdependence with others in Christ. It should not be based on consumerism (what do we get out of it?), convenience (what demands the least from me?), or commonalities (where are the people my age, ethnicity, culture, style, etc.?) but on commitment to work towards seeing one another become like Christ. It is in this context that we can grow in Christlikeness, and it is in the church that pastoral care operates.

---

[105] Matthew 16:25
[106] John 14:15ff.; Acts 1:5,8
[107] 2 Corinthians 5:17; 4:5-6
[108] 2 Corinthians 3
[109] Ephesians 1:14; 2 Peter 3:13
[110] 1 Corinthians 12:12-14; Ephesians 2:15

REFLECTION

- How does this gospel understanding of the person of God shape the way you live, how you think of other people and how you care for them?

Servants of the triune God: motivation, methods and means

The gospel begins with God the Father in creation, centres on God the Son in redemption and reaches completion with God the Spirit in restoration. In pastoral care we offer ourselves to God, Father, Son and Holy Spirit, in his work in others. This triune fellowship shapes our motivation, method and means.

Motivation: the compassion of the Father

We act out of our hearts. My motivations are a mixture of self-seeking and selflessness because my character is a mixture of sin's desolation and the Spirit's restoration. God's actions also flow from his heart, but he is flawless and utterly consistent. He loves because He *is* love.[111] He acts justly because He *is* light.[112] To care for others, then, we must share God's heart and grow towards his character. From God's providential care, we learn to honour people as precious individuals created and loved by God. From God's Father heart, we learn to feel for others as he does.

The heart attitude we need in pastoral care is often described as 'empathy'. Empathy (from Greek en-, 'in', and pathos, 'suffering') means sharing *in* another person's suffering; putting ourselves in their shoes. This may sound like a great quality for pastoral caregivers, but the concept of empathy is problematic for three reasons.[113]

---

[111] 1 John 4:8
[112] 1 John 1:5
[113] For a discussion of the limitations of empathy from a psychologist's perspective, see Kwon, 2017

Firstly, empathy overwhelms. In a crisis, decisive action is needed. If you enter into a care-seeker's suffering, you may be paralysed along with him. A degree of emotional 'distance' is needed. This does not mean developing a hard heart that is so calloused it cannot feel. It does mean recognising that your role in this moment is to be strong where the other person is weak. In ongoing relationships, too, you cannot carry the burdens of everyone you care for. As Chapter 4 will explain, you must stay emotionally and spiritually healthy to be able to help others. Otherwise, you could develop so-called 'compassion fatigue'. Empathy may not help with that.

Secondly, empathy misleads. When people say they 'empathise', they are not truly feeling the other person's emotions, as if there were some psychic link between them. They are imagining what they might feel like or remembering what they felt like in a similar situation. That is not always helpful. I might think someone is 'overreacting' because I coped differently. I may advise a course of action that 'worked' for me when it may not be best for them. It is often deeply unhelpful for people to be told, 'I know what you are feeling'. Every experience is different, and every person is unique, so people react differently to circumstances that may look similar.

'Empathy' may blind us to needs and perspectives that differ from what we expected. It is more honest, and less threatening, to say, 'I can only imagine how you must feel', or to recount how you felt at a similar time in your own life and allow the person to identify resonances with your experience. Only God is truly empathic. Nothing is hidden from the Father's sight.[114] Christ experienced every temptation.[115] The indwelling Spirit knows us from the inside. This knowledge can be hugely helpful for suffering people. We can honestly say, 'God knows exactly how you feel'.

Thirdly, empathy feeds prejudice. It favours those who are most like us, with whom we can identify, and neglects people of different backgrounds and cultures. Such favouritism or partiality is a sworn enemy of faithful care, the antithesis of God's character and one of the most frequently condemned qualities in the New Testament.[116] When we are seeking to

---

[114] Hebrews 4:13
[115] Hebrews 4:15
[116] Acts 10:34; Romans 2:11; Galatians 2:6; Ephesians 6:9; Colossians 3:25; 1

guide people through conflict and relational difficulties, empathy is unhelpful. Intense feelings cloud our view, making accurate moral judgements difficult. Only God is utterly fair and impartial, but we must learn to be like him.

Rather than empathy, the quality we need to motivate pastoral care is 'compassion' (Latin *com*, 'with', and *pati*, 'to suffer'). Compassion is tender love arising from identification with suffering.[117] It is not merely concern from a distance – that would be 'pity' – it comes close, alongside the suffering person. It is never idle either. It motivates appropriate help without clouding judgement or paralysing. Compassion allows us to care for people with whom we cannot empathise because we cannot get inside their world or have had no similar experiences. We grow in compassion not by focusing on the other person, but by attuning our hearts to the 'Father of compassion'.[118] We learn to love others as he loves them.

Methods: servant relationships like the Son

Our methods in pastoral care must follow the example of the Son. Entering the experience of others, Jesus embodied humility and vulnerability. Despite our imperfections we, like him, share the humanity of those we care for. We know weakness and temptation. You need not pretend to be free from struggles when you care for others. You can be what Henri Nouwen called a 'wounded healer', ready 'to offer your own faith experience and to make your doubts and hopes, failures and successes, loneliness and woundedness, available to others as a context in which they can struggle with their own humanness and quest for meaning'.[119]

Christ-like pastoral care means coming close to people in their need, aware of our weakness and dependence on our heavenly Father. The pastoral caregiver understands herself to be Christ's servant for the sake of

---

Timothy 5:21; James 2:1,9; Jude 16 (ESV)
[117] Nouwen, 2014, p.43
[118] 2 Corinthians 1:3
[119] Nouwen, 2006, p.10

others, following his example of being, 'among you as one who serves'.[120] We can learn much about pastoral care from the Lord Jesus. He knew how to listen well, to ask great questions and to give good answers. He always saw people in their whole need and treated them with dignity as people loved by his Father yet needing restoration into relationship with him.

Means: Spirit-led pastoral care

Christ's care for people had a clear goal: that they might know, trust and love his Father by following and learning from him. Jesus' work is continued by the Holy Spirit, who aims to make people like Jesus, so they know, trust and love the Father as Jesus does. Only the Spirit can make people like Christ. We are helpers and counsellors; the Spirit is *the* Helper, the Counsellor, like Jesus.[121] We proclaim Christ; only the Spirit can unveil people's hearts so they see God's glory in Christ.[122] We sow seeds of gospel truth; only the Spirit germinates it in hearts.[123] We pray for God's will to be done; the Spirit intercedes perfectly for people according to God's will.[124] We remind people of God's love for them; the Spirit pours God's love into hearts, working it into lived experience.[125]

Our powerlessness to change people can breed discouragement and frustration, but the Spirit's power to transform hearts should give us hope and inspire us to persevere. As Jeremy Pierre and Deepak Reju write, 'Coming alongside people in impossible circumstances will be a constant reminder to the pastor of his need for the God of the impossible'.[126] The Spirit who changes people's hearts also guides us as we care for them and the Scriptures are the means through which he brings this change.

---

[120] 2 Corinthians 4:5; Luke 22:27
[121] John 14:16
[122] Ephesians 1:17-18
[123] 2 Corinthians 4:6
[124] Romans 8:26-27
[125] Romans 5:5
[126] Pierre and Raju, 2015, p.31

People of God

It should be obvious from this brief consideration of our motivation, methods and means in pastoral care that a gospel-shaped pastoral caregiver must be a believer in the Lord Jesus Christ and that her effectiveness will be directly related to her relationship with the living Lord Jesus. Usefulness in pastoral care is much less about our giftedness and skills than it is about our character and faith. If you want to care well for others, lean closely into your Father's arms of compassion, follow closely after your Lord in his service of others, and depend heavily on the Spirit's power at work in and through you.

REFLECTION

- How can you cultivate greater compassion for others? Do you need to take time to be refreshed in your appreciation of God's love for you so you can learn to love others?

- Why is it important that our understanding of pastoral care is shaped by the compassion of the Father, the example of the Son and the work of the Spirit?

CHAPTER SUMMARY

The gospel assures us that the effectiveness of pastoral care does not depend on us, but on God. We become effective pastoral caregivers when we work in faithful relationship with the triune God. Authentic pastoral care is God-like, Christ-centred and Spirit-led. It is motivated by a heart of compassion in relation to our Father, proceeds through Christ-like methods in servant relationships, and depends on the means of the Spirit who guides us and transforms others. All true Christian pastoral care leads people to greater trust in, love for, and obedient service to God, the one true Shepherd.

CHAPTER 3 - DISCUSSION QUESTIONS

1. Why is a true understanding of God's character (love and holiness) and qualities (power and wisdom in providential care) vital for faithful pastoral care?

2. Do you recognise the problems with the concept of 'empathy' outlined in this chapter? How can you cultivate true compassion without being overwhelmed by others' pain?

3. How is the example of Jesus helpful for us as we seek to care for others? What limitations or dangers are there in making this our standard (recognising His unique qualities as God incarnate)?

4. What would it look like for your practice of pastoral care to be focused on the Spirit's agenda of bringing people to maturity in Christ and dependent on his power at work in them?

4. PEOPLE IN COMMUNITY

It was three years to the day since the commissioning service when the principal of Sam's seminary quoted Paul's words to Timothy as he prayed for the graduating class: 'Do your best to present yourself to God as one approved, a worker who has no need to be ashamed, rightly handling the word of truth'.[127] Those words impacted Sam especially deeply because earlier that morning his parents had given him a card containing the same verse. He took his responsibility as a preacher seriously. After all, that is what he believed it meant to handle the word correctly. He glanced up at the card, now pinned in the centre of the noticeboard above his desk. Sam sighed, then immediately felt guilty. 'Surely a pastor shouldn't feel this way!', he thought. After the 'honeymoon' period with the church, the pressure of a multitude of decisions had descended on him, from the colour of a new carpet to the renaming of the youth club. He felt like the CEO of a small company and the unseen work of sermon prep often felt rushed between all the other meetings.

The church members had welcomed Sam warmly, but this past year had been a steep learning curve. Work as an assistant pastor in another church had not prepared him for the politics of committee meetings or the rumblings of low-grade conflict between people with long histories and equally long memories. There always seemed to be something urgent and he felt he lacked time to assess what was most important. The idea of identifying a voluntary pastoral care worker came from Beth. She said that pastoral care was where the need seemed greatest. If Jude would take some of the

---

[127] 2 Timothy 2:15

responsibility for visitation, Sam could reclaim more time for sermon preparation. But Sam had a niggling feeling that it was not so simple. He had read a blog post that suggested that pastors needed to handle the word well 'in the pew as well as the pulpit'. Was the writer correct that his ministry of the word was as important in conversations with individuals as in his preaching? That thought triggered another guilty memory. He believed that he should be mentoring one or more people with leadership potential, but he had never got round to arranging that. Maybe Beth was right that, if Jude took the role, he could start to rebalance his workload. Sam opened a commentary to begin his sermon prep. Just then, his phone rang. It was Jude!

The Challenge of Church

Sam felt pressure from two sources: the programmes of the church, which he was expected to sign off on, and the people in the church, whose relationships were not harmonious. If you have been involved in church for any length of time, you will recognise the picture. Churches can be riven by conflict and are often intensely busy. At times, the church might seem to work against pastoral care. Negative experiences with church might even cause some of the problems people seek your help with. Sadly, many Christians could tell tales of hurtful experiences – conflicts, betrayals and disappointments. These are especially painful when they happen in the context where they expected to find harmony and comfort. Some of these walking wounded have abandoned church whilst continuing to profess faith in Jesus. Others have abandoned the faith altogether. What are we to make of this? What should we expect from the community we call a church? We need to see the Church in gospel perspective so that we neither set our hopes too high, leading to endless frustrations, nor allow our expectations to be too low, so that we settle for something less than God's desire.

REFLECTION

- Do you struggle with mixed motivations? How can you handle these so that they do not paralyse you and you do not give in to the wrong motives?

Church in Gospel Perspective

The way we communicate the gospel can make it sound as if the Church is an add-on or after-thought. The call is to personal faith in Jesus – that much is true and vitally important – and then it is up to you to decide what commitment to make to a church – that is not entirely true and potentially dangerous. We need to think about Church in gospel perspective if we are to understand the part community plays in pastoral care.

God rules – invited into the eternal community

A Christian understanding of community begins with the person of God and, specifically, with the realisation that God exists in eternal community. Father, Son and Spirit relate together in perfect loving harmony. We cannot comprehend this reality we call the 'trinity', but we see it described in Scripture, especially when we eavesdrop on Heaven's family conversation in the Gospel records of Jesus' prayers. We get a hint of it in Genesis, when God converses with Himself about the creation of humankind in a way that does not happen when anything else is created.[128]

It is clear that life in loving community is vital for human beings as God's image-bearers in the statement that it was not good for Adam to be on his own without a suitable mate.[129] Humankind was to multiply from a community of two in a bond of marriage.[130] Community was to be born out of community. Remarkably, God walked with Adam and Eve in the Garden like a friend talking a daily stroll.[131] Their marriage community was made complete by communion with their Creator. God's intention in creation was that we should live in community with one another and with him. God invited human beings into his eternal community.

---

[128] Genesis 1:26
[129] Genesis 2:18
[130] Genesis 1:28
[131] Genesis 3:8

4. PEOPLE IN COMMUNITY

We rebelled – individualism and idolatrous communities

Sin fractured the relationship between Adam and Eve and their relationship with God. Their marital harmony turned into conflict.[132] In subsequent generations, it set people against one another. Rivalry and competition. Jealousy and envy. Distrust and hatred. All symptoms of our heart's rebellion against God and each antithetical to community. Sin destroys community because it sees other people either as rivals to be eliminated or idols to be worshipped. In the opening chapters of Genesis, these twin temptations are clearly displayed.

Cain kills Abel in a prime example of rivalry.[133] Cain resented his brother and was jealous of the acceptance of his sacrifice, so he killed him, thinking that the removal of his rival would open the path to his own advancement. Community was abandoned for individual supremacy.

The tower of Babel exemplifies idolatrous worship of human potential.[134] The builders resented God's purpose of spreading out across the world, so they grouped together, seeing their interrelationship as a means to their collective glory. True community was replaced with an idolatrous community.

These two stories share a common principle which has marked human relationships ever since. In both cases, other people become a means to our own end, either our advancement by subjugating them or our protection by cooperating with them. Human beings remain capable of altruism – an echo of their likeness to their selfless Creator – but we are inexorably prone to selfishness, pride and greed.

God rescues – covenant community

God's rescue plan was always about forming a community and never only about saving individuals. God called Abraham – an individual – so he

---

[132] Conflict and unhealthy ways of relating between the sexes are implied by Genesis 3:16, however the verse is interpreted.

[133] Genesis 4:1-16

[134] Genesis 11:1-9

could form a great nation – a community deriving from him – that would bring blessing to all the families of the earth – all the many communities of people.[135] God bound himself to Abraham's family in covenant promises. Israel would be a community of people with God, not in the immediacy enjoyed by Adam and Eve in the Garden, but in this relationship of loving care they would have the security they had sought at Babel and there would be blessing enough for all, with no need for conflict.

For people to live harmoniously in this covenant community, they had to cut off their own desires for supremacy. The cutting of the body in the rite of circumcision for male children was an image of the metaphorical cutting off of the flesh in denial of selfish desires. The rest of Genesis shows how sin worked destruction within this family community. Poor parenting – especially favouritism – compounds the selfish actions of individuals with disastrous consequences. In the midst of this mayhem, rare selfless acts bring hope, culminating in Joseph's protection of his family despite his brothers' betrayal.[136]

Reading on into Exodus, God forges Israel, rescued from slavery in Egypt, into a nation. A nation of an estimated million and a half people could not be governed as a cohesive community through parenting alone, so God graciously gave them his Law through Moses. The nation pledged allegiance to God and promised obedience to his law in a renewal of the covenant.[137] Again, however, the hope of blessing for the world through this nation-community was spoilt by their sin. Tribalism and idolatry blighted Israel's history until God exiled the nation from the land. Even after that purifying experience, they were stubbornly resistant to the idea of being a light to all nations. If God was going to have community with people, they thought, only Abraham's physical descendants could be in it. Indeed, only the respectable within the nation could be in the community. There was no place for those who were branded 'sinners'. No restoration for those who stumbled. A fence constructed around the law, supposedly to keep people from breaking God's commands, became a barrier excluding people from the community simply because they did not conform to

---

[135] Genesis 12:1-3
[136] Genesis 50:19-21
[137] Exodus 20

human traditions.

Into this narrow, self-serving idea of community, Jesus spoke. He rejected the idea that inclusion among God's people was based on physical descent from Abraham.[138] He claimed that those who knew God would receive his words as God's truth and people could only come to the Father through him. He formed around himself a new community, choosing twelve disciples to symbolise a new beginning for the twelve-tribed nation of Israel. He told these disciples, who he designated as his authorised representatives (the meaning of the word 'apostle'), that he would build his church. The word translated 'church' refers in Greek translation of the Old Testament to the assembly of the nation of Israel. This new assembly or community would begin with Peter, who was the first to testify that Jesus was the Messiah.[139]

The community of the apostles would become the nucleus of the community we know as the Church. Jesus instructed the apostles about how this community should live together, teaching them the values of God's kingdom and explaining that grace and forgiveness as well as a commitment to truth and purity would be core values.[140] Above all, this community would be marked by obedience to his command to love one another as he had loved them, which would be the prime evidence that they belonged to him.[141]

We respond – covenant commitment

A response of faith to the gospel is a transfer of allegiance from self and whatever idols we have worshipped to the true and living God who calls us into covenant with himself. In this covenant we are also bound to the others who are in covenant relationship with God. Together as God's children we become brothers and sisters. In other words, a person becomes a member of the one true Church when he becomes a Christian. Church is

---

[138] John 8:31ff.
[139] Matthew 16:18
[140] Matthew 5-7; 18
[141] John 13:34-35

not an add-on to the gospel – 'you're saved now, so find a church to join' –
but integral to it – 'as a child of God, you are now part of God's family, as a
believer in Jesus, you are part of his body, as someone indwelt by the Spirit,
you are now united with other Christians in the Spirit'. In this sense, joining
the Church is not distinct from the response of faith we make to the gospel.

There is, however, an important caveat. The response to the gospel
expected in the New Testament is not merely belief in Jesus in one's heart,
but confession of him with one's mouth.[142] For the first Christians, this
public confession accompanied baptism. That is often the case today as
well. When new believers are baptised, they normally confess their faith in
Christ, either through describing their own journeys to faith or by
responding to questions they are asked. In church traditions that baptise
infants, a confession of faith may be made by the child's parents instead,
expressing their hope that the child will grow to believe in Jesus. Important,
baptism is performed by a representative of the Church. It is not simply a
declaration of personal faith, either present or hoped for, but a sign of
inclusion among the covenant people of God and a commitment to identify
with a specific community of Christians who understand themselves to be
the Church in a location.[143]

God restores – the community of the Spirit

As Jesus approached the cross, he told the disciples they would not be
left alone like orphans. They would not have to figure out how to live the
life he called them to or be the community he envisaged. The Father would
send the Holy Spirit to remind them of what Jesus had taught, reveal new
truths to them, and bring Jesus' peace into their experience.[144] The Church
is formed by the Holy Spirit. We cannot understand God's restoration of

---

[142] Romans 10:9-10
[143] This kind of community is often called a congregation. It is common for
people to refer to it as a 'local church'. I prefer to reserve that terms for the whole
Church in a region or city, which is normally bigger than one congregation,
constituting all those in the area who are believers in Jesus and all of the
congregations they gather in.
[144] John 14:18, 26

people without appreciating that the Church is the context in which it occurs.

When Christ returns in glory, all his people – both those who have died and those who remain alive – will be gathered together with him.[145] Until then, only God can see the Church in its entirety. In this sense, the Church is invisible to human eyes. Similarly, the New Testament teaches that God's new creation has already begun in the lives of those who are in Christ,[146] but it will only be revealed in fullness when Jesus returns in glory. We could say the same about the Kingdom of God, which is not seen fully yet, but will be on that day. When Christ returns, his people will be made perfectly like him and will share in his glory. Until then, the Church will be as imperfect as the people who comprise it.

The Church is invisible, but it becomes visible in the communities of believers who gather to obey Jesus' command to love one another, to follow the Spirit into truth and to worship God in words and actions. These communities do not perfectly represent the holiness to which God calls the Church, but in them people grow towards holiness. The Spirit continues his work of making them like Jesus, primarily through other Christians who help them along. Pastoral care is a restoration work of the Spirit through people within and among whom he dwells.

The Spirit can grow his fruit in people through their individual devotion and prayers, but the command to "be filled with the Spirit" was issued to a church community rather than to an individual.[147] The Spirit's fullness can only be experienced fully in community because it is there that we experience the unique gifts he has given to other individuals, which complement those he has given to us. In a church community responsive to him, the Spirit moves freely to make people like Jesus and to make Jesus known through them.

---

[145] 1 Thessalonians 4:16-17

[146] 2 Corinthians 5:17

[147] Ephesians 5:18 – this command is surrounded by other commands that are clearly to the community rather than just the individuals who comprise it.

REFLECTION

- Do you think we place enough emphasis on commitment to a church community? From your experience, what makes it easy or difficult to believe that the Church is the context of spiritual restoration?

The Promise of Christian Community

Christian community is trinitarian. It is formed around Jesus, in loyal obedience to his command to love one another as he loved us and to forgive one another as he forgave us. It is formed by the Spirit, who reminds us of Jesus' commands and enables us to obey them. It is formed for the Father, to whom it prays as Jesus taught and whose eternal purposes it seeks to serve. Church is essential in gospel-shaped pastoral care because it is an integral part of the gospel. We must appreciate the promise of Christian community.

A community of faith, hope and love

The earliest Christian communities were deeply attractive. Luke's account of the very first one, in Jerusalem, reveals its distinctive features.[148] It was grounded in the gospel of God the Son: formed from people who had believed the apostle Peter's message and enacted it in baptism, sustained by the apostles' ongoing teaching of the gospel, and regularly enacting the gospel in the Lord's Supper. It was formed by the powerful presence of God the Spirit: in awe of his works and thankful to him, its members praised God and sought his direction in prayer. It was sustained by commitment: its members were 'devoted' to meeting together to engage in the core practices that enabled them to grow in their faith and they shared time, homes, food and possessions in tangible expressions of mutual care. None of this is to say that there were no issues in that congregation – we need only read on into Acts to see that there were – but the result of this kind of community was that they had "favour with all the people. And

---

[148] Acts 2:41-47

the Lord added to their number day by day those who were being saved".[149]
Luke's account tells us what matters most in a Christian community.

The New Testament epistles never shy away from the problems that
arose in the early churches, but they also paint a picture of an attractive
community resulting from the gospel and the Spirit. They call Christians to
mutual care, urging them to consider 'the interests of others' and 'Bear one
another's burdens'.[150] One of the longest passages about Christian
community, Ephesians chapters 4 and 5, describes three key qualities: truth,
love and holiness. Gospel *truth* is believed and shared so that members put
away falsehood and speak truthfully to one another.[151] This truth is shared
in *love*, so members reject bitterness, malice, covetousness and anger and
promote kindness and tenderness, refusing to slander and readily forgiving
one another.[152] The outworking of truth and love is holiness: stealing and
sexual immorality are forbidden and people are called to work hard in
God's service with thankfulness and submission.[153] Truth, love and holiness
are also exhibited in the church's gathered worship as its members praise
God and instruct one another.[154] These three key qualities relate to the
three features of the Jerusalem church in Acts 2. It was grounded in gospel
truth, held together by *loving* commitment, and energised by the Spirit of
holiness.

We can also relate truth, love and holiness to the three cardinal Christian
virtues the apostle Paul expounds earlier in Ephesians – faith, hope and
love.[155] Sharing *faith* in God's *truth*, we learn to trust one another, accepting
and being accepted, forgiving and offering forgiveness, serving and being
served, teaching and being taught. Our *hope* in God inspires our hopes for
each another's *holiness*. We know the transformation God can bring now
and will complete in future, so we seek mutual growth towards godliness.
From our experience of God's *love*, arises love for one another, enabling us
to mourn and rejoice together on life's journey. In this community of faith

---

[149] Acts 2:47
[150] Philippians 2:4; Galatians 6:2
[151] Ephesians 4:15-16, 25
[152] Ephesians 4:26-27, 31-32
[153] Ephesians 4:28; 5:3-4
[154] Ephesians 5:18-21
[155] Ephesians 1:15-19

in God's truth, love from God's love, and hope for God's holiness, we can be vulnerable in our weakness as we seek God's power.

Real commitment and *realistic expectations*

Congregations are not always the communities of faith, hope and love they are called to be. Alternative, counter-gospel values from the surrounding culture seep into our thinking about church. Hunger for self-fulfilment displaces faith in Christ, so we walk away when we are offended or challenged, even if the challenging idea is gospel truth. Consumerism, with its promise of gratification now, replaces hope in God's holiness, so we shop around for the 'best offering' of programmes for our families. Individualism overrides love, so we suspect and reject authority rather than submitting to godly leaders, while some leaders are ungodly in their own pursuit of selfish gain. Such values feed an anti-commitment spirit that is inimical to gospel growth. People become discouraged, and discouraged people find it hard to trust, to love and to hope for better things. I believe the Church's greatest need today is to rediscover a deep commitment to shared pursuit of truth, love and holiness.

Deep commitment only grows amidst realistic expectations. We must not approach church with false expectations that relationships will be smooth and people will never fail. People will only work through differences and disappointments if they expect such problems to arise and believe that resolutions are possible. Henri Nouwen reminds us that, 'community is not always easy. In every community the healing of acceptance happens and deep betrayals take place'.[156] Pointing to Judas' betrayal of Jesus, Nouwen says we will inevitably find 'someone in the community who betrays your trust or hands you over to something painful or unwanted. As soon as you have community, you have a problem'. He argues we must not expect a community to meet our deepest emotional needs. Perfect love is found in God alone. When we expect others to love us flawlessly, we make idols of them.

Only people who look to God for security, acceptance and meaning can

---

[156] Nouwen, 2006, p.113-114.

commit to community. Pastoral caregivers can help people towards realistic expectations of Christian community. By assuring them in the security of God's love, they can strengthen them to contribute fully. Gospel-shaped communities accept people as they are but challenge them to take responsibility under Christ for their growth in him and service for him. Here, every person's contribution, however limited, is valued. Members of such communities treasure and invest in the relationships they have rather than giving up because they are not all they could be. Only when we rein in our expectations can our communities stick together through the tensions and conflicts that inevitably arise. Dietrich Bonhoeffer reminds us that 'It is not the experience of Christian brotherhood, but solid and certain faith in brotherhood that holds us together. […] We are bound together by faith, not by experience'.[157]

Bonhoeffer has a special warning for church leaders, who often call people to give more time, money and effort to an unrealistic vision they have set. He warns that, 'God hates visionary dreaming; it makes the dreamer proud and pretentious'.[158] A Christian community cannot be led through demands. The only worthy place to lead from is gratitude. Leaders must learn to love the actual people they lead more than they love their ideal vision of what those people 'should be'. In doing so, they discover God's grace for the people who most need their patience, forgiveness and help. Indeed, they realise that they need patience, forgiveness and help from others too.

Bringing people to church and church to people

In a community of faith hope and love we can develop intimate and trusting relationships. That is not, however, the only reason why Church is vital in pastoral care. The Church's distinctive practices, as seen in Acts 2, also form and reform God's people in faith and faithfulness. In baptism, the gospel is enacted (death and resurrection) and people are included in the Church. The Lord's Supper re-enacts the gospel each time it is celebrated

---

[157] Bonhoeffer, 1954, p.39.
[158] Bonhoeffer, 1954, p.27.

and leads us to renew communion with God and others. It is, therefore, essential, to find ways for people in our care to participate in baptism and communion.

Joining with other believers to hear God's Word proclaimed and proclaiming truths together in congregational singing also sustains and deepens our faith. If care-seekers cannot come to church gatherings, we may be able to bring the gathering to them by live streaming services to their home, bringing them recordings or arranging a small gathering of believers in their home. Similarly, people who are confined to home can participate in the prayer life of the congregation if we keep them informed of needs.

REFLECTION

- How can you contribute to helping your church become increasingly the kind of community it should be?

- How can you help others to have realistic expectations and high hopes for the relationships in your church?

Groups of Caregivers and Levels of Care

There are pastors. There is *pastoral* care. Logic dictates there must be a connection, yet the role of pastors in pastoral care is not always clear. Part of Jude's hesitation about accepting the pastoral care role was her sense that something described as 'pastoral' must be the responsibility of people recognised as 'pastors'. Sam, for his part, struggled to see how pastoral care fitted into his role as a pastor among other responsibilities and felt inadequate to do it alone. Pastoral care cannot be confined only to recognised pastors, but we must understand their distinctive role if care is to be truly pastoral. It may help to recognise three groups of caregivers and five levels of care so that we can structure pastoral care effectively in our congregations.

4. PEOPLE IN COMMUNITY

Three groups of caregivers

Within the church community of shared faith, hope and love, the New Testament epistles sets expectations for the way Christians relate to each other. The frequent phrase 'one another' gives shape to these relationships. Christians are to:

- have the same care for one another, meaning they suffer with those who suffer and rejoice with those who are honoured (1 Corinthians 12:25-26);

- serve one another in love (Galatians 5:13);

- carry one another's burdens (Galatians 6:2);

- teach and admonish one another with all wisdom (Colossians 3:16);

- encourage one another and build one another up (1 Thessalonians 5:11);

- confess their sins to one another (James 5:12);

- show hospitality to one another (1 Peter 4:9).

Taken together, these commands expect believers to use their resources and time to respond to the needs of their brothers and sisters. *All* believers have a *responsibility* in mutual care.

Alongside this responsibility on all believers, the New Testament teaches that God gives believers opportunities to respond to the needs of others and diverse *gifts* to enable them to do so. The church community is described as a body, with Christ as the head and each member as a part of it. There is diversity within unity. Each believer has a unique contribution to make. No individual can do everything necessary for the health of the Church. Some of the gifts God has given are listed in 1 Corinthians 12 and Romans 12. None of them equates directly to 'pastoral care', but several have a part to contribute in pastoral care, including:

- messages of wisdom and knowledge (1 Corinthians 12:8);

- helping (1 Corinthians 12:28);

- serving (Romans 12:7);

- exhorting or encouraging (Romans 12:8);

- acts of mercy (Romans 12:8).

The fact that these gifts are given to some believers, does not absolve others of responsibility to care. All believers should share wisdom and knowledge, help, serve, encourage and be merciful to one another. It seems, though, that God gives some people additional capacities, abilities and opportunities in these areas and those people should take additional responsibility for fulfilling them. *Some* believers are *gifted* for care.

The third group we can identify in the New Testament are those given by Christ to the Church as shepherds and teachers. In this book I will call them 'pastors', although they are known by different names in various church traditions, including elders, ministers, priests, overseers or bishops. The noun 'pastor' or 'shepherd' (Greek *poimenas*) is only used once in the New Testament to describe these people,[159] but the Church is twice called a 'flock' (Greek *poimniō*) to be shepherded (Greek *poimanate*) by elders or overseers.[160]

The Lord Jesus used one parable, concerning a lost sheep, to describe both his own love for individuals who have strayed from God [161] and the responsibilities of Christian leaders towards seemingly unimportant 'little ones'.[162] One of his last recorded words in the Gospels was his commissioning of Peter to tend and feed his lambs.[163] This same Peter later wrote to elders in the Church, describing himself as their 'fellow elder', urging them to 'shepherd the flock of God that is among you, exercising oversight' until the 'Chief Shepherd' returns for his flock.[164] The role of elders and overseers in shepherding the flock is an intrinsic part of the Lord's design for his Church.

Pastors have a responsibility under Christ to guide his people in faithfulness to the gospel. They must oversee the relationships between people in the Church and its activities. This must include overseeing the provision of pastoral care. In particular, they must make sure it stays pastoral, meaning that it is focused on the goal of all pastoral ministry,

---

[159] Ephesians 4:11
[160] Acts 20:28-35; 1 Peter 5:1-4.
[161] Luke 15:3-7
[162] Matthew 18:10-14
[163] John 21:15-19
[164] 1 Peter 5:1-4

which is equipping God's people for the works of service he calls them to so that the body grows to maturity in Christ-likeness.[165] As Chapter 1 said, shepherds love their sheep and feed, restore, protect and guide them. Pastors, as shepherds of souls, love the people in their churches and feed their souls on God's Word, restore them into relationship with God and others, protect them from false teaching and Satan's schemes, and guide them in obedience to God, disciplining them if they go astray. Pastors may be *few*, but their role is vital for the effectiveness of the whole church community in its service of God.

There are, then, three categories of people who contribute to pastoral care: **all** believers care for 'one another'; **some** are specifically gifted to care for others; and a **few** are recognised as pastors of the flock. These distinct contributions can be related to different aspects of pastoral care.

Five levels of care

We can distinguish five kinds of caring relationship within pastoral care, which can be placed on a scale from less intensive to more intensive.[166] I use five 'C' words for these levels, which are summarised in Table 2.[167] The first and most foundational level of care is the 'one another' support of the *community*. This progresses to *companionship* when a caregiver commits to more focused presence with a person in a particular need. Such companionship may develop into *comfort* as the caregiver listens to the person in need and affirms biblical truth. The next level, *counsel*, is when it becomes clear that the person needs more focused engagement with Scripture and application of truth to their needs. Some cases need the most intensive level, *coaching*, which refers to a committed relationship over a considerable time of deeper investment into the life of the person needing care.

---

[165] Ephesians 4:11-13

[166] Wayne Oates (1992, p.42ff.) also suggests five 'levels of pastoral care', although his scheme is somewhat different from the one advanced here.

[167] These same words may be used in different ways by other authors, so it is important to treat them as shorthand for my definitions rather than technical terms.

Table 2   *Five levels of pastoral care*

	Level	Description	Providers
Less intensive	Community	Brothers and sisters caring for each other in everyday life with its needs and challenges	All
	Companionship	Supportive presence with and provision for someone facing a challenge beyond the normal	All + Some
	Comfort	Hearing a person's story and confession of sin and assuring them of gospel truth	All + Some + Few
	Counsel	Bringing biblical guidance to people through issues in their thinking, relationships and emotions	Some + Few
More intensive	Coaching	Acting as a guide and mentor to a person over a longer period of time for their growth in Christ	Few

These levels of care can help us distinguish the roles of *all* believers, *some* gifted believers, and the *few* who are pastors. *All* believers should be involved at level 1 (community) on a regular basis and most believers will often be involved at levels 2 (companionship) and 3 (comfort) as needs arise for people to whom they are close. The gifted *some* will provide much care at levels 2 (companionship) and 3 (comfort) and may act at level 4 (counsel) in some cases under the oversight of the *few* who are recognised pastors. If the *all* and *some* are fulfilling their parts, these *few* will be relieved of heavy responsibilities at levels 1 to 3 and freed to focus the time they have available for pastoral care on levels 4 (counsel) and 5 (coaching) for a smaller number of people whose needs are more complex or long-term. This is not to say that pastors should not engage at all in level 1 care. They are also among the *all* and need to give and receive encouragement in the community.

In this scheme, care at levels 4 and 5 is provided by people designated
by the Church with responsibility for pastoral care, whether pastors or
other gifted people working under their guidance. Such people should be
trained in skills needed for pastoral care and must work in accountability to
one another. Importantly, involvement in pastoral care is not a distraction
from the pastor's function as a teacher in the Church. Rather, it is an
expression of it, since counsel and coaching do for individuals, couples and
families what preaching does for the whole flock. In such relationships, the
pastor-teacher applies truth specifically to people's needs.

Relating the five levels to the four ministries of pastoral care

The five levels of care can also be related to the four ministries of
pastoral care, as illustrated in Figure 2.

Figure 2   *Pastoral care relationships, ministries and levels in cura animarum*

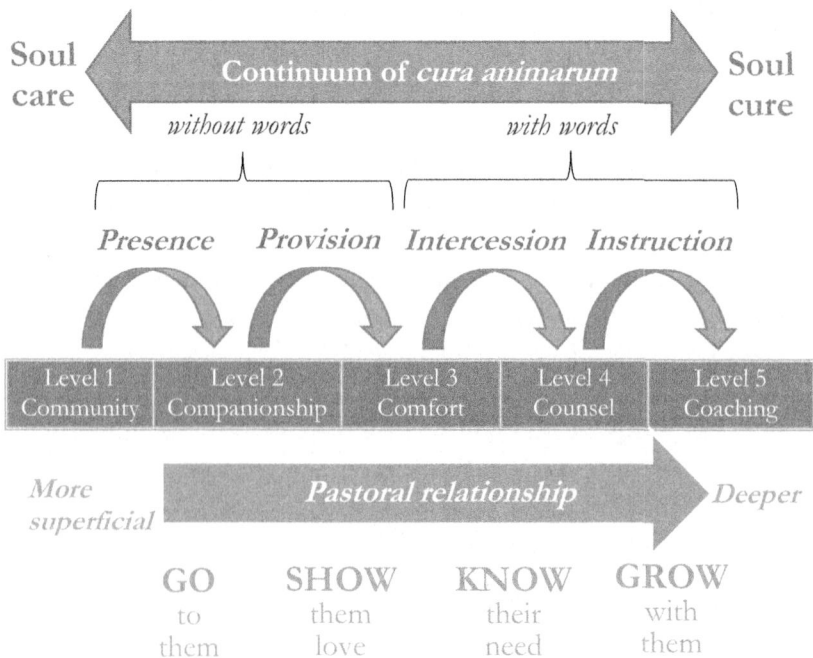

Increasing need for each indicates that care is shifting into the next level. Provision happens routinely in *community*, but those who need increasing provision probably need level 2 care, *companionship*, within which presence becomes more intentional.

If it becomes clear that the person or family unit requires increasing pastoral presence, they are moving into level 3 care, comfort, in which caregivers will intercede more with and for them, often reminding them of Scripture's promises in prayer.

This intercession may lead to a realisation that they need level 4 care, counsel, in which instruction becomes more prominent. If their response to instruction is slow or they would benefit from longer, more structured instruction, they would benefit from level 5 care, coaching.

Importantly, soul care through the 'without words' ministries of presence and provision does not disappear in the higher levels of pastoral care. Nor should soul cure through the 'with words' ministries of intercession and instruction be entirely absent at the lower levels. All four ministries should occur as needed in all pastoral relationships, but the degree of soul cure increases and the pastoral relationship deepens as we move through the levels.

It is also important to remember that the four ministries of pastoral care are not necessarily provided by the same person or group of people. The 'some' who are particularly gifted in pastoral care but not recognised shepherds will play a crucial role in seeing that people in need move smoothly between levels and along the continuum from care to cure.

Structuring pastoral care in church

Having identified five levels of pastoral care and three groups involved in it, we can now think about how we ensure that pastoral care is provided effectively in a congregation. Three questions can help us do so. How we answer them will depend on the size of the congregation and the people who comprise it.

4. PEOPLE IN COMMUNITY

Who provides pastoral care?

In some congregations, a single pastor or small group of pastors, perhaps including elders who are not employed by the congregation, may be able to provide all pastoral care at levels 4 and 5. Gifted members (the *some*) can provide care at levels 2 and 3 spontaneously as needs arise, without any need for this to be organised formally. This can only work effectively if the congregation is small enough for everyone to know everyone else and if the pastor watches attentively over the needs of the flock.

In a larger congregation it becomes impractical for all its members to know each other and there is a risk that some needs are not noticed. There are two main ways to compensate for this. One is to organise a pastoral care team comprising the gifted *some* to coordinate care at levels 2 and 3. It is often best for this team to be led by a gifted pastoral care coordinator rather than a pastor so that the pastor can focus on providing level 4 and 5 care. The alternative is to arrange care at levels 2 and 3 through small groups, each one led or co-led by one of the gifted *some*. In some cases these groups will be arranged geographically, in others by grouping together people with similar interests or serving in specific areas. Given the diversity of gifting in the body, however, I suggest that more diverse groups will be more effective in providing mutual care.

Whether a congregation has a pastoral care team or arranges care through small groups, caregivers should be able to refer people needing level 4 or 5 care to a pastor as necessary. If a pastoral care team is established, the team members or coordinator should meet with the pastor or pastors regularly. If care is structured through small groups, the leaders may meet periodically with the pastor or, if there are multiple pastors, each small group may also have a pastor within it.

Whatever structures are put in place, three subordinate questions are worth considering:

- **What training will the caregivers have?** Pastors and others with significant responsibility for pastoral care should be trained in foundational principles of pastoral care and have access to conferences, seminars and books for ongoing refresher training. It is often helpful for the key people to discuss anonymised or fictionalised case studies as a way to share wisdom and develop best practice.

- **How will accountability be maintained?** It is always advisable for caregivers to be accountable to one another. A pastoral care team should be a team, learning to share responsibility together and to encourage each member of the team. Caregivers must also understand that they are accountable to the pastor or pastors who have a responsibility to oversee them.

- **Who will care for the caregivers?** Everyone needs care at times and caregivers often need encouragement and support both within the congregation from one another or from the pastors. External mentors or advisers can also add value to their work. This is especially important for pastors, who are often overseeing others and not receiving care themselves. They should seek a mentor or pastoral supervisor, either formally or informally, who can provide advice, pray for them and help them reflect on their experiences.

How is care accessed?

Care provision in a congregation can be thought of in terms of the colours of a set of traffic lights.

1. RED: reactive care in crises

A red light is a crisis requiring an urgent response. Unexpected crises, for example a sudden death or a road traffic accident, can arise any time. In a small congregation, the pastor may be the single point of contact in emergencies. Even if this is feasible, however, it may not be advisable. The pastor should be able to have protected rest days and frequent pastoral calls will also distract from a pastor's focus on prayer and ministry of the word exercised through preaching and pastoral care at levels 4 and 5 care. Having a single contact person can also encourage unhealthy dependency on one person and exclude other gifted individuals. It is, therefore, better to have a rota for emergency contact including several pastors or gifted individuals.

A rota allows those who participate to be prepared to respond when they are on duty, for example ensuring availability of a car or driver, avoiding all alcohol, and keeping a Bible at hand. The name and contact number of the 'duty' person may be publicised on a weekly bulletin or online. Alternatively, there may be a single mobile handset or number that can be rotated between caregivers. Other forms of communication, such as email or mobile messaging, are not advisable for emergencies as the sender often has no way of knowing if they are received and they do not allow for immediate clarification of details the responder may need to know, such as the exact location of the emergency.

Three steps for responding to a pastoral crisis can be remembered using the A-B-C acronym used in first aid situations:[168]

A – Airway. Provide an 'airway' for the person to tell you what has happened. Speaking on the phone may be adequate, but it is often helpful to go to be with the person. Listen attentively to understand the situation and identify immediate priorities. Do not ask unnecessary questions – there will be time later to find out more details – simply focus on getting the information you need to decide what urgent response you should make.

B – Breathing. The person may be paralysed by shock and you may be deeply unsettled, but a cool head and warm heart can bring focus. Take a deep breath – both literally and metaphorically – and encourage the person in need to do so too. Break the problem down into its component parts so you can decide what needs to be done about each. For example, what people are directly involved, where does each of them need to be and what do they need to keep them safe and enable them to do what needs to be done?

C – Circulation. You must respond actively to the crisis, circulating the news to appropriate people, with permission so that confidentiality is maintained. You can mobilise emotional, spiritual or practical support to ease the burden on the people in crisis. You should not shoulder all responsibility alone. Get people praying for you and consider whether and when to refer the matter to a pastor if you are not one.

---

[168] Similar steps are proposed by Margaret Whipp (2013 p.77), who adapted them from Switzer and Stone.

2. AMBER: proactive care as needs arise

An amber light refers to issues that are not at crisis point but are affecting a person negatively. Some crises are not unpredictable, but are the culmination of a problem that has developed gradually, such as a death after lengthy terminal decline, a walk out from a marriage that was 'on the rocks' for some time, or a crisis of faith in someone who has not engaged in church community for weeks. In a healthy church community, such evolving needs should be noticed, and action taken to prevent crisis point. We need to watch for warning signs such as a change in physical demeanour or mood, non-attendance at activities a person was previously committed to or comments about being under pressure or finding it hard to cope. Helpful interventions may include initiating level 4 or 5 care (counsel or coaching), putting practical support measures in place, or assigning a gifted pastoral caregiver to be the main 'contact person'. Proactive care needs resources. To be able to respond to developing needs in a timely fashion, caregivers must have time and energy. It is important that they are not over-committed to regular programmes in the church.

Proactive, 'amber light', care is also often needed after the immediate phase of a crisis has passed, for example, caring for bereaved people after the funeral, continuing to support a family after a member is discharged from hospital, or coaching someone after a crisis of faith has turned the corner. It is, therefore, important that those who respond to crises know who to refer people to if they are not best placed to provide the ongoing care.

In smaller churches, people may know each other well and share life together in trusting relationships, so people may notice evolving needs naturally and know who to speak to if they cannot respond themselves. In larger congregations, there are several mechanisms to identify needs and link them with proactive care. I will suggest five, which can be used together or alone.

The first mechanism is *visitation*. The practice of regularly visiting every individual or family in the church was a major feature of classical Protestant pastoral care. It still has great potential to ensure everyone is known and listened to, often in their natural context. Regular visitation can enable pastoral caregivers to build relationships and get a sense of a person's, or family's, life patterns. The traditional pattern of unannounced visits to the home may still work in some contexts, but it may require modification for contemporary lifestyles. It is highly advisable to arrange a time to visit in advance and to clarify who you want to meet with (e.g., an individual, a couple, or the whole family). Visits to homes may be complemented with visits to workplaces, walks in a park, invitations to one's own home, or meetings in coffee shops, especially for people who are more private, seldom home, or living in a house of multiple occupancy. Traditionally, visitation was organised geographically, with parishes divided into regions assigned to individual caregivers. It is now rare for everyone in a congregation to live or work in one area, so a different way of organising visitation may be preferable. For example a group of similar people (e.g., young or older people, ethnic minorities, people with chronic illness, in hospital or in care homes) may be cared for by someone whose gifting, personality, training or experience is most relevant to their needs.

A second approach to proactive care is a *pastoral care clinic*, which is a set time when a designated pastoral caregiver is available for phone conversations or in-person appointments.

A third strategy utilises *small groups* as the front line of pastoral care. Small group leaders keep in contact with those in their group, including anyone who stops coming unexpectedly, and identify any pastoral care needs. If this strategy is adopted, it will be important to ensure that people who cannot or choose not to join a small group are not forgotten.

Specific need ministries are a fourth mechanism for proactive pastoral care, usually supplementing more general provision. These group-based programmes support people with needs related to specific issues such as divorce, bereavement, parenting, and marriage. High quality materials are available for many such needs. This can be a great way for people to use diverse gifts and life experiences to help others. It is wise for a congregation to cooperate with other congregations nearby to ensure these ministries are accessible regularly and for each major need.

A final strategy for proactive pastoral care is to identify *specialists* with skills or training in particular needs who can be designated as champions for that need and made accessible to the congregation. Specialists should normally be given fewer responsibilities in general pastoral care provision to free them to focus on the people who most need their help.

There are many ways to organise proactive pastoral care, but the fundamental need is for a mechanism whereby every individual is known and developing and ongoing needs are spotted and the person linked with the best source of pastoral care.

3.   GREEN: preventative care

The green light means that there is no evident pastoral need. We may be tempted to think that pastoral care is not needed in such cases, but that is mistaken. The best kind of care is often preventative. Building believers in their faith can help them avoid issues that arise from sin and can strengthen them to be more resilient when crises or problems arise. Pastors should consider how the regular activities of the church can best grow mature disciples. This will include commitment to corporate prayer and teaching, learning and applying Scripture through Sunday services, discipleship programmes and small groups. It also includes encouraging people to put the 'one another' commands into action so that level 1 care is a reality. Many pastoral problems can be averted if a congregation is encouraged and if people are habitually forgiving one another.

What are the limits of congregational pastoral care?

No pastoral caregiver can provide for every need that might arise in a person's life. Indeed, no congregation can meet every need either. It is important to be able to signpost people to other sources of care when we reach our limits or their needs are more complex than we can handle alone. People responsible for coordinating pastoral care in congregations should be aware of additional care (for example specialists or specific need groups) available in other nearby congregations, through denominations or networks, and from professional counsellors, charities and statutory bodies (including family doctors, psychiatric services, benefits agencies and social services).

It may be helpful to compile a list of numbers and websites detailing such services so you can easily sign-post people. Preparing this in advance allows you to decide which services you trust enough to recommend them, for example limiting your list to other congregations that align with your beliefs or identifying counsellors who are sympathetic to the Christian faith.

Signposting is important, but it is also important to remember that pointing a person to another source of help does not absolve the pastoral caregiver or congregation of responsibility for the person in need. Whatever help can be given by professionals and experts outside the congregation, there will also be a need for the kind of care that can uniquely be found within a congregation bound together in faith, hope and love. Only in this kind of community will people know you well enough to see progress you are making and to speak truth in love to you. Only there will people stick with you through your time of greater need and through times when you are under less pressure. Only there can true mutual care happen, so that you bring your contributions to the needs of others as well as receiving from them.

Pastoral caregivers should, therefore, keep in touch with those they refer to others and should, wherever possible, seek to integrate the various kinds of care a person is receiving. This may entail communication with external care providers, with the care-seeker's permission, or at least asking the person how they have been benefiting or not from the other sources of care.

REFLECTION

- Are you, or should you be, one of the 'all', the 'some' or the 'few'? What does that mean for your involvement in pastoral care?

- How can you become better equipped for the levels of pastoral care you believe God is entrusting to you?

CHAPTER SUMMARY

The Church is created in Christ by the Spirit to be a community of faith, hope and love whose members have deep commitment and realistic expectations. In this context, people grow together towards maturity in

Christ. God has given the Church shepherds under Christ the Chief Shepherd to guide, protect and feed the sheep. These pastors have a specific role in providing pastoral care, overseeing the work of those who are gifted for pastoral care and nurturing a culture of mutual care. They oversee pastoral care at five levels from community, through companionship, comfort and counsel, to coaching, and should focus their own involvement on the deeper levels of care. A congregation should be organised for reactive, proactive and preventative care through means appropriate to its size and composition.

CHAPTER 4 - DISCUSSION QUESTIONS

1. Is mutual care through 'one another' ministry strong or weak in your church or organisation? How could you encourage it to become more normal and effective?

2. What do you understand to be the distinctive role of pastors in the Church? In your context, how can they stay focused on these core responsibilities?

3. Consider each of the 'five levels' of pastoral care. Which, if any, do you think should be the responsibility of the recognised shepherds alone, or at least closely supervised by them?

4. How is pastoral care currently structured in your church or organisation and how could it be improved? What is clear and what is unclear about responsibilities and processes?

5. Which external sources of help would you refer people to if they have complex needs? On what basis do you trust these sources of help?

5. PEOPLE WITH LIMITATIONS

As she hung up, excitement was growing in Jude. It had been a brief conversation. She had acknowledged Sam's email and said she would like to chat about the role. Sam sounded upbeat when he thanked her and offered to meet her in a coffee shop the next evening. Knowing how tightly pastoral care was regulated in her workplace, Jude had asked Sam for a copy of the church's guidelines to read over before they met. After a momentary silence, Sam confessed he wasn't sure there was one. Jude was tempted to express a concern about that but, not wanting to discourage her youthful pastor, she said, 'Okay, see you tomorrow evening then'. She could explore the limits of the role when they talked.

Jude worried about Sam. He was clearly passionate about Jesus and committed to teaching Scripture, but he was young, with limited life experience. Thinking that way made her feel old! She was only ten years his senior, but her very different journey through life made that decade seem worth two or three. Sam also seemed to have little evident support. The church in which Jude grew up had a strong team of elders. Sam had none. Jude also realised she wasn't sure what exactly Sam did in terms of pastoral care. He didn't seem to do regular visitation to everyone the way Derek, the previous minister had. That thought stopped her sharp. Painful memories and guilt that she hadn't spotted the signs. Derek had often visited her house. His habit of visiting single women at home hadn't seemed a big deal. Nothing untoward had happened with her. But the damage done by his dismissal when it came to light that he was having an affair with another unmarried church member cast things in a different light. She was glad Sam had suggested meeting in a coffee shop rather than her home. Jude prayed he would never go the way Derek had.

The Challenges of Abuse and Misuse

Abuse means literally to use something for a purpose for which it was not intended. When we speak of a person being abused, we are implicitly saying that person was made for something other than what has been done to them. An abuser does not treat other people as an end in themselves. Rather the abuser uses them as means to their own end. This is always wrong and always harmful.

Abuse can take various forms depending on which aspect of a person's being has been harmed or how the abuse occurred, including physical, emotional (or psychological), material (or financial), and sexual. Modern definitions of abuse also include discrimination and neglect. Abuse is, rightly, recognised as wrong in our modern societies and Christians should agree. High profile scandals and countless personal stories have shown us how destructive it is. It should be obvious that abuse has no place in pastoral care. Indeed, in a Christian context behaviours that may not be regarded as abusive in wider society should be seen as abuse, such as a consensual affair, because they misuse our own bodies and those of other people, which become a means to our gratification.[169] This is not to suggest that consensual sins are as damaging as non-consensual ones, but that Christians ought to have a higher standard even than our society in how we treat other people.

It is not enough that pastoral caregivers avoid abusing people. They must also be careful not to misuse what God has entrusted to them. As people of God, we should be committed to using every gift, resource, and opportunity for God's purposes. We misuse our time and our bodies if we serve idols rather than God or even if we engage in Christian ministry in a way that is unnecessarily harmful to our health. We need to know our limitations and to serve within limits.

---

[169] This is strongly implied in 1 Thessalonians 4:3-6, which describes sexual immorality both as misusing our own bodies and misusing our brother or sister.

Limitations in Gospel Perspective

If we are to avoid sins of abuse of others and misuse of ourselves, we must understand our limitations. These, as with every other aspect of faithful pastoral care, flow from the gospel.

God rules – stewards but not kings

God alone is eternal, all-powerful, all-knowing and self-sufficient. Every created thing is dependent upon him for its being. God is the sovereign creator and sustainer of all things. In the beginning, he created the universe from nothing by the power of his Word.[170] Within his creation, human beings were created to be stewards over creation under God (see Chapter 5 for more on this theme). Our first parents were given dominion over everything that lives on this planet.[171] We can rightly be described as the pinnacle of creation, but we are still created beings. We must, therefore, recognise the limitations that result from our createdness. Unlike God, our knowledge is limited. We need to communicate – speaking and listening – to work towards understanding in relationship to other people. We need to breathe, eat and drink to sustain our bodies with energy and nutrition. We must sleep and rest to replenish our energy. We grow tired. God does not. These limitations are not a result of sin, but aspects of our created nature. We must learn to work with them.

Genesis Chapters 1 and 2 describe two additional limits God explicitly set on humankind for our good. These were not limitations arising from the way he created them, but limits set by his words to them. Firstly, they must not work on the Sabbath and must treat it as different from the other days. Sabbath was to be a reminder of their created nature and that God's work of creating and sustaining was foundational to their own work within God's creation. The other limitation was the prohibition on eating the fruit of the tree of the knowledge of good and evil, which was accompanied with the warning that death would follow if they disobeyed. Both limitations are

---

[170] See the repeated phrase 'God said …' in Genesis 1
[171] Genesis 1:26

evidence of God's gracious provision for his creatures and his intention that they would live not only by their natural instincts alone but by his word. These commands made them morally accountable to God and called them to live by faith, trusting in what God said, and in faithfulness, obeying him.

We rebelled – rejection of limits

Adam and Eve sinned by rejecting the limitation God set on their actions when they ate the forbidden fruit of the tree of the knowledge of good and evil. The technical word for this is that they *transgressed*, meaning they over-stepped a line. In doing this, they thought they could be free to become more than they were. The serpent's lie said they would become like God.[172] In fact, they became less than God intended for them, experiencing the constraints of sin and its consequences. Distrust and suspicion blighted their relationships. Communication became tainted by deceit and malice. Their bodies became prone to disease and death. The curse God placed on creation had implications for Adam and Eve too. Work became harder and less fruitful than originally intended. Their environment became hostile to them.

As sinful human beings we have new limitations in addition to those that arise from creation. We are even more prone than Adam and Eve were to temptations of all kinds and we can easily convince ourselves that what is wrong is right. We can be tempted to abuse others or to misuse our own bodies. When we do so, we become weaker to resisting the temptation in future. We may even tell ourselves that we are powerless to do otherwise. This may be an excuse to absolve ourselves of responsibility, but there is also a very real sense in which sin enslaves us and becomes our master. We must, therefore, recognise our weakness and set limits to guard against temptation. God has graciously given us more limiting commands than Adam and Eve had too, which are recorded in Scripture. These are necessary to show us what is right and wrong since our sinful minds cannot discern such truths reliably. God did not give his commandments to curtail our freedoms but to set limits that can keep us from the destructive results

---

[172] Genesis 3:5

of sin and protect others from the harm we may cause them. God's law is good, acting as a restraint when we obey it and revealing our need of his forgiveness when we do not.

God rescues – the perfect humanity of Christ

Jesus was both fully God and fully man. We need to remind ourselves of this paradoxical truth often, especially when we read the Gospels. As a human being, Jesus shared all of the limitations our bodies experience as a result of creation. He needed to eat, rest and sleep. He modelled for us the nature of perfect humanity, constantly listening to his Father, always obeying and never transgressing. He lived healthily within the limitations of humanness. He never transgressed the limits of Sabbath, although he restored its true meaning, or of any other command of God.

Our sinless Lord Jesus did not, however, experience the unhealthy limitations that come from our experience of sin. He never abused another person and never misused his own body, resources or time. Indeed, he was abused by others who misused their power and position. He willingly submitted to this abuse in obedience to his Father and for our redemption. He won the victory over sin and death that we could not. He has taken our place, dying for our sins and triumphing over death by his resurrection, so that we can be set free to live for God.

We respond – gladly embracing limits

The gospel calls us to turn away from our illusion of freedom without Christ and to acknowledge our sin. To repent means to acknowledge where we have been wrong in our beliefs and behaviour, admitting that God's limiting commands were right all along, and to submit ourselves to God's judgement. When we repent and trust in God, we step back within the limits he has set. Trusting in Christ means committing to live within those limits in dependence on his grace to forgive us and the power of the Holy Spirit to change us. Faith means gladly embracing the limitations God has set in creation and the limits God has set in his Word. As pastoral caregivers, our commitment to work within limitations is an act of worship.

It is part of our discipleship.

God restores – transcending our limits

The gospel proclaims that real change is possible. There are no limitations to what the Holy Spirit can do in a person's life other than his good and perfect will. He will overcome the limitations that result from the Fall and from sin and transform the believer to become more like the Lord Jesus. That happens to some degree in this life, but it will be completed when Christ returns in glory. Wonderfully, we can become agents of his restoration work in others. Our words and actions can be used by him to teach others God's truth and show them God's love. He empowers us to do this, but he does not override our humanity and the limitations that come from creation. He may do miraculous things through us as he did through Jesus, but we will still grow tired and we will not be omni-competent. Indeed, that limitation is not a result of sin, but of our created nature. Even after the Spirit's work of transforming us is complete, we will always be limited in our knowledge, our energy and our presence (you can only be in one place at a time!) To deny these truths is a form of idolatry. To transgress the limitations of your created nature is no less sinful than breaking a command of God is.

We must acknowledge our limitations as caregivers. Wonderfully, however, God transcends our limits in three ways. Firstly, he can meet with the person in need in an immediate, direct way without using us. The Holy Spirit can prompt a person as they read the Scriptures and pray. Indeed, we should be praying that they will become aware of his prompting, and we should rejoice when it happens. We can also be reassured that when we are an imperfect representation of Christ, the Spirit can overcome our deficiencies. Indeed, if he could not, we would be utterly useless, since even our best moments are imperfect.

The second way in which the Spirit overcomes our limitations is by storing up the transforming grace people need until Christ's return. We are limited by time, but God is not. We must remember that people will never be the 'finished product' this side of glory! We may labour with them for a lifetime and see relatively little change, but God can carry on his work beyond our lifespan and even into eternity.

The third way in which God will transcend your limitations is by using other people. God does not create superheroes. He has distributed gifts diversely among his people. You have certain abilities and resources (everything God has given you), but you do not have every gift people need. Some of your limitations as a pastoral caregiver are simply because you do not have the knowledge, wisdom, resources or time that this person needs. Working in a team and as part of a caring community is a vital way to recognise this truth and to allow the Spirit to work holistically for the good of the other person by mobilising the gifts of varied believers.

It is not always easy for us to know which of our limitations as caregivers result from creation (how God has made us) and which result from our fallenness (how we have messed ourselves up). Personality traits influenced by creation can be used as excuses for character flaws which result in sin. Either way, depending on co-workers can help us recognise our limitations and their strengths can make up for our weaknesses. As pastoral caregivers, we should also recognise the benefits of setting limits on our actions and thoughts to keep us in a healthy pattern of service and away from obvious temptations. When we work with others, we need to establish 'boundaries', which are 'limits that allow for a safe interpersonal connection'.[173]

REFLECTION

- What limitations are you aware of as a pastoral caregiver? Which of these are due to creation (how God has made you) and which result from the Fall (the effects of sin on you)? How can you learn to work within these limitations and to trust in the Spirit to overcome them?

---

[173] Harbaugh, Brenneis and Hutton, 1998, p.77

Boundaries Preventing Misuse of Self

The scenario of Derek, Jude's former pastor, leaving ministry because of a sexual scandal is fictional, but it is not unrealistic. You may have observed or heard of pastors who resigned or were removed for this or other reasons such as misuse of finances or power. Reliable statistics are hard to come by, but it is safe to say that many others leave ministry because of burn out. We need to understand the roots of drop out and how to set limits that protect our own well-being.[174]

Roots of drop-out

Two root problems result in drop-out from pastoral ministry and pastoral care.

Root 1: Inattention to heart

Lack of attention to our own soul health is a sure route to drop-out. We must take seriously the biblical warning that, 'The heart is deceitful above all things, and desperately sick'.[175] Temptations from money, sex and power – long recognised in the history of the Church as the three areas most likely to derail us – grow in the hidden recesses of our emotions and thoughts. They are fuelled by structures and cultures in Christian organisations that can feed the ego and trade in the currency of reputation. Character flaws can be hidden behind personal charisma and management competence.

The priority of character in ministry is clear in Scripture. In lists of qualities of people who should be recognised as overseers, only two concern competency – ability to teach and to lead a household well – the rest are character traits that should be evident to everyone, especially their

---

[174] For more on this subject, I highly recommend *Zeal Without Burnout* by Christopher Ash (2016), *Reset* by David Murray (2017) and *Rhythms of Grace* (2012) and *Working from a Place of Rest* (2010) by Tony Horsfall.

[175] Jeremiah 17:9

families and non-believers.[176]

Leaders must be *godly*, exhibiting consistency in sincerity, holiness and gentleness. Their motives should be *pure*, not driven by love of money or a desire for personal gain, but selfless in hospitality and good deeds. They should exhibit *self-control* in relation to sex, alcohol and temper. So, people with big personalities must learn to moderate them for the sake of others. If they cannot, they should not be considered for leadership. Faithful dependence on God and growth in godliness are the foundations from which we submit our personalities and gifts to God for his use. Pastoral caregivers should be people who are themselves growing in the ways we want to see others growing.

Root 2: inattention to health

The second root of drop-out is failure to remember our basic human needs for sleep, healthy food, friendship and rest. Eager to meet others' needs or discouraged and tired, we may neglect our own well-being. We may even think that is virtuous. Does the Bible not call us to labour hard and use our limited time to maximum effect? If missionaries and ministers in the past could do so much, should we not be able to as well? But we are careless in our reading of Scripture and history. Warnings against laziness and unproductiveness are balanced with Christ's call to walk unburdened in his easy yoke.[177] Ministry for the passionate and productive apostle Paul was limited by daylight hours, long travel periods, and slow communications. Jesus modelled a healthy pace by regularly drawing apart to commune with his Father. Some historic 'heroes' harmed their families through overwork or died prematurely because of poor attention to their well-being.

Let me state my case clearly: failure to maintain healthy patterns of self-care is not heroic or godly; it is idiotic and idolatrous. If we hope to last a lifetime in ministry, times of intensity should be infrequent and must be

---

[176] 1 Timothy 3:2-12; Titus 1:6-9
[177] Matthew 11:30

offset with times of replenishment. 'Ministry' done in a way that denies our own humanity takes the place of God and is harmful to us and others. If we are going to care well for others, we must learn to live healthily in God's care for us.

Self-limiting as worship

Setting limits to protect our well-being should not be confused with love of self, which is forbidden in Scripture.[178] Self-love feeds abusive and manipulative behaviours and excuses laziness or overwork. Self-limiting acknowledges the biblical truth that my body is not my own to treat how I will.[179] Self-love feeds indulgence of ungodly desires and neglect of healthy appetites. Self-limiting learns from the Creator to turn every desire or appetite towards its proper end in his glory. Self-love is idolatry. Self-limiting is worship. To recognise your limitations is not unloving towards others. As Christopher Ash helpfully writes: [180]

> love does not mean always jumping when somebody calls. There are crises; but there are also many pastoral needs that can perfectly well wait until after your day off. [...] A wise measure of self-preservation and the drawing of boundaries around our time is not the denial of love, but the outworking of wisdom.

We can think of self-limiting as worship in relation to each of the three persons of the Godhead. The Father's compassion and strength never fail. He searches every heart and never slumbers. You, on the other hand, need to be renewed in his compassion and strength. Secure in his providential care, you can develop a rhythm of living consistent with the truth that nothing of eternal significance depended on you.

The Son is the perfect pastor. Our Good Shepherd laid down his life for the salvation of his sheep and intercedes constantly at his Father's right

---

[178] Some people call this limit setting 'self-care'. I prefer to avoid that term because I fear it may lead us too close to the kind of self-love we must avoid. If others use it with awareness of the risk of self-love, however, it need not be problematic.

[179] 1 Corinthians 6:20

[180] Ash, 2016, p.60-61.

hand for his people. You will face the same restrictions in your human nature that Jesus knew during his ministry on earth, so why would you expect to work in a way that he could not? You are not, however, risen yet and you cannot intercede ceaselessly for others!

The Spirit is the ever-present Comforter. He brings real and lasting change in lives and intercedes for God's people according to His will. You, on the other hand, have a limited understanding of God's will and cannot transform hearts.

Self-limiting is worship because it gladly acknowledges that God is God and you are not.

Advice for self-limiting

Good self-limiting pays attention to your heart and your basic needs.

Response 1: attention to heart

Your heart is kept pure through faithful dependence on God. Only he can sustain your confidence that he can bring life where you see no hope and will remain faithful through death itself. Jesus' words to his disciples in John 15 reveal five guiding principles for fruitfulness in pastoral work. Firstly, we need to know we are made clean by Jesus not ourselves (verse 3). Secondly, our Father prunes us through our difficulties for greater faithfulness (verse 2). Thirdly, we are utterly dependent on Christ (verse 5). Fourthly, our resources are the Word internalised in us and prayer according to God's will (verses 7-10). Fifthly, our service must be motivated and sustained by love for others that arises from God's love for us (verses 12-13).

Meditating on such truths can sustain us when it gets tough. The greatest thing you can do for those you care for is to stay close to their Good Shepherd. This means setting limits in your life that create space for time to read Scripture, to pray and to enjoy God's presence. It also means staying in close fellowship with other believers in a community of faith, hope and love where you can grow and be supported.

Response 2: attention to health

You must also pay attention to all aspects of your well-being. Some principles for health in four aspects of your being are:

- *Physical* – adequate rest and sleep, regular exercise, balanced diet, healthy body weight, sufficient fresh air and sunlight, moderate alcohol consumption, avoidance of excessive caffeine or other stimulants, keeping screen time within sensible limits and avoiding too much light from screens close to bedtime, and compliance with sound medical advice.

- *Mental* – evaluating thoughts and feelings (see Chapter 6), maintaining a healthy routine, keeping in touch with family and friends beyond ministry and talking with them about feelings, weekly sabbath rest, limiting social media use, recognising and countering compulsive and addictive behaviours.

- *Social* – investing in quality family time, building and sustaining healthy, restorative friendships centred not only on ministry but on shared interests, engaging in the church community with simplicity, authenticity and vulnerability, recognising the limitations and dangers of social media.

- *Spiritual* – recognising and confessing sin regularly to God and embracing his grace and forgiveness, submitting to godly overseers, engaging regularly in communion, listening to and singing truthful songs of praise, developing good habits of daily meditation on Scripture and prayers of thanksgiving and adoration as well as intercession for others.

REFLECTION

- How can you recognise the difference between self-love and self-care? Pray for wisdom and insight into this distinction in your own life and attitudes.

- What unhealthy practices and habits have you developed and what changes do you need to make to ensure you stay healthy in every respect?

Boundaries Preventing Abuse of Others

If we are to avoid abuses of others, we must commit to ministry in 'simplicity and godly sincerity'. [181] That means our values should be known and our adherence to them should be visible.

Boundaries: what and why?

Boundaries promote safety and consistency by setting intentional limits on actions, words and ways of thinking. A faithful pastoral caregiver knows there are some things he will not do or say and some thoughts he will not entertain. Boundaries will not prevent the issues that can destroy pastoral relationships – Satan's schemes, the flesh and opposition from the world – but they make it easier to recognise temptation, to control desires, and to defend against accusations. Far from being negative, boundaries are a positive statement about the value of people and 'protect the essential nature of persons and things'. [182] They form what has been called a 'therapeutic frame',[183] within which we can focus on care-seekers' needs, just as a picture frame enhances the image and keeps one's focus on it.

Boundaries should not be created arbitrarily. They should emerge from our convictions. Boundaries provide protection for three things:

- **Care-seekers** – the first duty of the caregiver is to ensure she does no harm to care-seekers. The 'power imbalance' [184] in pastoral relationships is not always evident to caregivers, especially if their self-esteem is low,

---

[181] 2 Corinthians 1:12
[182] Mahlberg and Nessan, 2016, p.20
[183] Lynch, 2002, p.62
[184] Lynch, 2002, p.61.

so that even well-intentioned people can easily harm others. Boundaries help to prevent this.

- **Caregivers** – compassion can lessen our ability to control our emotions and it is easy to confuse one emotion for another. No caregiver is above temptation. As the apostle Paul warns, 'let anyone who thinks that he stands take heed lest he fall'.[185] Boundaries can protect a caregiver from temptation. Staying within boundaries can also reduce the risk of spurious accusations of inappropriate behaviour from malicious people who want to destroy your reputation or vulnerable who may misread situations.

- **Church** – the harmful impact of scandals, especially concerning sexual misconduct, involving representatives of churches is well-known. That should trouble us, because the reputation of the gospel and of Christ is inextricably tied to the reputation of the Church. Wrong-doing should never be covered up – to do so would be a denial of the gospel – but boundaries should be transparent, and transgressions should not be tolerated. Boundaries can increase confidence that the Church genuinely cares about people and create a culture within which it is more difficult for predatory people to operate.

How do boundaries work?

Boundaries are not optional guidelines to be taken or left. A boundary should never be transgressed knowingly. It is important, therefore, to follow three basic principles when establishing and following boundaries. Firstly, boundaries must be clear and appropriate. The aim is not to bind people unnecessarily, but to free them to act wisely. Guidelines should, therefore, be easily understood, remembered and applied. Churches should have agreed guidelines, but individual caregivers may wish to add ones that reflect personal values without undermining these.

Secondly, boundaries are no substitute for wisdom. Guidelines cannot cover every scenario and caregivers must learn to exercise 'appropriate

---

[185] 1 Corinthians 10:12

autonomous ethical judgment'.[186] Caregivers must not assume that staying within the standards guarantees ethical behaviour. Our moral duty is not simply to avoid sin, but to maximise love for God and for others. We must not only ask what is forbidden, but what is the very best action we can take for God's glory and others' good.

Thirdly, boundaries should be followed with accountability in three directions. First to those you care for by making your guidelines freely available to them and providing an avenue for them to report concerns to your supervisor. Second, to the pastor or pastors of the church, or your fellow pastors if you are one, who should supervise your work. Third, I recommend having at least one additional trusted Christian accountability partner who can ask you regularly about adherence to boundaries. This may be your spouse if you are married. If you are unmarried or your spouse cannot be an accountability partner, it should be someone for and from whom you do not expect romantic feelings. You should share with your overseer(s) and accountability partner as soon as possible if you think you may have breached any boundaries or otherwise acted unwisely.

A Contract of Care?

Counsellors and psychotherapists often work within a written contract that includes details such as: location, frequency and duration of sessions; cost of the service; and confidentiality guidelines. Such contracts are seldom used in church-based pastoral care. Routine use of contracts would change our relationships away from those of brothers and sisters or fellow-disciples. They could also impede effective pastoral care, since situations are never the same, needs change unpredictably, and encounters often happen in homes as well as church buildings. Pastoral-caregivers need to be flexible.

A contract of care may, however, be beneficial in some situations:

- If there is a reasonable concern of additional risk to either the caregiver or care-seeker, for example when working with people at risk because of intellectual or physical disability or who have a history of violent

---

[186] Pattison, 1999, p.379.

behaviour. The difficulty with this factor is ensuring consistency, so that favouritism and unfair treatment are avoided.

- If a care-seeker expects a contract or finds clarity about expectations beneficial, for example because of a mental health problem, impairment of memory or dependence on practical support with personal needs or childcare covered in the contract.

- If a pastoral caregiver is engaging in level 5 care (coaching) through a process that would benefit from being time limited and structured, with a formal commitment from the recipient.

When a contract of care is in operation, the caregiver must not work outside it without renegotiating it.

REFLECTION

- Why are both innocence and wisdom important in pastoral care and how do boundaries promote both?

- What organisational and personal boundaries do you have around your practice of pastoral care? Are they adequate or do you need to develop better ones?

Establishing Boundaries

I highly recommend that every church or Christian organisation should have a code of practice that is available to everyone. Even where this is in place, individual pastoral caregivers may benefit from a personal code of practice that supplements it without contradicting it. This section outlines the major areas to be considered when setting organisational and personal boundaries for pastoral care. Codes of practice should call caregivers positively to the highest standards rather than simply prohibiting obviously harmful behaviours.

Safeguarding

All churches and Christian organisations should have regularly reviewed policies concerning safeguarding of children and adults at risk. These should include guidelines about recognising signs of abuse and mechanisms for reporting suspected abuse. You must always operate within this policy.

Confidentiality

Confidentiality must be respected in pastoral relationships to establish trust and honour care-seekers. Information must not be shared with anyone else without the prior consent of the care-seeker unless there is a legitimate exception for safeguarding reasons. As Pastoral Care UK states, confidentiality 'does not need to be confused with secrecy i.e. concealing information which could be significantly harmful to others or collusion i.e. explicitly or inherently cooperating with illegal or unethical behaviour'.[187] In three circumstances confidentiality must not be maintained:

1. When the caregiver is required by law or a Court of Law to disclose information to police or a court;
2. When an individual, especially a child or vulnerable adult, is or may be, at risk of harm or injury;
3. When there is reason to believe a person is at risk of harming himself or herself.

These limits of confidentiality should be clearly stated in pastoral care guidelines and explained to care-seekers if the caregiver expects that such information may be disclosed. If you become aware that confidentiality cannot be maintained, you should encourage the individual to report the information to the proper authorities themselves, perhaps offering to accompany them if doing so does not put you at risk. If they will not agree to do so or you are unsure that they will, you must report it yourself. It is preferable to gain the person's permission, but you have a legal and ethical obligation to report concerns even if consent is not given.

---

[187] ACC, 2016, 7.4.

5. PEOPLE WITH LIMITATIONS

If a pastoral caregiver wishes to share needs for prayer with others or to seek advice from a supervisor or another pastoral caregiver, the caregiver should ask the care-seeker for permission to share details. This is advisable even if you intend to share the need without naming them, since others may be able to figure out who you are speaking about. If you genuinely need advice about what to do and cannot ask for consent or it is not given (especially if safeguarding is a concern), share anonymously with one trusted individual who is also bound by confidentiality.

Another aspect of confidentiality concerns the spouses of married caregivers. Some pastors have a standard practice of keeping details of pastoral care interactions confidential from their spouses. I am not convinced that this is best. In principle, it is best to have few secrets from one's spouse and in practice a spouse can be a valuable source of support, accountability and insights from the opposite sex. I suggest it is good practice to share routinely with your spouse about the broad details of your pastoral work and in more detail on more complex situations in which you believe they can contribute helpfully. You should, however, only do so if he or she understands confidentiality principles and commits to abide by them. You should also be careful not to overload him or her. Most importantly, you must not assume that care-seekers will expect or understand that you share with your spouse, so you must ask for their permission. If it is not given, you must either maintain absolute confidentiality, meaning you do not share details with your spouse, or explain that you cannot provide the person with pastoral care, in which case you should refer them to someone who can if possible.

If sharing with spouses is standard practice in your church or organisation, its code of practice should specify that married caregivers may share with their spouses but the church or organisation should also ensure that those spouses are subject to the same confidentiality principles. If sharing with spouses is not the standard practice in your church or organisation but it is something you intend to do, you should explain this approach to care-seekers yourself and be sure that your practice does not violate the code of practice in your church or organisation.

Confidentiality also applies to records of pastoral conversations, whether paper or electronic. Written records should be stored in line with data protection legislation, only for the purpose they were made for and the time they are needed for. It is generally wise to keep pastoral care records to a minimum, only including the details you need to prompt your memory and make sure details are accurate and not including identifying features (e.g., names or addresses) unless absolutely necessary. Keep any notes securely – paper notes are best kept in a locked drawer but should certainly never be left sitting around where they may be read accidentally and electronic notes should be password-protected.

Sexual and relational misconduct

Sexual and relational misconduct is one of the most serious transgressions possible in pastoral care. Its impact on the victim can be devastating and its reputational harm to the Church is rightly severe. Scripture clearly presents marriage as the only legitimate context for sexual activity.[188] That principle should be enough to keep Christian caregivers from sexual or romantic relationships with care-seekers, but Carrie Doehring adds another reason:[189]

Because of the power differential between themselves and the caregiver, careseekers cannot give authentic or meaningful consent to such relationships [...]. Without this consent, such sexual relations are on the same continuum of coercive sexual relations as sexual abuse and assault. While the desire for sexual conduct during an intense pastoral care session may be experienced in the moment as consensual by either or both parties, [...] such relationships are always harmful.

If eroticised behaviour or conversations develop in a pastoral relationship, or if the caregiver begins to fantasise about the possibility, the caregiver should break contact immediately and take measures to ensure they cannot develop further, including passing the responsibility for pastoral care to another caregiver.

Pastoral caregivers should also have clear boundaries concerning face-

---

[188] By 'sexual activity', I mean any activity between two or more people that results in sexual stimulation, especially those involving genital contact.
[189] Doehring , 2006, p.58-59

to-face meetings with care-seekers. I find helpful Billy Graham's policy (also known as the Modesto Manifesto after the California town where Graham adopted it) of never meeting privately with a woman other than his wife or a biological relative. This principle could be extended to people of the same sex if there is any possibility of same-sex attraction. It is seldom impossible either to meet in a public place or, if privacy is important, to bring one's spouse or a second caregiver. Insistence by a care-seeker on absolute secrecy is a warning sign. When privacy is necessary and you cannot have a third person present, you can still avoid absolute secrecy by using a room with a window in the door and sitting in a position where you are clearly visible through it. In this case, you can be seen but not easily heard. You should also ensure there is at least one other person in any building you meet in who knows where you are meeting and that someone else (a colleague or accountability partner) knows you have a pastoral appointment.

If these standards cannot be met, for example in an emergency, you should take extra precautions to avoid physical contact, to limit the one-to-one contact to the minimum possible time, and to inform your accountability partner what happened.

Physical contact

Physical contact can communicate care, but has obvious risks of misinterpretation, temptation and abuse. The following suggestions for appropriate use of touch in pastoral care are adapted from Judith Shelly:[190]

- You should not touch someone if there is a clear risk of transmitting infection between parties.

- You should ask for permission before touching, reading both the verbal response and body language of the other person, aware that the power imbalance may make it hard for them to say no.

- Do not proceed if you are concerned they might feel forced.

---

[190] Shelly, 2000, p.118-119

- Knowledge of cultural background and personality may help you know in advance what level of contact will be appreciated. East Asian introverts probably prefer none beyond an initial handshake; extravert Latin Americans are likely to expect hugs.

- In general, avoid touch if you are alone with another person.

- Beware the danger that some people may think that your touch conveys healing or blessing, especially if accompanying prayer.

If you think contact is appropriate, be careful where you touch:

- Stick to the hands, arms, back and shoulder.

- Always avoid breasts, genitals, buttocks and thighs.

- Avoid any suggestion of flirtatious touching by keeping your hand still (e.g., not stroking or patting).

- Avoid playful physical contact, such as tickling or wrestling.

- Be aware of your emotions and avoid even innocent touch if you think romantic feelings or dependence may be developing.

Financial misconduct

Money is another area in which pastoral caregivers must be above reproach and beware any suggestion of inappropriate financial gain through pastoral care. Boundaries in this area may not be as clear-cut as those concerning sexual misconduct, since some caregivers may be legitimately remunerated by a church or directly by clients, but some principles are important, including:

- Always maintain a clear distinction between your own money and funds belonging to a church or Christian organisation.

- Know how you will handle a financial gift and tell anyone who gives you one what you will do.

- Have a clear principle about who pays for coffee or food if you meet in a café and keep what you order to a reasonable level if the other person is paying.

- Keep a record of every gift you receive.

- Ensure all taxable income is declared.

- Set limits on the value of gift you would accept.

- Have guidelines on how gifts are declared.

- Consider what you would do if a recipient of care suggests leaving a financial legacy to you.

Misuse of power

As I have already mentioned, there is an inevitable power-imbalance in a pastoral relationship. If caregivers are unaware of this, they may inadvertently coerce care-seekers. Sexual and financial misconduct are more likely to lead to scandal than other misuses of power in pastoral relationships but bullying and manipulation can also harm care-seekers. Gordon Lynch writes that, 'ill-timed, insensitive and morally judgmental pastoral responses are also generally damaging to care-seekers' well-being'.[191] Principles for offering guidance without domineering will be discussed in Chapter 10.

Dual relationships

Relationships between caregivers and care-seekers may not be one-dimensional. A pastor may also be the patient of a doctor who seeks his support. An elder may be a cousin of a care-seeker's wife. A caregiver may also teach a care-seeker's children. In a close-knit church community such 'dual relationships' are almost inevitable. They need not be problematic; indeed, they can be beneficial. When you recognise one, you need wisdom to decide whether you are the right person to offer care. Both parties need to be comfortable with the arrangement and you must ensure you avoid conflicts of interest and maintain confidentiality.

Always remember that favouritism and partiality conflict with God's

---

[191] Lynch, 2002, p.71

character, are roundly condemned in Scripture, and have no place in the Church.[192] In pastoral care, aim to keep the focus on the pastoral relationship above other relationships. As Mahlberg and Nessan advise, 'What is called for is clear prioritization, giving priority to the role one has assumed for the church, informed by the values of the culture of God. This requires a great deal of self-awareness'.[193]

Limits of expertise

Pastoral caregivers must recognise the limits of their ability to help. We need wisdom to recognise when we need to point someone to another source of help, whether a more experienced pastoral caregiver or pastor, a professional counsellor or a medical professional. As suggested in Chapter 3, it is helpful to be aware of these other sources of care and to have a list of contact points so you can easily signpost people to them. Above all, avoid giving an impression of competence in areas in which you have no training.

Communication

Given the multiple means of communication at our disposal, especially the ability to send private messages and images, boundaries around communication are essential. In the digital age, boundaries against sexual misconduct concern virtual relationships as well as physical ones. The possibilities for hiddenness are deeply concerning for those who care for others, especially given reportedly high rates of people in ministry ensnared by pornography usage. So-called 'sexting' – sending sexually explicit messages and images – opens a world of potential manipulation and abuse that did not exist historically.

Gospel-shaped communication should always be transparent and pure. It should be factual, courteous and non-flirtatious. We should work hard to

---

[192] Romans 2:11; James 2:8-9; Jude 1:16
[193] Mahlberg and Nessan , 2016, p.47.

avoid potential misinterpretation, including in our use of emoticons, slang and non-verbal gestures such as winks and nods. As an aspect of confidentiality, we should take care not to forward emails or copy others in without the consent of the care-seeker or to leave other communication from them (e.g., thank you cards) in open view. It is, however, advisable to make these accessible to an accountability partner.

Consider installing parental controls on devices used for pastoral communication, whether personal or owned by the church. Give your accountability partner the password and consider giving them access to your browsing history or installing accountability software.[194] Such measures are, of course, no substitute for transparency in accountability relationships, but they can helpfully reduce the risk of straying into dark places.

Strictly private communication with a care-seeker in writing, images or video should be avoided. An accountability partner should have access to messages arranging or following on from meetings wherever possible without breaching confidentiality. Doubtful communication (e.g., containing flirtatious language or provocative images) should be reported immediately to an accountability partner, before any escalation. If it happens, consider blocking the contact immediately. Communication that begins to slide towards flirtation, flattery or sexualisation should never be trivialised.

REFLECTION

- Think through each of these types of boundaries and set your own standards. Seek advice from your accountability partner and overseer(s) on what you have decided and ask them to keep you accountable.

---

[194] For accountability software see xxxchurch.com or covenanteyes.com

CHAPTER SUMMARY

Self-limiting and setting boundaries around pastoral care are acts of worship and expressions of wisdom. Pastoral caregivers should not neglect their hearts and health if they want to be faithful to God and effective in caring for others. Boundaries protecting others from the risk of harm express love for God and others, and can protect care-seekers, caregivers and the reputation of the Church and the gospel.

CHAPTER 5 - DISCUSSION QUESTIONS

1. Why do you think drop out is so common among Christian leaders? What can you do to make the work of leaders in your church or organisation easier and more sustainable?

2. Why is it important to see self-care as worship? Share honestly about times when you have not cared for yourself in ministry and what lessons you are learning that might help others.

3. Review together any existing guidelines for pastoral care in your church or ministry. Do they cover all the necessary points and are they clear and adequate? If not, how could they be improved?

4. Share one or more personal boundaries you would add to the agreed boundaries in your church or ministry, which other people may also find helpful.

SECTION 3

WHY?

GOSPEL-SHAPED NEEDS

6. MADE FOR GOD

It was Wednesday – Sam's day off – but not just any Wednesday. This date had been circled in red on the calendar since the appointment was confirmed a couple of weeks ago. Twenty weeks – the 'big scan'. He peered at the blacks, whites and greys, trying to discern shapes. Then, suddenly, a hand popped into view. It looked perfect, if a little fuzzy. Sam was truly in awe. It was hard to believe what was happening inside Beth's swelling belly. It made him think of Psalm 139. Beautiful words about God's involvement in knitting the body of the unborn child together and making plans for its future. His imagination conjured a toddler in a garden, a university graduation, a wedding day. A thousand hopes and dreams for someone he could barely see and couldn't yet touch.

Over evening dinner, relieved by a positive report and celebrating the passing of Beth's morning sickness, the couple wondered who their child would be. All they knew so far was that it was a girl. Whose nose would she have? Would she be an extravert like mum or an introvert like dad? Would she be clever? Musical? Good humoured? Would she have a disability or be prone to illness? How would they nurture her and how would parenthood change their own identities? Beth confessed she wasn't sure she was ready to be a mum. Sam was more relaxed and said she was too hard on herself. They agreed that, whatever happened, they would never be the same people again.

The Challenge of Self

Who am I? The child Beth was carrying would face that question, just as countless generations before her had. Her ancestors took their sense of identity from external sources – their family, ethnic group and nationality. Moral standards, too, derived from outside – from cultural norms, religious teachings or the law of the land. In the Western world into which Beth's child would be born, all these factors still exist, but they are no longer regarded as certainties. Western culture has experienced what Canadian philosopher Charles Taylor calls a 'massive subjective turn'.[195] We no longer have an agreed story of who we are and how we should live. The only place left to turn is inward. Be true to yourself. Discover your authentic self, then let yourself grow into the best version of you.

The goal of this journey of discovery and development of the self was called 'self-actualisation' by German psychiatrist Kurt Goldstein. American psychologist Abraham Maslow placed this at the pinnacle of his influential 'hierarchy of needs' as the supreme need of each individual, while pioneer of person-centred counselling Carl Rogers described the drive to self-actualise as the 'curative force in psychotherapy'.[196] To help us on the path to this goal, parenting and educational theories, social policy and psychology aim to boost our self-esteem through unconditional, non-judgemental, positive regard.[197] Self-actualisation depends, of course, on having freedom in a liberal society to choose your own path as an autonomous individual. So, the hallmark values of contemporary Western societies are liberty and autonomy.

In practice, the autonomy-authenticity-actualisation project of contemporary Western culture does not deliver what it promises. We find ourselves torn between various 'selves': the 'subjective self' I understand myself to be; the 'objective self' others see; the 'social self' I think others see; and the 'ideal self' I would like to become.[198] I am told to love and accept myself, disregarding others' opinions. Sadly, despite, or perhaps because of, the emphasis on self-esteem boosting, mental health problems

---

[195] Taylor, 1991, p.26

[196] Rogers, 1961, p.350-351

[197] For an excellent Christian critique of the self-esteem boosting project and its failure to deliver what it promised see Harrison, 2013

[198] Parrott, 2000, p.18

are increasing, especially among younger people. [199] The situation is not helped by the image-obsessed world of social media world and the shaming at a distance it enables. For all our efforts to discover and actualise the self, it remains a tricky concept.

REFLECTION

- To what degree do the people you provide pastoral care to value authenticity, autonomy and self-actualisation? What about you?

- What are your thoughts about psychology? Have you found its ideas helpful in coping with your own challenges or helping others?

Humankind in Gospel Perspective

Amidst the confusion of our hyper-individualistic, inward-focused culture, the gospel calls us to a different understanding of ourselves. It challenges us to understand human identity in gospel perspective.

God rules – accountable image bearers

Human beings are, indisputably, remarkable when compared with other lifeforms on earth. Only we blush with embarrassment, weep with compassion at others' grief, and faint with fear or shock.[200] The gospel grounds our exceptionalism in creation. We were made of the physical stuff of the cosmos and share 'the breath of life' with animals, but we were also made in God's image – to make his glory, wisdom and authority visible – and commissioned to govern the earth.[201] Our special qualities are

---

[199] Nuffield Trust (2018) https://www.nuffieldtrust.org.uk/news-item/striking-increase-in-mental-health-conditions-in-children-and-young-people

[200] For more about the uniqueness of humankind, see my article, *Are we just naked apes?*, on my personal website www.paulcoulter.net/apologetics.

[201] Genesis 1:28-30; 2:7

endowments from our Creator to enable us to fulfil this purpose.

God designed it so that subsequent generations do not come into being through direct acts of creation by him. Rather, he created a process of 'procreation' that involves human choices and actions. With the sole exception of the virgin conception of Christ, no human being after Adam and Eve came to be without a decision by at least one human being to take an action that could result in conception. God's good purpose was for the complementary powers of male and female to come together as 'one flesh' physically for procreation in the context of a marriage partnership under God in which they become one in their souls.[202]

It is not just as a collective species that we are special to God. Each individual has dignity and worth because the divine image is inherited in an unbroken line stretching back to our first parents.[203]. There has never in history been anyone just like you. Wonderfully, you have potential to know God's love and to love him in return, not merely as an instinctive response but by choice. God made us morally accountable to him so that the essence of human existence would be faith. Adam and Eve were called to trust that God is good and truthful, obey him and enjoy his loving provision. This is still the biblical vision of a fulfilled human life. Autonomy is, therefore, a dangerous lie. It is good for people to be free from domination and oppression from other human beings, but rejection of God's rule is not liberation and the path to self-actualisation, but degradation and the slippery slope to self-destruction. We were made for God and only in him can we find true life.

We rebelled – dignity and depravity

In a unilateral declaration of independence, Adam and Eve rejected God's rule. Every subsequent generation has followed suit. God declared the consequences – exclusion from his presence, labour in producing food, pain in childbirth, conflict between the sexes and eventual death.[204] God's

---

[202] Genesis 2:23-25
[203] Genesis 5:1-3
[204] Genesis 3

'curse' and our sin have affected our environment and biology for many generations, so that we inherit imperfect genes that predispose us to disease and **ungodly desires. Fallen human beings** are a paradox. We remain image-bearers but no longer perfectly represent God's likeness.[205] We are a mixture of dignity – amazing achievements and compassionate care – and depravity – despicable deeds and callous cruelty. Without God, we struggle hopelessly to reconcile these traits. The philosophies we devise are either biocentric – devising gods from the powers of nature or thinking of ourselves as an insignificant part of biological life, mere animals, powerless to resist our desires – or anthropocentric – worshipping powerful human beings as gods or seeing ourselves as the centre of the universe, god-like masters of our own destinies. The autonomy-authenticity-actualisation project is just the latest version of the anthropocentric lie. It is idolatry of the self.

Sin is all-pervasive. Our root problem is not wrong actions contradicting God's laws, or even wrong desires that lead toward them, but wrong worship because we reject our Creator and turn to false gods.[206] The primary false god, or idol, of contemporary Western culture is the self. It is the object of our devotion. Self-love leads to other false loves – of possessions, praise, position and pleasure.[207] We even reject the pointers to truth God wove into creation.[208] We suppress the signs of God's power and wisdom in this universe, insisting on atheistic origin theories.[209] We ignore the witness of the conscience against our wrongdoing until it becomes numb like cauterised flesh.[210] Without God, I cannot discover a true identity. Whether I look outward or inward for authentic self-understanding, I will be misled. Cultures, nations and even religions may contain some truth but are corrupted by false human philosophies. The heart, however, is an even worse place to look for understanding. It is 'deceitful above all things, and desperately sick, beyond anyone's ability to

---

[205] Genesis 9:6
[206] Romans 1:18-32.
[207] 2 Timothy 3:1-5
[208] The apostle Paul writes of these in Romans Chapters 1 and 2.
[209] Romans 1:21ff.
[210] 1 Timothy 4:2

understand other than our Creator.'[211]

Sinful human beings are riddled with self-deception. David Benner writes that we 'settle easily for pretence, and a truly authentic self often seems illusory'.[212] Unable to see ourselves accurately, we generalise from specific attributes to make a false judgement about ourselves. A strength catches my attention and I conclude I am great. Or I focus on a weakness and decide I am worthless. Arrogance or abasement. Gods or beasts. Attempts at self-actualisation are doomed to fail. We lack the power to become who we want to be and the self-understanding to see what we should be.

These negative psychological effects of sin, however, are not our greatest problem. They are part of sin's effect on us, but the essence of sin – the root of these issues – is our rebellion against God. The growing tendency among Christians to describe sin as brokenness is an unhelpful accommodation to a culture that seeks to absolve us of responsibility. We may be broken, but we are also the breakers. We are affected by sin, but we are also sinners. Sin is a personal offence against God. It provokes God's intense, just anger, so that we are, 'by nature children of wrath'.[213] We were made for God, but we have turned from him and made gods of our own imagining, bringing on ourselves just condemnation. We need rescued!

God rescues – loved and redeemed

From among the rebel masses of humanity, God formed a people with a new identity. He called Abram – whose name meant 'exalted father' – and re-identified him as Abraham – the father of many. The humbling process of long years of childlessness showed that Abraham's greatness would not come through his own achievement but God's work in his ageing body and that of Sarah, his wife. She too had a re-identification from her previous name Sarai. The pattern of divine name changing skipped a generation past

---

[211] Jeremiah 17:9
[212] Benner, 2004, p.15
[213] Ephesians 2:3

their son Isaac, to resurface in their grandson Jacob. His identity change was the most dramatic of all. The man who was 'deceiver' by name and by nature was transformed through encounters with God to become Israel, one who wrestles or prevails with God.

From Abram/Abraham, through Jacob/Israel, God made a nation whose distinctive identity would be in the fact that they belonged to him. A covenant nation that bore his name and through which his glory would be seen. A nation of people who acknowledged sin and trusted him for forgiveness through sacrifice. God's own people. He disciplined them, instructed them, and comforted them, sending prophets to remind them of his love and justice. They would not listen, so he moved in judgement to purify them. The perpetual story of Israel was like that of the man whose name the nation bore – wrestling with God, but never prevailing over him and having to realise the hard way that it is not we who triumph through our own struggles, but he who triumphs for us and brings us into his victory. The prophets looked forward to a new age of the Messiah when God's Spirit would transform the hearts of his people.[214] God's law would be written not on stone tablets but in human hearts.[215]

At the right time, God sent his Son to live as a human being, confirming the unique dignity of humankind and showing us both the true nature of God and authentic humanity. His death in our place, bearing our sin and taking the wrath of God, made possible what the sacrificial system could only point to – the forgiveness of sins and direct access to God. His resurrection conquered death and broke the claims of sin, Satan and death over us. Astoundingly, the union of God and man in Christ Jesus, who is fully God and fully human, is permanent. Jesus lived, died, rose again, and ascended to heaven as a human. He remains human and will still be human when he returns in glory. He is the beginning of a new humankind restored in relationship with God.[216] If the greatest need each human being has is forgiveness of sins and a restored relationship with God, the only way we can receive it is through the sacrificial death and triumphant resurrection of

[214] Isaiah 44:3-4; Ezekiel 36:26-27; Joel 2:28-29
[215] Jeremiah 31:33

[216] Ephesians 2:15

the Lord Jesus.

We respond – living by faith

Authentic humanity is found in Jesus alone. We can only attain it by being in him and becoming like him. The gospel calls us to turn from idols to serve the true and living God.[217] We must abandon anthropocentric and biocentric philosophies for a theocentric view – acknowledging that God is, and always has been, the centre of existence. This response sets believers apart from, and sometimes at variance with, former sources of identity – family, culture or religion – but it restrains us from the urge to look inwards instead and points us upwards. We lay down our demands for autonomy to follow a higher authority. We stop trying to justify ourselves and admit that God has been right all along. We run into his arms of mercy and acknowledge that Jesus Christ is indeed Lord. We experience new birth by the Spirit into a new life and embark on the journey of restoration by the Spirit whose goal is to form the character of Christ in us. We abandon the autonomy-authenticity-actualisation project and embark on God's repentance-regeneration-restoration project.

The gospel tells you that you are more than your past. You are not defined by your genes, your environment, your upbringing, or even your choices. Through faith in God, you are regenerated – born again with a new identity as God's child. Under the cross, God's judgement purges your past failures and purifies your past successes and God's grace meets your present need. The cross and resurrection of Jesus are not only historic events on which our faith is grounded, but realities into which we enter as we trust in Christ. This is the call of discipleship and the truth enacted in Christian baptism.[218] Through faith in Christ, we receive forgiveness of sins and new birth by the Holy Spirit into a new relationship with God as Father.

---

[217] 1 Thessalonians 1:9

[218] Mark 8:35ff.; Romans 6:4

6. MADE FOR GOD

God restores – help and hope

To be a Christian is to be 'in Christ'. As part of God's new creation, we no longer view ourselves or others as the world does: 'The old has passed away; behold, the new has come'.[219] In the fullness of God's new creation, to be revealed after Christ returns, Revelation says we will receive a stone with 'a new name written on it'.[220] We will know then what only God knows now: our true identities. Until then, we may never understand ourselves fully, but we can discover more as we grow to know God more. As John Calvin wrote in the opening section of his famous *Institutes*, 'true and solid wisdom, consists almost entirely of two parts: the knowledge of God and of ourselves'.[221] The latter depends on the former. To know ourselves, we must first know God.

God's gracious acceptance as his beloved children, frees us from fear of self-condemnation and rejection by others. His truth dispels our illusions like the rays of the sun breaking through a mist that shrouded our minds. We learn to think about ourselves, 'with sober judgement, each according to the measure of faith that God has assigned'.[222] Tim Keller describes this as the freedom of self-forgetfulness, which is when we are not motivated by the opinions of others or our own desires.[223] Love of the self shrivels and love for God grows in its place. People who know this freedom in Christ set no limits on how God might transform them. They grow towards Christ-likeness in God-awareness, self-awareness, and character. When this happens to us, we do not lose our individuality. Indeed, we 'become more uniquely our own true self'.[224]

God's repentance-regeneration-restoration project continues through the same dynamic that brought us into relationship with him: repentance from sin and trust in God's truth. God's grace teaches us to control our desires and direct them towards their proper goal in his glory.[225] God's

---

[219] 2 Corinthians 5:16-17
[220] Revelation 2:17
[221] Calvin, 1989, I.1.1
[222] Romans 12:3
[223] Keller, 2012
[224] Benner, 2004, p.15
[225] Titus 2:12

Word cuts into our hearts to reveal our inner motives with greater clarity.[226] The Spirit revives and sharpens the testimony of conscience, convicting us of sin and righteousness, exposing Satan's lies.[227]

The flesh – the person we were and still would be without God – kicks and screams against this, spurred on by the world's clamour and the devil's lies. It tries to drag us back towards the idolatry self-love, but the Spirit resolutely leads us in the opposite direction, towards life, goodness and wholeness in God's truth and love. We must choose to follow him. The answer to the destructive 'big ego trip' of boosting our self-esteem is what Glynn Harrison calls the, 'bigger than your ego trip', when Jesus eclipses the self.[228] To live authentically, according to the gospel, means dying to self and living for Christ. We were made for God and by the Holy Spirit we can live for him.

REFLECTION

- How does this gospel account of human nature differ from perspectives commonly held by non-Christians?

- How has the pursuit of self-actualisation rivalled the pursuit of God in your life and experience? How can you refocus your life on knowing God more? Talk to your heavenly Father about this.

Gospel healing for the self

God's repentance-regeneration-restoration project is directly opposed to our culture's autonomy-authenticity-actualisation project. Pastoral caregivers need to know how the gospel brings healing to our sense of

---

[226] Hebrews 4:12
[227] John 16:8
[228] John 3:30; see Harrison, 2013, p.186ff.

identity. They also need some understanding of how the gospel relates to the other major place modern people tend go for healing in their mental and emotional lives, psychology.

Love of self, God and others

Before I consider the relationship between psychology and pastoral care, I want to correct a potential misunderstanding about love of self. Some Christians point to Jesus' command to 'love your neighbour as yourself' as support for the idea that love for oneself is biblical.[229] 'If we don't love ourselves, how can we love others?', they argue. But that misunderstands the command. They have unwittingly adopted the cultural value of love for self that is key to the autonomy-authenticity-actualisation project. In its original Old Testament context, the exhortation to neighbour love rounds off a list of commands to look after the needs of others, treating them justly without deceit, hatred, vengeance or bitterness. [230] These commands describe the way of thinking that Jesus commended in his 'golden rule': 'whatever you wish that others would do to you, do also to them'.[231] So, the command to 'love your neighbour as you love yourself' does not mean that you need to learn to love yourself so that you can love others. Rather, it means you should treat others according to the standard with which you know you would like to be treated.

We need no encouragement to love ourselves. Every breath we take is an act of love for self. Sinners routinely default towards self-protection, self-preservation and self-justification. We make excuses for ourselves that we would not allow to others. We selfishly gather more than we need while others lack. Our problem is not too little love for self, but too much. Even self-neglect can result from love for self. A person can dislike himself while still loving self. His neglect expresses a belief that if the self is worthless everything is pointless. His declared self-loathing actually expresses a kind of self-love because he bases his assessment of himself on his own

---

[229] Matthew 22:39
[230] Leviticus 9:9-18
[231] Matthew 7:12

judgement. There is nothing bigger to give life meaning. No one more authoritative to tell him otherwise. His hope for salvation, if he has any, is in himself or other 'selves'.

Self-love leads to death via conflict and disappointment. Its only cure is to love God with one's whole being. In doing that, we learn to receive his good gifts for our own well-being and to love others enough to share them freely. Love of God and others brings life, peace and joy. Self-actualisation is not the pinnacle of our needs. God's restoration is. Maslow's hierarchy of needs may have its uses, reminding pastoral caregivers to see care-seekers and themselves holistically and to care for every need. How can a hungry person engage with deep spiritual ideas? How can an insecure person care selflessly for others? We must not, however, allow such humanistic theories to reinforce the predominant view in our culture that people are basically good, and that their deficiencies result merely from unmet needs. We must help people see that their most basic need is also the pinnacle of needs: restored relationship with God through repentance and faith.

Psychology and Pastoral Care

When people experience troubled emotions and disordered thinking, they often look for help to psychological theories. Many of these are rooted in the work of Austrian neurologist Sigmund Freud. His philosophy was thoroughly biocentric. An atheist, he believed we are highly evolved animals and much of our behaviour is irrational, arising from basic instincts in an unconscious self (the *id*) of which we are barely aware. Problems arise from conflict between the *id* and the conscious self (the *ego*). Unhelpful feelings of guilt compound this conflict, as a punitive third aspect of self (the *super-ego*) forms a sense of conscience and passes judgement on the *ego*. For Freud, guilt is never helpful because there is no universal law or lawgiver. Healing from guilt is not found by seeking forgiveness but through resolving one's internal conflict. Freud's ideas have found a lasting place in popular discourse. Just think how often you or others around you have asked whether something may have influenced them at a 'subconscious' level.

More recent psychological theories reject Freud's sharp distinctions between rational and irrational behaviours, but still hold to the basic idea that issues in the unconscious can affect us negatively. Therapies, therefore, aim to help clients dig beneath layers of shame and guilt conditioned by the expectations of others. One technique is to ask them to transfer thoughts, feelings and images on to the therapist so they can be expressed and addressed. Transference on to the therapist is said to help towards self-understanding, while transference on to others is thought to be a major source of interpersonal struggles. For example, we may feel hostility towards our boss or spouse not because of anything intrinsic to them but because we project on to them our negative feelings towards an overbearing or abusive parent. Belief in the value of getting suppressed feelings out in the open also underlies the popular notion that emotions should be expressed so you can get things 'off your chest'. Since the unconscious is said to be formed in infancy, a great deal of emphasis is placed on childhood experiences, including family dynamics. Personality is believed to be fixed by adulthood, although its extremes may be moderated.

Various schools of psychology have developed since Freud. Psychiatrists, psychotherapists and counsellors often combine insights from more than one. But care is never value-free and these psychological theories and therapies rest on basic convictions about human nature and healthy thinking. Christian psychiatrist and counsellor Richard Winter explains that the major theories exhibit the two distorted understandings of human nature that I have explained above as biocentric and anthropocentric. Some theories, like Freud's, are rooted in naturalism – the belief that only the physical world exists. They tend to 'dehumanize people, defining us as less than we really are and seeing us as complex machines or animals with little responsibility or significance'.[232] Other theories are influenced by humanism or by eastern mysticism. They 'tend to deify human nature by saying that we have all that we need within us to become godlike through our own efforts, or that we are already God if we could only realize it'.[233] Used uncritically, these approaches could lead people further into sinful thinking and behaviours even if they report greater peace of mind or stability of

---

[232] Winter, 2005, p.20-21
[233] *Ibid.*

emotions.

The foundational values of the therapist are highly influential in psychiatry and psychology. Popular psychology found in books, magazines and websites is often pseudo-scientific or non-scientific. Even academic psychology is significantly shaped by the values of theorists, including whether they believe God or other spiritual powers can be at work. Psychological investigation is inevitably less reliable than physical sciences because thoughts and emotions are often intangible, unclear and conflicted and they are only accessible through communication, which can be dishonest, unclear or confused. Even the process of communicating our emotions affects them, sometimes reinforcing and sometimes challenging what we feel. Clients may lack self-awareness or intentionally deceive therapists. Furthermore, there is no agreed method in psychological research to parallel the accepted scientific method in physical sciences.

None of this is intended to say that psychology contains no truth. We can expect some helpful insights from psychology because of what theologians call 'general revelation' – truths we can know by studying creation and heeding the conscience. We must recognise, however, that general revelation has limitation. It cannot expose sin accurately because our minds are corrupted by self-love. It may show what human psychology is like now in its fallen state, but cannot explain how it came to be this way or what it should be like. It is utterly incapable of discovering a path to salvation, which comes only through Christ. For all of this, we need the 'special revelation' in words and flesh that God has given in the Bible and in Christ. Scripture must be allowed to speak on its own terms. Its truths must shape and correct our emotions and thoughts.

Evaluating psychological ideas

The principle that Scripture is supreme over psychology is central to pastoral guidance as I will explain in Chapter 10. We can integrate ideas from psychology into pastoral care, but in doing so we must ensure that they do not subvert or distract from the gospel.[234] To illustrate how to do

---

[234] Other authors arguing for the integration of insights from psychology with

that, we can evaluate the ideas of the unconscious and transference against the gospel as well as the Freudian idea that guilt is only a product of internal conflict.

Exploring the unconscious

What are we to make of Freud's idea of the unconscious? The Bible distinguishes between intentional and non-intentional sins,[235] but it holds people responsible for both and there is no suggestion that the decision to commit either is not consciously made. You may be quicker to forgive my hurtful actions if you know they were not intended, but I cannot excuse my sinful behaviour on the basis that I did not realise I was sinning. The Bible's warning that our hearts are 'deceitful above all things' and beyond understanding means we can accept that our minds have hidden depths of which we lack full awareness.[236] But Freud's belief that these depths are hidden because they function in a primal part of the brain we cannot access is not supported by Scripture, which attributes them, instead, to sin. Without Christ, we are deceived in Satan's lies and myths of our own concocting, given over by God to 'strong delusions'.[237] Internally conflicted desires can certainly contribute to our troubled emotions and disordered thoughts, but worldliness, rebellion against God and demonic powers also play their part.[238] We do not need to embark on attempts to unearth our hidden depths, as if doing so will help us. Rather, we need God's light to shine into the recesses of our hearts to expose sin and bring new creation.

The idea of the unconscious too readily becomes an excuse for sin – 'I'm sorry you were offended, but you shouldn't be because I didn't mean it' – or a cause for self-condemnation – 'I thought my motives were right, but maybe subconsciously I was acting selfishly'. Self-examination is

---

gospel truth under the authority of Scripture include Carr (1997, p.37), Cornick (2000, p.376) and Goodliff (1998, p.175). For a more general survey of ways of relating psychology to theology, see Johnson, 2010.

[235] See, for example, Leviticus 4
[236] Jeremiah 17:9

[237] 1 Thessalonians 2:11
[238] James 4:1-10

healthy, but introspection is not, especially if it leads us to think of ourselves as endlessly at the mercy of an unconscious *id* we can never fathom or control. The delusions that bind us can be dispelled by the truth of the gospel. The mind led by the Spirit will not be thoughtless but focused by love. Rather than excusing our actions because our motivations were 'subconscious' we should ask the Holy Spirit to show us our sinfulness and guide us in God's will. The most important conflict within the believer is not between *id* and *ego* but between flesh and Spirit.[239]

Embracing true transference

An understanding of a second psychological concept – transference – may have some benefit in pastoral care. It is important for pastoral caregivers to recognise when their emotional responses shaped by past experiences colour teir reactions to care-seekers. We will also be wise not to take personally hostility expressed by care-seekers and to remember it may actually be aimed at someone else. More significantly, however, we can understand God as the one who invites us to transfer our anger and confusion on to him. Rather than making ourselves the object of transference from others or allowing others to become our object of transference, we can learn to turn every emotion onto God. To him we can express every emotion, however dark, as the psalms model without fear he may be overwhelmed.

As we do this, we remember the ultimate and true transference. The sins of others that provoked our negative emotions and the sins we have committed because of them or in provoking others have already been transferred on to Jesus on the cross.[240] That objective transference frees us from the burdens of sin, guilt, vengeance and aggression. It can break the destructive cycle of subjective transference in our relationships. Knowing that Christ bears our sorrows enables us to be patient as others express what may have been buried for a very long time. We can also point them to him and help them realise that healing is not found in expressing emotions but in trusting in Christ. To express emotions to others without first

---

[239] Galatians 5:16-17
[240] 1 Peter 2:24

filtering them through the cross could be a grave sin against them. We are called to speak only what will build others up, not what will make us feel better.

Exposing our shame

A third aspect of psychological theories is perhaps the point at which it is most important for pastoral caregivers not to be misled. How are we to handle feelings of guilt and shame expressed by care-seekers? Global cultures can be described as either shame or guilt cultures.[241] Societies that are more collectivist have been called 'shame cultures'. Actions are judged by the 'loss of face' they cause the family. Those who deviate from expectations are inadequate and should feel ashamed. Western societies, more individualistic in orientation and influenced by Christian values, have traditionally operated with 'guilt cultures'. Actions are judged by the fact that they break laws. Law-breakers have done wrong and should feel guilty.[242]

Contemporary Western society can no longer be said to operate as a guilt culture. External moral authorities, including ideas of right and wrong derived from Christianity, have been rejected. Freud's idea that guilt feelings are just pathological consequences of internal conflict has been embraced. Dismissing the idea of true guilt, psychology has contributed to a greater focus in our culture on managing negative emotions. As Ian Bunting writes, 'today most people tend to seek help not because they "feel bad", but because they "do not feel good"'.[243] As guilt has declined, however, shame has increased. Younger people are less concerned about disobedience than nonconformity. Social media compounds the problem. Crippling shame results from 'unfriending' or trolling. In traditional collectivist cultures, shame could draw errant people back into conformity with a community in which they belonged. In our hyper-individualistic culture, there is often no path to restoration because communities are temporary without deep

---

[241] Hiebert, 1985, p.212ff.
[242] Collins, 1988, p.136ff.

[243] Bunting, 2000, p.387

commitment.

The Bible describes both shame and guilt as consequences of sin, but guilt precedes shame. After eating the forbidden fruit, Adam and Eve tried to cover their nakedness and hide from God.[244] They felt shame. But this subjective experience resulted from the objective fact that the fruit was forbidden by a divine rule. They were guilty of breaking God's command. We feel shame in God's presence because we are guilty before him. In gospel perspective, guilt is 'real'. It is not merely a product of internal conflict, but a proper response to alienation from God and necessary to lead us to grace. People who feel little guilt but great shame, need to realise that shame is meaningless without guilt and cannot be overcome unless guilt is dealt with. It should not, ultimately, matter what other people think of us if we are innocent. The gospel declares 'no condemnation for those who are in Christ Jesus' and 'Everyone who believes in him will not be put to shame'.[245]

The gospel calls us beyond subjective experience into objective realities. Gospel-shaped pastoral care aims to align feelings with God's character and will revealed in Scripture. It brings us before God as responsible people, wounded and wounders, calling us to repentance and faith. Christian physician and psychologist Paul Tournier explained that growing awareness of God's character often intensifies guilt because our faults become more obvious by contrast.[246] Nevertheless, he insisted, 'it is not guilt which is the obstacle to grace', but 'the repression of guilt, self-justification, genuine self-righteousness and smugness'. [247] Acknowledging our guilt does not diminish us. Rather, as **Dietrich Bonhoeffer wrote,** 'the one real dignity that man has [... is that] though he is a sinner, he can share in God's grace and glory and be God's child'.[248] Denial of guilt demeans us and leaves us with no hope of forgiveness. Chapters 9 and 10, will return to these vital issues of guilt and shame in the context of pastoral listening and guidance.

---

[244] Genesis 3:7-8
[245] Romans 8:1; 10:11
[246] Tournier, 1986, p.41
[247] Tournier, 1986, p.136
[248] Bonhoeffer, 1954, p.106

REFLECTION

- How does the idolatry of self-love express itself in your life? Ask God to reveal it to you more fully and confess it to him.

- What is your experience and understanding of psychology? How can you integrate insights from psychology with the gospel in pastoral care?

CHAPTER SUMMARY

In contrast to our culture, which tells us that our greatest need is to self-actualise and that the pathway to that goal is through authenticity and autonomy, the gospel tells us our most profound need is to be restored into relationship with God through faith in Jesus Christ. We have great dignity as people created in God's image but are also depraved because of sin. We need divine forgiveness, so we must repent: recognising our sins; receiving God's pardon; restoring relationships where possible; and reducing the likelihood of future sin. We must surrender our autonomy to Christ's Lordship and so find true authenticity in becoming like Him. The call of discipleship is not actualisation of self, but denial of self in love of God and others. Psychology can provide useful insights and tools for helping people with troubled emotions and thoughts, but we must understand the values that underlie psychological theories and evaluate their claims against the gospel.

CHAPTER 6 - DISCUSSION QUESTIONS

1. Do you recognise the values of authenticity, autonomy and self-actualisation in our culture? Share about ways you have seen them in popular culture or in the lives of people you know.

2. To what degree have these cultural values influenced the way we organise our churches and their activities, including pastoral care? How can we ensure we don't reinforce them?

3. How can you recognise and correct the idolatry of self-love in yourself and others.

4. What is your understanding of what it means for human beings to have dignity as divine image bearers and depravity as sinners? What does this mean for your expectations as you care for others?

5. Choose an idea from psychology (in this chapter or from your own experience) that you are either unsure about or have found helpful. Help each other to understand it and evaluate it against the gospel.

6. How does the gospel truth of the transference of our sins and their consequences onto Jesus help us to help others with negative emotions and disordered thoughts?

7. Do you recognise the shift from a concern with guilt to a sense of shame in our culture? How can we recover a gospel perspective on guilt and shame?

7. MADE FOR WHOLENESS

As she walked to her meeting with Sam, Jude was almost ready to say yes, but she had a niggling concern. She was fairly confident she knew how to support people in need. She could hold a hand and absorb others' intense feelings. When her mother was terminally ill, she had not shied away from her suffering. At least, her mum's physical pain had not deterred her, difficult as it was. What she had struggled with was the question mum asked repeatedly as the cancer ravaged her body, 'Why doesn't God just heal me or take me home?' Jude had not known how to respond then and she still did not. How could she provide pastoral care if she had nothing to say?

Other Christians had given mum their answers. A cold chill ran over Jude as she recalled them. The retired minister who visited had one response: 'God's ways are mysterious, but everything is part of his good plan for us'. He spoke gently, but his words made Jude angry. She still did not know if that anger was directed at God, the minister or the tumour, but, whichever, she just could not see cancer as a good thing or understand how it could be part of God's plan. A different answer had been suggested by a childhood friend of her mum who reconnected through Facebook during her last months. She shared a link to a healing ministry led by a 'prophet' who claimed, 'Healing is your birth right! Claim it by faith!' That angered Jude too. She had known many godly Christians who experienced illness and some who had died. Was this man saying they were all lacking in faith? The minister saw the illness as an act of God; the healer saw it as the work of Satan. Either way, it felt like mum was being judged for lack of faith. The minister thought she should have more faith to find peace. The healer thought, if she had more faith, she could experience healing. Jude decided she needed to talk this through with Sam before she could say yes.

The Challenge of Suffering

Jude's experience with her mother is not uncommon. Suffering is universal in human experience, 'intrinsic to the sphere of life'. [249] In the normal course of events, our first breaths come through the pangs of labour and our final breaths cause the anguish of grief. Between these two points, our lives bear greater or lesser burdens of suffering, both physical and mental. Despite, or perhaps because of, this universal experience, suffering is often the greatest conundrum for people of faith and the strongest accusation sceptics level against faith. Even mature believers experiencing severe suffering may feel God is distant. Ironically, people who deny God in good times may blame Him when bad things happen.

At the heart of the problem of suffering are questions about God's nature. 'How can a loving God allow this?', or, 'Is he powerless to intervene?' On the lips of the sufferer, the questions often boil down to one word: 'Why?' This question reflects our instinctive desire to make sense of our experience. When things seem meaningless, we realise how little control we have over life. This is especially unsettling for followers of our culture's autonomy-authenticity-actualisation project. It is unsurprising, therefore, that people living in countries with the greatest environmental, political and economic stability are most likely to question God's existence because of suffering.[250] Their habitual illusion of control over their destiny is shattered by the stark reality of mortality. Paradoxically, then, those who have greater means to lessen their experience of suffering find it a greater offence.

There is historical record of Europeans questioning God's existence because of suffering before the eighteenth-century philosophical revolution known as the Enlightenment. Human reason was made supreme and divine

---

[249] Farley, 1996, p.204.
[250] See Sobrino, 2004, p.140

revelation was doubted, making atheism a serious intellectual option. C.S. Lewis famously expressed this process as putting 'God in the dock' to be judged by human sensibilities.[251] That is not to say that no one judged God before the Enlightenment. Blaming God is as old as sin. Adam and Eve started it when they believed the serpent's lie that they could do a better job than their Creator. As apologist Os Guinness writes, 'So long as the world's last sin remains unconfessed, the buck will keep on passing and passing, and the final finger always points at God'.[252] What changed with the Enlightenment was that the God we had previously blamed was dismissed as a figment of human imagination. Paradoxically, the angry atheist rants against someone he says does not exist.

Yet the problem of suffering does not diminish when God is removed from the equation. Atheists struggle to explain why death feels unfair or why the suffering of innocent people provokes outrage in us. They may theorise that such responses have some 'evolutionary basis', but that explanation seems implausible for the person who experiences grief or injustice. Where does a concept like justice come from if there is no Creator and lawgiver? Suffering is a problem for every human being. How are gospel-shaped pastoral caregivers to handle their own suffering and that of others?

REFLECTION

- Have you ever asked 'Why?' because of your experience of your own suffering or that of someone else? Did it express sin, fear or faith?

- How would you answer the person who asks, 'How could a good God allow such suffering?' What would you want to know about the person's experience and situation before responding?

---

[251] Lewis, 1972
[252] Guinness, 2015, p.54.

Suffering in Gospel Perspective

Suffering in all its forms is a central issue in pastoral care because it is usually an experience of pain that causes people to reach out for help. We must understand what the gospel says about suffering.

God rules – goodness and power

From its opening verses onwards, the Bible presents God as the all-powerful Creator and sustaining ruler of the universe. Recognising this truth, Christians cannot dismiss the problem of suffering by suggesting that God is unable to do anything about it. Someone might argue on this basis that, since God could do something about suffering, the fact that he does not must mean that he does not care. This claim is also incompatible with the Bible, because, again beginning with Genesis 1, Scripture consistently reveals God to be good and generous, caring for his creation and, supremely, for human beings who were made in his image. Still, the experience of suffering, especially when those who suffer appear to be innocent, casts a shadow for many on their understanding of God's character.

When we seek to understand God's character, we must beware our tendency to major on one quality over another. For example, we cannot think of God as loving and gracious without also recognising that he is truthful and just or vice versa. When we do that, we end up with a false god rather than the God of Scripture. The true and living God is loving *and* truthful, gracious *and* righteous, merciful *and* just. These twin truths are expressed in his words to Israel,[253] echoed in Israel's praises to him,[254] evident in the character of Christ,[255] upheld in the cross,[256] and taught by the apostles.[257] God's goodness is absolute and his will for his people is

---

[253] Exodus 34:6
[254] For example in Psalm 34:4-5; 85:10; 86:15
[255] John 1:14
[256] Romans 3:26; 5:8
[257] For example, 1 John 1:5 – 'God is light' (meaning he is full of truth and justice) – must not be divorced from 1 John 4:8 – 'God is love'.

'good and acceptable and perfect'.[258] Part of our struggle with holding God's love together with his justice relates to our limited understanding of love and inability to comprehend God's wisdom. God's love always seeks what is best for his beloved and God's wisdom is such that only he ultimately knows what that is. We tend to think that love for another means seeking their happiness, but how do we know what happiness is and what should we do if our beloved's happiness would lead to someone else's unhappiness? God wants more than our immediate happiness – he wants our eternal good – and only God knows the full extent of the consequences of every one of our possible actions and their potential outcomes.

At the same time as acknowledging God's wisdom in ruling the universe, we must consider the nature of how he rules. We must acknowledge that God is sovereign, but that does not necessarily mean that everything that happens is planned by him. What God causes – his 'directive will' – need not be identical to what God allows – his 'permissive will'. God allowed human beings to disobey him, and he permits the consequences of their actions to unfold. In the language of Romans Chapter 1, God has given us up to our own desires.[259] He did not cause us to reject him or to desire what is wrong, but he does not normally forcibly intervene to stop us following the path we have chosen. God may cause suffering directly by acting in judgement on his enemies and in discipline of his children, just as he is recorded as doing in Scripture, but he is never the source of evil or the cause of sin.[260]

God allows us to suffer, but he does not permit unlimited evil or indefinite suffering. This principle operates both cosmically and individually. Cosmically, God has set an end point for suffering in the coming fullness of the new creation, in which those who trust in him will participate. Individually, the book of Job shows that God sets limits on the duration and extent of the suffering of his people. The world we inhabit may seem bad, but it would be much worse if God were not restraining the evil of Satan and human beings by his Spirit and the preserving, salt-like

---

[258] Romans 12:2.
[259] Romans 1:24,26,28
[260] James 1:13; 1 John 1:5

presence of his people.[261] Within our confused and confusing stories, God is working out his grand story that ultimately makes sense of them all.

We rebelled – sin's consequences

God's story tells us how suffering became part of human experience in the first place. Suffering started with sin. The Bible recounts the origins of human sin clearly, but it does not explain definitively how evil originated. We know that Satan, who was personified in the serpent in Genesis 3, was in rebellion against God before Adam and Eve sinned, but we are not told how or when Satan turned to evil. Many Christians believe that he was previously a beautiful and powerful angelic being who rebelled against God, bringing many other angels with him to become demons, but biblical support for this claim is not certain.[262] What we do know is that Satan is a created being who is opposed to God and who seeks to lead human beings astray through lies, but who cannot rival God's knowledge, wisdom or power and has been defeated through the cross and resurrection of Jesus.

Evil came into human experience by eating the fruit of the tree of the knowledge of good and evil. From that act, all human suffering flows, either directly because of sinful human actions or because of the effects of the curse God placed on the world. It would be wrong to say that every painful experience is a divine judgement for a specific sin – the suffering of righteous Job debunks that myth – but there would be no suffering if humankind had not sinned. Much human suffering is caused directly by intentional sins – people speak and act in harmful ways towards others. Another quantity is caused indirectly by human failure to do good we could do or through unintentional sins – curable diseases go untreated, drought, famine and exposure result from bad government. Much suffering is

---

[261] 2 Thessalonians 2:6-7

[262] The claim that Satan is a fallen angel is based on interpretations of several passages: the idea that the war in Revelation 12 occurred before the Fall of human beings; the identification of the fallen star of Revelation 9:1 with Satan; the theory that the 'Day Star' in Isaiah 14:12 refers not only to the king of Babylon but also in a secondary sense to Satan; and Jesus' reference to seeing Satan fall from heaven like lightning in Luke 10:18. Taken together, these passages may well refer to the banishment of a rebel angel and his followers, but we cannot be certain.

generated, prolonged or intensified by greed, wars, violence, foolishness, carelessness, bad lifestyle choices, pollution, abuse, neglect, bitterness and unforgiveness.

If human suffering raises questions about God's power and goodness, 'man's inhumanity to man' testifies abundantly to the limits of our own power and goodness. Humankind stands in the dock and is found wanting. Considering the human responsibility for suffering forces us to think not only about the suffering we experience but also the suffering we cause to others. I may be the victim of horrendous injustices at the hands of others, but I am also guilty of injustice towards others. More fundamentally, I am in rebellion against God. Suffering tells us something is wrong with the world, but it also tells us something is wrong with us. We suffer because of sin, and we cause suffering because we sin. Similarly, much of our mental anguish results from patterns of thinking founded on lies, or refusal to accept or trust the truth. At times we can only blame ourselves for this because we make choices and allow habits to form that we know are ungodly and do not encourage faith to grow. At other times, we cannot identify a reason for our struggle to trust or our troubled emotions are fruit of past traumas and present discouragement. In any case, there is only one place to turn – to our loving and powerful Creator.

God rescues – the suffering God

The Bible makes it abundantly clear that God is not distant from or unconcerned about human suffering. His righteous anger is kindled against the sins that cause suffering. His tender concern for those who suffer because of injustice and oppression is clear in the words of Old Testament prophets like Amos and of John the Baptist and Jesus.[263] He does not reject those who cry out to him. Rather, he promises to save them and calls them to himself.[264] Jesus, God made flesh, puts the question of God and suffering into a fresh perspective. No one could accuse him of indifference to pain. He condemned those who oppressed others and brought dignity,

---

[263] Luke 3:7-15; 4:18-19
[264] Isaiah 5:1-2; Joel 2:32; Romans 10:13

healing and restoration to suffering outcasts. More than that, Jesus himself suffered in every sense, emotionally and physically. As author Dorothy L. Sayers, wrote, God 'can exact nothing from man that He has not exacted from Himself'.[265] A gospel account of suffering must, inevitably, lead us to the cross.

The cross says many things about human suffering. It shows that God works out his purposes through weakness rather than power and that suffering need not be shameful. Indeed, Christians boast in the sufferings of Jesus and the death to self that is our experience when we trust in him.[266] The cross also assures us that suffering can result from faithfulness to God. Jesus suffered in obedience to God and sometimes we will too. God can use suffering to refine our character and enfold us in his love.[267] The cross confronts us with the cost of discipleship, reminds us of the cost of salvation from the sin that causes suffering, and brings living power to endure the rejections, sacrifices and loneliness the journey to growth inevitably entails.[268] The cross reveals God as the one who suffers more from our sin than we do and Jesus' endurance through the cross provides an example of how to face unjust suffering.[269] Making sense of these lessons, though, is the fact that Jesus was bearing our sins,[270] taking God's wrath in our place,[271] and offering himself as one sacrifice for sins for all time.[272] Christ's cross is the ultimate response to suffering because it dealt with the root problem that caused it, human sin. His resurrection from the dead proved that his death defeated death itself not only for himself but for those who will respond to him.

We respond – nothing wasted

The gospel calls us to repent of sin, to trust in God and to obey him, not

---

[265] Sayers, 1949, p.4.
[266] Galatians 6:14
[267] See 2 Corinthians 12:7-10 and Hebrews 4:15-16.
[268] For more on this read Brennan Manning (1985).
[269] 1 Peter 21-23.
[270] 1 Peter 3:24.
[271] Romans 3:25.
[272] Hebrews 10:12

just once but daily. When we turn to God, we bring everything to him – our hopes and fears, praise and puzzles, joys and pains. As we do so, we learn to trust in his promises. The gospel does not promise a life free from suffering. Christians are not immune to the shared suffering of humankind in this sin-scarred world. Indeed, obedience to God may even increase suffering through hostility from others and the intense inner struggle against sin and Satan. The lifelong pattern of Christian faithfulness is not just of turning away from sin but also from the temptation to sin when under pressure. In suffering we find temptation, but we also find an opportunity for growth.

Without God, suffering is pointless and meaningless – a cruel twist of fate before death's release. With God, even the toxic soil of suffering can grow good fruit. Job's faithfulness through his unjust suffering vindicated God. Jesus said the suffering of a man born blind was an opportunity not to apportion blame but for God's work to be done in the man and Jesus glorified.[273] The apostles assured us that the fire of suffering can refine faith and forge godly character.[274] Experience affirms this paradox. Suffering and the awareness of death is often what makes people realise they need God. Believers often testify that, 'the God who is Immanuel is equally in those moments we would never choose as in those we would always gladly choose'.[275]

Importantly for pastoral care, knowing God through suffering does not equate to understanding God's purpose in it, at least at the time. The recognition that God does not cause evil and works for our good does not remove the question Jude's mother asked: why am I suffering this way right now? Such questions do not always indicate rebellion against God. They may simply express fear in the face of pain. Often, they verbalise faith, like the questions of Job, the Psalms and Habakkuk or Christ's anguished prayers in Gethsemane. Questions directed to God, no matter how despairing or angry, still reflect trust in him as the only hope for rescue. When we encounter them in others, we should not be unsettled, or assume they have 'lost their faith'. We know such questions addressed to God can

---

[273] John 9:1-5
[274] Romans 5:3-5; 1 Peter 1:6-7
[275] Benner, 2004, p.41-42

be paths to growth.

One popular image thinks of God weaving all the threads of our lives into a beautiful tapestry of which we currently see only the loose threads on the back. Such images are helpful, but amidst pain we seldom have even this degree of clarity about what God is doing. Like the disciples who asked Jesus why the man was born blind, we seldom receive answers to the 'Why' question beyond the general promise that God is at work. Like Job, when we come to God in grief, we are more likely to receive an overawing revelation of his majesty than a reason for our tragedy. Sometimes we will gain understanding because God will reveal it to us during the event or, more often, as we reflect after it. More often, as time passes, our perspective on the suffering changes and we learn something new and unexpected about God.

Unanswered questions need not cause interminable mental turmoil. As Henri Nouwen writes, 'Our lives are not problems to be solved but journeys to be taken with Jesus as our friend and finest guide'.[276] The questions of life can be lived even if they remain resolved. In God's repentance-regeneration-restoration project, unresolvable puzzles can give way to unfathomable peace.[277] We need not stop seeking understanding, but through pains and joys we pursue Christ, longing to know him more. On this journey, we may even find that questions that once seemed important disappear. As Henri Nouwen writes, 'Sometimes, in living the questions, answers are found. More often, as our questions and issues are tested and mature in solitude, the questions simply dissolve'.[278] God may answer our questions, they may dissolve, or perhaps they will never go away in this life. Whichever is the case, there is hope because God restores.

God restores – there is hope

God's ultimate limit to evil is the fixed date when he will put all things

---

[276] Nouwen, 2006, p.6
[277] Philippians 4:6-7
[278] Nouwen, 2006, p.13

right.[279] On this 'day of the Lord', all people will answer to him and everything will be laid bare.[280] There will be no more 'buck passing', excuses or deceptions. Those who have taken refuge in Christ will be vindicated as God finally judges justly and totally. Christians are born again into a living hope because Jesus is risen.[281] We are already God's new creation and we await our home in a renewed heavens and earth where there will be, 'no more death or mourning or crying or pain, for the old order of things has passed away'.[282] In these sure and certain promises of Scripture we can rest from questioning.

The Bible clearly teaches that total physical healing is not possible until the day of the Lord. We are already justified – declared right with God – through Jesus, but the redemption of our bodies awaits the future day of resurrection.[283] In the meantime, God is working all things together for our 'good', not in some nebulous sense of 'good' that we might try to define, but the specific good of our being 'conformed to the image of his Son'.[284] Unlike the minister who visited Jude's mother, Scripture does not say that everything that happens to us is good, so we need not try to believe that a specific experience must be. God's actual promise is more powerful. He is transforming everything, working good from every experience, including those that are utterly bad. He will not allow anything to stand in the way of his good purpose for His people.

The totality of our restoration is future. We will be like Jesus when we see him.[285] On that day, all creation will breathe a sigh of relief as it gazes on God's children in the glory of their Saviour.[286] The wonder is not merely that suffering will be no more, but that the glory revealed on that day was forged in the furnace of suffering. On that day we will also know God as

---

[279] See Proverbs 10:27; 11:21; 12:21; 13:25; Ecclesiastes 12:9; Romans 2:1-16
[280] 2 Peter 3:10
[281] 1 Peter 1:3
[282] 2 Peter 3:13; Revelation 21:4
[283] Romans 3:24; 8:23
[284] Romans 8:28-29

[285] 1 John 3:2
[286] Romans 8:19

we are known by God.[287] For now, it is as if we are looking into God's purposes in a poorly polished mirror. Much remains unclear. On that day, it will become clear. The tapestry will be turned around and we will see the beauty of the story God has been weaving.

Christians have hope of future total restoration, but we also have the real possibility of healing and restoration in the present. The degree to which we expect healing now is a crucial question that I will address later in this chapter. For now, it is enough to say that God brings comfort to suffering people and that comfort is primarily embodied in his people. God sends us into his world as carriers of the message of Christ's redeeming power and the embodiments of his love. Bringing hope and help, we become part of God's answer to the problem of suffering. In pastoral care, we help suffering people to trust more in God, to prioritise their growth in Christlikeness, and to depend more upon the Spirit as they repent, believe and obediently wait for God's glorious future. We testify to the fact that life is not, as our culture claims, about maximising fulfilment or happiness in our brief time before death. There is eternal meaning that transcends the challenges of living God's way now.

REFLECTION

- How does this gospel account of suffering differ from perspectives commonly held by non-Christians?

- Which aspects of the gospel perspective on suffering do you find easy to believe and which do you struggle with? Meditate on the portions of Scripture referenced in this section, especially Romans 8:18-30, and ask God to strengthen your confidence in his good purposes as you work with others.

---

[287] 1 Corinthians 13:12

7. MADE FOR WHOLENESS

Health, Healing and Help

As we saw in Chapter 1, it is impossible to have a clear understanding of care without convictions about the nature of need, health and help. In this section, I will discuss the nature of health and healing in light of everything we have discovered so far about the gospel and then propose the kind of help we can offer.

Health and its absence

The word 'health' is widely used in everyday speech – health services and systems, healthcare workers, mental health problems – but we may never have paused to ask what it means. The Old English word *hal* is the root of the word health, but it also gave us 'whole' and 'holiness'. That suggests a broad understanding of health as wholeness. To be healthy is to have a 'whole life' – one in which nothing is lacking and all the parts work together for their intended purpose. Widely accepted modern definitions of health recognise that it embraces various dimensions – physical, mental and social. [288] Increasingly, healthcare professionals also recognise that health does not only mean the absence of disease; it entails positive well-being. What is often missing, though, is spiritual well-being.

Jesus showed us the meaning of health through his ministry on earth. He often used the Greek word *sōzō* to describe the result of his work in people's lives. It can be translated 'saved', but 'made whole' is an alternative. It appears 54 times in the Gospels, referring variously to physical healing, deliverance from demonic influence, and salvation from sins.[289] Christ's work in people's lives, for example with the demonised man in the country of the Gerasenes [290] or the woman with abnormal bleeding,[291] restored wholeness by dealing comprehensively with sin and its effects, including physical sickness, social alienation, emotional disturbance and death. Yet Jesus identified spiritual restoration as the priority for people when he

---

[288] World Health Organisation, 1946
[289] See, for example, Matthew 9:22; Mark 5:34; 10:52; Luke 8:48; 17:19; 18:42
[290] Luke 8:26-39
[291] Mark 5:25-34

described his healing of a paralysed man as proof of his authority to do the greater work of forgiving sins.[292] Later in the same chapter, he described himself as a physician for people who are sick, paralleling that image with the fact that he had come to call sinners to return to God.[293] Jesus' miracles demonstrated the nature of God's kingdom – freedom from sin and its consequences and restoration to wholeness in every sense – but he affirmed that our greatest need is a restored relationship with God through forgiveness of sins. Only through new birth can we enter the kingdom in which lives are truly made whole.

In gospel terms, restored relationship with God through Christ is the core of spiritual health. Indeed, without the new birth of the Spirit, we are dead in our sins.[294] However we might define health, being spiritually dead certainly is not it! The gospel identifies spiritual life and health at the core of a whole human being. Around this core, health must mean that all aspects of oneself – body (physical health), thinking and emotions (mental health) and relationships (social health) – are brought under the lordship of Christ. It is living consistently with the truth of God revealed in Christ in every dimension of our being. We can, therefore, define health in gospel perspective as: wholeness in the truth.

Wholeness in the truth

I have defined health as wholeness in the truth. Both aspects of this definition – wholeness and truth – require further explanation.

Health is wholeness

An understanding of health as integrated wholeness can help us avoid unhelpfully separating different aspects of health. We are not compartmentalised and ill health in any aspect of our being, if it continues long enough, will cause harm in other aspects. Physical disease can lead to

---

[292] Mark 2:1-12
[293] Mark 2:17
[294] Ephesians 2:1

mental ill-health, spiritual malaise and social alienation. Similarly, mental illness can profoundly impact spiritual well-being, physical health and social functioning. Realising these interconnections, we can think of the absence of health in three different senses: *disease* is the problem doctors measure, define and describe; *illness* is the experience of the one who is unhealthy; and *sickness* is the way the unhealthiness impacts his life in relationship with others.[295]

The same disease can result in different illnesses and sicknesses for different people in different social settings. Doctors may describe an illness or sickness without a disease diagnosis as 'psychogenic' and others may dismiss it as 'hypochondria', but its impact on the person may be no less real than something with an obvious physical cause. Individual health cannot be considered in isolation from relational networks and belief systems. The pastoral caregiver must identity which aspects of health are compromised and determine how each can best be addressed. She knows her focus is where the gospel's priority is, on soul health in relationship to God. Her part is soul care and cure, but she will also value the parts others play in body care.

Health relates to truth

The relationship between health and truth is also vitally important. We recognise this instinctively when it comes to physical health: I am physically healthy if each of the organ systems of my body is working within normal limits to fulfil its purpose in harmony with the others. Medical science provides excellent tools to health professionals – blood tests, X-rays, scans and biopsies – to determine when something is wrong with the body. These work by comparing what is seen or measured in the person's body with the normal range. Truth matters in physical health. From Scripture, we understand that God made our bodies to operate in a certain way and that ill health occurs when that purpose is compromised. From a gospel perspective, physical health means a body functioning as God designed.

We may acknowledge a similar definition of social wellbeing: I am

---

[295] Marinker, 1975, p.81-84

socially healthy if I am behaving within acceptable limits to fulfil my contribution to society in harmony with others. People may have different ideas about what acceptable limits of behaviour are and what contribution a given person ought to make to society, but the goal of social harmony with each person limiting his or her actions for the sake of maintaining it is likely to be non-controversial. We do not, however, have the same kind of agreed definitions of 'normal' behaviour and healthy relationships that we have for physical health. In large part this is because we do not have a methodology akin to physical science to measure such things. The Bible teaches, however, that God designed us for relationships based on love for others like his love for us. The 'acceptable' limits of my behaviour are not determined by me or by society, but by God, while the contribution I should make to society is whatever God intends for me. From a gospel perspective, social health means loving as God loves.

When it comes to mental health, I suggest that we need a similar definition to those I have given for physical and social health: I am mentally and emotionally healthy if my thoughts and feelings are consistent with what is true. This definition is, however, less likely to find support in our wider culture than my definitions of physical and social health. When people on the street speak of mental health, they often mean positive affect – feeling happy. It should not be difficult to see that this definition is inadequate, because there are circumstances in which we should not feel happy, and to do so would seem like detachment from reality. More helpful definitions of mental health focus instead on ability to cope and function – consider, for example, the emphasis placed on resilience, which is the ability to bounce back from tough experiences. The problem with this approach, though, is that it is not necessarily interested in truth. It would, of course, recognise that someone with psychosis, whose thinking is clearly disconnected from reality, is mentally ill, but it is not concerned with whether our beliefs about questions like God's existence or right and wrong are true or false so long as we are able to moderate our emotions enough to live without professional support.

The problem with relating a definition of emotional and mental health to truth is that there is no agreed understanding of what is true when it comes to non-physical things. From a gospel perspective, however, we know that there is truth revealed in Jesus. Understanding this, I can recognise that my emotions have a purpose and there are normal, healthy limits of emotion which are necessary for the balanced and harmonious function of my soul. My thoughts, too, can be measured by correspondence to what is real and true. According to the gospel, thoughts and beliefs that are healthy and good are those that correspond with God's truth. From a gospel perspective, mental and emotional health means feeling and thinking as God does.

Table 3   Definitions of health

Concept	Short definition	Expanded definition
Health	Wholeness in the truth	Integration of one's whole being under Christ's lordship in consistency with the truth of God revealed in Christ
Physical health	Body functioning as God designed	Each organ system is working within normal limits to fulfil its purpose in harmony with the others
Social health	Loving others as God loves	Behaving within God's limits to fulfil my God-given contribution to society in harmony with others
Mental and emotional health	Feeling and thinking as God does	Thoughts and feelings consistent with what is true as revealed by God in Scripture and in Christ
Spiritual health	Worshipping as God commands	Whole life – body, soul and relationships – offered to God for his service in thankful response to his grace

We can also add a definition of spiritual health, although here we will be unlikely to find any agreement with people who do not accept the gospel. I am spiritually healthy when my loyalty and desires find their focus in their proper end – the person of God – and when I practice repentance and faith habitually. From a gospel perspective, spiritual health is when I worship as God commands. This definition reminds us once again that spiritual health is the core concept from a gospel perspective, since worship embraces all of the other dimensions of health. We worship by offering our bodies to God as living sacrifices to fulfil his will.[296] We worship by loving God with our whole being and our neighbours as ourselves. We worship by directing every thought and emotion to God and allowing his Spirit to transform our thinking and feeling. We offer our whole selves to God for his service in gratitude for his grace to us.

Emotions, thoughts and mental health

It is important to think a little more about mental health, because it comes so close to the distinctive concern of pastoral care for soul health. Furthermore, the relationship between spiritual health and mental health is often poorly understood. Awareness of mental health issues has increased in recent years, but it is still often the poor cousin of physical health in both healthcare and society. Reactions to 'I have cancer' or 'I have broken my leg' are likely to be more sympathetic and less awkward than to 'I can't see a point in life'.

Sometimes the stigma surrounding mental ill health can be compounded in Christian settings due to poor understandings and misguided theological assumptions. People may imply, for example, that physical illness is not the sufferer's fault, whereas disordered thinking is, so that a godly Christian should not experience mental illness. This is simply wrong. Most illnesses, both physical and mental, are caused by a combination of factors, some within our control and others outside it. Mental illness may result or be made worse from a physical disorder – imbalanced hormones in the body or neurotransmitters in the brain – and some people appear to be predisposed to poor mental health because of their genes or upbringing, just as some people are to heart disease or diabetes. At the same time, our mental health can be negatively impacted by experiences and by patterns of thinking we choose to indulge in, just as diet and other lifestyle factors contribute to physical health problems.

Gospel-shaped pastoral caregivers should follow the heart of God in responding to every person who suffers with compassion. It may be helpful to determine what factors have contributed to a person's illness so that we

---

[296] Romans 12:1-2

can work to counter them, but our basic approach will be the same whatever factors are at play. We can draw alongside the suffering person in the ministry of presence. We can respond to his material needs in the ministry of provision. We will pray for his healing in the ministry of intercession. We will seek to help him towards truth in the ministry of instruction. We can assure people that mental struggles are not in themselves sinful and should not be a cause of guilt.

We will also recognise that struggles in our emotional life can lessen our resistance to temptation. We can encourage people to seek all of the forms of help available to them. Some forms of mental illness, especially when experience is disconnected from reality in psychosis, require complex and long-term treatment by medical specialists. Other forms, like depression and anxiety, may benefit from medical input, including medication, or may be treatable through talking therapies. Alongside any such professional help there is a meaningful role for pastoral caregivers to offer friendship.

Mental health refers to wellbeing of the mind. Some people prefer to speak of 'mental and emotional health' in recognition that people can face challenges with their emotional well-being as well as their thoughts. I think this can be helpful, but also caution against making too sharp a distinction between feelings and thoughts. To do so could be another indicator of our tendency to have a fragmented understanding of people rather than an integrated view. We tend to think of 'thoughts' and 'feelings' as separate phenomena. Even in Christian preaching and writing it is commonplace to hear 'head' and 'heart' being used to refer to separate things. The reality, however, is that both feelings and thoughts occur in our brains. Scripture refers to the heart as the seat of both emotion and reason. When we speak of the two as if they were distinct, we are reflecting a false dichotomy that arose from human philosophies rather than Scripture or sound scientific research.

Feelings and thoughts are closely related. Feelings or emotions are our instinctive reactions to experiences. They are often unsought and can be overwhelming. Thoughts are the interpretations we place on our feelings as we reason about them. We might call thoughts 'processed emotions'. That might cause us to think that thoughts are superior to emotions and the person who is led by reason is better than the one who follows her

154

instinctive 'gut reaction'. That would be too simplistic. The fact is that our processing of emotions is often incomplete and it may end with us justifying our instinctive emotional reaction. Our sinful hearts are expert at finding excuses for ourselves. 'I know my reaction wasn't nice, but I have a right to be angry, and she really deserved some of her own medicine'. This is a far cry from biblical truth. The outcome of processing our emotions will only be as sound as the values we use to evaluate them.

It is fair to say that Christians should be led by thoughts more than emotions. It is always dangerous to react without evaluating. 'I couldn't help myself – the feeling just overwhelmed me' is not a valid excuse. Yet we should not delude ourselves into thinking that logical people are always wiser than more emotional ones. Feelings can be just as true as thoughts, and they can be equally aligned with God's heart too. What matters is that we allow God to rule over our emotions and our reason. We pray that we might feel as he feels and think as he thinks. We allow the words of Scripture to shape our thinking so that we submit our feelings and thoughts to his will. I say no to what is ungodly and yes to what is good, true and pleasing to God.

Growth towards Christian maturity entails the transformation and renewal of our minds, enabling us to discern God's will and to make accurate judgements about our contribution to serving it as he has gifted us.[297] I need to evaluate and test my thoughts for truthfulness. This process of evaluating emotions and thoughts follows biblical wisdom, which tells us to guard or keep our hearts 'with all vigilance' because 'the springs of life' flow from them.[298] It **entails** three steps, which can be remembered through the classic movie director's phrase 'lights, camera, action!':[299]

- First, allow **lights** to shine on your heart, seeking to bring your emotions and thoughts into perspective so that you do not make assumptions or act without thinking. These lights include the words of Christian friends,

---

[297] Romans 12:2-3
[298] Proverbs 4:23
[299] Similar schemes for heart keeping are found in Lane and Tripp (2006), Chester (2008) and Anderson (2000).

the prompting of the Holy Spirit in your conscience, and, above all, the words of Scripture.

- Second, focus your mental **camera** to take an honest 'selfie' of the specific sins, false thoughts and spiritual snares in your life. It is often helpful to write down this assessment so that you can see progress made over time, or lack of it.

- Third, take **action** by committing yourself to seek growth and establishing habits that reinforce obedience. Appropriate actions may include apologising to someone who bore the brunt of an uncontrolled emotional response, seeking accountability from a godly friend, or finding a positive way to control your emotions such as praying, going for a walk or practising controlled breathing.

Healing – possibilities and challenges

Questions surrounding healing are commonplace in pastoral care. We must have a clear perspective on how and when God heals.

When does God heal? Total healing, but not yet

God heals totally. This is a thoroughly biblical truth. God described himself to Israel as, 'the Lord, your healer'.[300] King David praised him as the one who 'forgives all my sins and heals all my diseases'.[301] The prophet Isaiah, in the most powerful predictive prophecy about Jesus' death, wrote that 'upon him was the chastisement that brought us peace, and with his stripes we are healed'.[302] Scripture is clear. God wants his people to have health in all its dimensions. Through the cross, God deals with both the sins of his people and their consequences, which include illness in all its forms. God forgives and he heals. On the basis of this fact, some Christians, like the healer Jude's mother encountered, claim that people who trust in God can experience healing from every disease. They may be sincere in saying this, but they are sincerely wrong. This approach is

---

[300] Exodus 15:26
[301] Psalm 103:3
[302] Isaiah 53:5

156

potentially hugely damaging. When healing does not happen, it crushes the faith of vulnerable people. Its error lies in a failure to understand how and when healing happens.

Faithful people suffer and die. Scripture clearly teaches that God's healing is not total in this life. Moses, David and Isaiah knew that God was healer, but each of them died. Every person Jesus healed, even those he brought back from death, is now dead too. His miracles were demonstrations of the kingdom's power, but their impact on the bodies of those who were healed was not permanent. That should not cause us to doubt that God's kingdom is eternal, because Jesus taught that the kingdom is both present now and that its fullness is future. Lack of physical healing is no reason to doubt God's power or faithfulness because God has not promised total physical healing in this life.

In our earlier consideration of suffering in gospel perspective, we saw from Romans 8 that justification and a restored relationship with God are our present experience, but that the redemption of our bodies is still future. We will not experience complete physical wholeness until we receive our resurrection bodies. The body I am typing these words with, like the one you are reading with, is weak, perishable and dishonourable. Through resurrection it will be transformed to be imperishable, powerful and glorious.[303] There is total physical healing through the cross of Christ, but only through resurrection and only when Christ returns.

When we consider social, emotional and mental health, we may have greater hopes for healing in this life. In theory, our thoughts and feelings could be perfectly aligned with God's truth and our relationships could be restored. These are certainly legitimate goals to strive towards and to pray for. In practice, however, things are not so simple for several reasons.

Firstly, feeling and thinking are not detached from our bodies, but happen within them, so while we live in these weak and perishable bodies, we will continue to have unhealthy emotions and thoughts because of imbalanced hormones and brain chemicals, misfiring neurones and

---

[303] 1 Corinthians 15:42-44.

incomplete understanding.

Secondly, relational restoration depends on two or more people, so even if I can put everything right on my side of the equation, there may still be difficulties due to the other person's refusal or inability to put everything right on their side.

Thirdly, even if two people have completely pure emotions and thoughts towards one another and are ready to forgive and exercise patience, circumstances outside them in this fallen world can make it impossible for them to be restored in relationship and the limited time available to them, limits of communication and our inability to forget past hurts can also hamper restoration of relationships.

We can long for total emotional, mental and relational healing in this life and we can expect significant progress in the right direction, but our souls will not be restored completely until we see Christ face to face. Just as with physical healing, we can trust God for total soul healing, but we will not experience it in any dimension until Christ returns in glory. God may bring healing to our hearts through dramatic leaps forward. When gospel truth penetrates into a recess of the heart that had been obstinately shut, the change can be astounding. Still, many Christians will experience chronic struggles with thoughts and emotions over a lifetime in the same way that they experience ups and downs in their physical health.

How does God heal? Miracles and more

Any healing we experience in this life is a foretaste of our ultimate restoration in the new creation. Physical healing now does not reverse death and its effects are for a limited time. Some Christians say miraculous physical healings were confined to the time of the apostles. I see no biblical reason to agree with them. I do believe, though, that we should be cautious about claiming a miracle on the basis of hearsay, as I have often seen Christians do. I am also concerned that many reported 'miracles' lack the hallmarks of biblical healings, which were dramatic, immediate and complete. In fact, such miracles are rare even in the Bible, being largely confined to times when God was doing something radically new in the history of salvation through leaders who needed authentication.

Most biblical miracles happened when Moses and Aaron were leading Israel out of Egypt, when Elijah and Elisha were beginning the prophetic pronouncement of judgement that would lead to exile, and when Jesus and the apostles were declaring the arrival of God's kingdom and entrance into it through the forgiveness of sins. It is sobering to realise that these miracles were as much about God's judgement as his deliverance. Most of those who benefited from them did not come to believe in him. We should not assume that healing miracles will be commonplace at every point in history, nor should we regard them as a necessary sign of the Spirit's work. The New Testament epistles offer no guarantee of physical healing, although they do keep open the possibility of gifts of healing operating in the church.[304] They do not, however, provide any basis for the phenomenon of individuals gifted to heal as sometimes seen in contemporary Christianity. Instead, the epistles send us to the elders of the church for prayer for healing.[305]

Another problem with focusing on healing miracles is that it lessens our appreciation for the varied ways in which God heals. Physical healing comes from God whether it is miraculous or not. The natural capacity of our bodies and minds to heal with time is a gift from him. So too is therapeutic healing through people who use the resources of his world and the skills he gave them to work healing in our bodies and minds. Even the death of someone who trusts in Christ is a kind of healing when we remember the promise that absence from the body means presence with the Lord [306] and the assurance of future resurrection. Discussions of divine healing too often focus on physical disease. We must think too of spiritual healing which happens as we come to faith in Christ and grow in faith in God's truth. Restoration of relationship with others, which is the subject of Chapter 7, is also a kind of healing, as is the correction of wrong patterns of emotion and thinking. Healing in these areas can appear miraculous when it is sudden and dramatic – like the person who never experiences a specific temptation again after their conversion – but it is no less a work of God when it is gradual and partial.

---

[304] 1 Corinthians 12:9
[305] James 5:14
[306] 2 Corinthians 5:8

What if God does not heal? Strength to endure

Our desire for healing in the present is understandable. We can pray for healing to happen now, but, above all, we pray for God's will to be done. We must recognise that he may give the grace of healing or the grace to endure without healing. We must accept God's answer to our prayers, whether it is yes or no. All the time, we keep our hope in the total healing to come when Christ returns. Endurance through suffering reveals God's power not through our strength but through our weakness. In pride, we fool ourselves that we are, or should be, greater than we are. Fundamentally, we like to feel like we have no need of God. This is ridiculous! Compared to God, our capacity, even at maximum health, is severely limited. Weakness is what drives us to God and when we get there, we realise that it is alright to admit that we cannot make it alone. That is the very essence of faith.

Sometimes we need physical or emotional weakness to grow spiritually. The lack of answers to the 'why' question of suffering teaches us dependence on God. We should not think that life would be better if we had every answer. As Eugene Peterson says, 'a solved life is a reduced life'.[307] The apostle Paul testified in his experience that God sometimes does not heal because he wants to teach us ongoing trust in his grace.[308] When God did speak to Paul it was not to tell him why he was suffering, but to assure him that God's grace would be sufficient for him. That assurance is better than reasons.

Help: walking with others on the road of suffering

Having presented a definition of health as wholeness in the truth and explored some questions surrounding healing, it is now important to consider what help we can bring to people who are suffering.

---

[307] Peterson, 1989, p.64.
[308] 2 Corinthians 12:7-10

Which view is needed now? The balcony and the path

We can consider the issue of suffering in two ways, which Alistair McGrath illustrates as views from the path and from the balcony.[309] The balcony view looks at suffering from a distance and sets it within the bigger picture of God's eternal purposes. It knows God's promises and sees his eternal consolation at the end of the road. The view from the path – how we think about suffering while we are experiencing it – is quite different. Clouded by pain and loss, its horizon is bounded by present experience.

The difference between these views is exemplified by two books by C.S. Lewis. The balcony view of the *Problem of Pain* (1940) brilliantly defends the existence and character of God, including the famous statement that pain is God's 'megaphone to rouse a deaf world'.[310] By contrast, in *A Grief Observed* (1961), written after Lewis's wife died from cancer and originally published under the pseudonym N.W. Clerk, an anguished Lewis writes: 'Talk to me about the truth of religion and I'll listen gladly. Talk to me about the duty of religion and I'll listen submissively. But don't come talking to me about the consolations of religion or I shall suspect that you don't understand'.[311] These words are a helpful reminder that the way we speak to people about painful experiences must be adapted to their ability to hear.

On the path of suffering, as Lewis discovered, it is often impossible to think clearly about anything, God included. Words about God's sovereignty over suffering and purpose in pain can sound like condemnation rather than comfort. People who are numb to everything cannot be expected to feel God's presence. People in crisis do not need a thesis on the purposefulness of suffering but the committed presence of a supportive person. Meaning and understanding may come later since. As David Benner writes, 'Most of us learn to discern God's presence by first looking for it in the rear-view mirror'. [312] As people begin to process their experience, a gospel perspective becomes ever more important. They will need a robust

---

[309] McGrath, 1992, p.71.
[310] Lewis, 1940, p.91.
[311] Lewis, 1961, p.38.
[312] Benner, 2004, p.42.

theology of suffering, but they also need help to bridge between it to the path. Theology must be integrated with lived experience. The church also has a vital role to play in preparing people for suffering by faithful teaching on the issue. A clear balcony view may help build resilience so that people enter the road of suffering with stronger confidence in God's goodness.

How can we help people endure?

One biblical promise that can assure us as pastoral caregivers and that we may share with those who are processing their suffering is that God will not give us more to carry in this life than we can bear with the grace he supplies.[313] Wholeness, as we learned earlier from Henri Nouwen, is not found only through healing, but also through walking with our unresolved problems and unanswered questions. Our Shepherd is with us both in green pastures beside quiet waters and in the darkest valleys, and he will protect and guide us until he brings us to his home where an abundant banquet of well-being awaits.[314]

Pastoral caregivers can do much to help people endure in faith and faithfulness by teaching and modelling good habits for wholeness. Endurance in faith and faithfulness requires us to maintain good mental health. The principles promoted by mental health charities contain much wisdom, reflecting how God has made us:[315]

- talk about your feelings;
- keep active;
- eat well;
- drink sensibly;
- keep in touch with people;
- ask for help;
- take a break;

---

[313] 1 Corinthians 10:13
[314] Psalm 23:5.
[315] Mental Health Foundation, undated.

- do something you are good at;

- accept who you are (we might qualify this as 'who you are in Christ'); and

- care for others.

Such advice is perfectly consistent with biblical principles. These simple measures can help people think clearly and maintain emotional stability. In that place, they can engage with gospel truth. I will return to this in Chapter 10 when I discuss pastoral guidance. In what follows, I will consider in light of the gospel three concepts that are frequently suggested in relation to mental health: resilience, mindfulness and gratitude. Insights into each of these concepts unearthed by research are catching up with principles revealed in Scripture and lovingly built into creation by our Creator for our good. They make sense within the gospel framework and the gospel should guide our engagement with them. We must not use them for selfish gain but as steps on the path of discipleship. Through these creation principles, the gospel calls us into the deeper new creation reality of relationship with God.

Resilience

Resilience is ability to bounce back from adverse experiences. Research suggests ten principles for developing resilience, each of which resonates with the gospel, as illustrated in Table 4.[316] The comparison shows how helpful Christian faith is in building resilience. It is important to emphasise, though, that we do not embrace the gospel because it is convenient or good for us, but because it is true. The fact that it makes so much sense of human experience is just one strand of evidence for its truth.

With the example of Christ, the power of the Spirit and the support of the Church we can endure through life's challenges. Indeed, Christian resilience can be sustained even when we cannot find any strength in ourselves. Whether I feel resilient or not, I hide in my mighty Saviour whose resilience is limitless. His power is made perfect in my weakness.

---

[316] TIME Magazine, 2015

Table 4 – Resilience from the gospel

Principle for resilience	Gospel perspective
An unshakeable set of core beliefs	The gospel is this core set of beliefs
Try to find meaning in stressful or traumatic experiences	There is ultimate meaning in God's sovereign purpose for our good in all things (Romans 8:28)
Try to maintain a positive outlook.	We have living hope and practise thankfulness and joyfulness (1 Thessalonians 5:16-18)
Take cues from someone who is especially resilient	We can look to the ultimate example of resilience in the person of Jesus (Hebrews 12:3)
Face things that scare you	We can face our fears in God's strength because He is with us (Joshua 1:9)
Be quick to reach out for support	The Church is a supportive community
Keep learning new things	We are called to be lifelong learners (disciples)
Don't dwell on the past	We know God's forgiveness and the hope of glory so we can forget past shames and successes as we pursue Christ (Philippians 3:13-14)
Maintain an exercise regimen	We are called to train physically and for godliness (1 Timothy 4:8)
Recognise and own what makes you uniquely strong	We recognise that our strength is in God and His unique purpose for us (Ephesians 6:10)

Mindfulness

The concept of mindfulness, which has become widespread in recent years, originated in Buddhism. Some advocates recommend Buddhist practices – meditation, yoga or tai chi – as pathways to achieve it. Christians should be sceptical of these practices and the spirituality behind them. We may even decide not to speak of mindfulness to avoid confusion. The basic concept of mindfulness is not, however, problematic. It means, 'Paying more attention to the present moment – to your own thoughts and feelings, and to the world around you'.[317] This mental discipline allows us to

---

[317] NHS Choices (2016) Mindfulness. https://www.nhs.uk/conditions/stress-anxiety-depression/mindfulness/#different-mindfulness-practices

experience afresh things we have taken for granted, to check thought patterns that might otherwise control us, and to recognise signs of stress and anxiety.

Mindfulness comes close to the devoted attentiveness Jesus commended Mary for in contrast to Martha's anxious busyness.[318] It also resonates with his teaching that we should focus on today's needs and leave tomorrow's worries for tomorrow.[319] Importantly, however, this discipline and the inner peace it brings is not an end in itself for the Christian. Rather, it is a way to maintain our focus on God's truth. Jesus commended Mary because she focused on him, not on herself, and he grounded freedom from anxiety in trust in our heavenly Father's provision. Focusing and clearing our minds should lead to meditation on Scripture and prayer to the God whose peace can guard our hearts and minds.[320] From that place of peace we commit to pursue his kingdom and righteousness above our own perceived needs.

Gratitude

Gratitude has been the subject of psychological research in recent years. Studies have shown its benefits physically (lower blood pressure, fewer aches and pains, better sleep), socially (increased empathy and reduced envy, resentment and aggression) and in performance (higher motivation and resilience).[321] There is a certain irony in these findings. Thankfulness is, ultimately, an illusion if there is no one to give thanks to. Again, these findings resonate with gospel truth! Christians have someone to thank and many things to be grateful for. As Revelation shows, we can join all Heaven

---

[318] Luke 10:38-42

[319] Matthew 6:25-34

[320] Philippians 4:4-9

[321] Konstantinovsky, M. (2017) '5 reasons gratitude is good for you', One Medical. www.onemedical.com/blog/live-well/gratitude/; Morin, A. (2015) '7 Scientifically Proven Benefits of Gratitude', Psychology Today. www.psychologytoday.com/gb/blog/what-mentally-strong-people-dont-do/201504/7-scientifically-proven-benefits-gratitude

in thanking God for creation, salvation and ultimate restoration.[322]

At the same time, we must accept that are times when we cannot feel grateful and things for which we should not be thankful. Telling people in deep pain to be thankful may be counter-productive, creating a vicious circle of worry about the negative impact of lacking gratitude and, thus, finding it even harder to give thanks. Thanksgiving is not intended to be a burden. God invites us to come to him for the rest we need to break the cycle of guilt and worry so that we can give thanks. As David modelled in Psalm 131, we can humble ourselves and refuse to concern ourselves with matters too great for us, calm our souls through childlike trust, and hope in the Lord now and for the future. We allow God to look after our ambitions, needs and desires.

REFLECTION

- To what degree do you think we can expect healing, or restoration of health in its various dimensions, in this life? How would you explain this to someone to whom you are providing pastoral care?

- How can you develop, model and teach principles for mental well-being in a way that leads to God?

CHAPTER SUMMARY

Suffering is universal in human experience. The gospel gives us both a 'balcony view' of the problem and resources for walking on the road of suffering with unanswered questions. It defines health as wholeness in the truth, with our bodies, minds, relationships and souls restored to what God intends for us under Christ's lordship. This wholeness will not be complete

---

[322] Revelation 4:9; 7:12; 11:17

until we are made whole in the new creation at the redemption of our bodies. Then we will have total healing, but we can experience partial healing now, including transformation in our thinking and emotions as we grow in the gospel. Pastoral caregivers can work with people in need to help them endure in faith and faithfulness and we can use creation principles in doing so, including Christian versions of resilience, mindfulness and gratitude.

CHAPTER 7 - DISCUSSION QUESTIONS

1. In pairs, role play answering the question, 'Why does God allow such suffering?' Assume the person you are answering is not going through a painful time at present. Share your responses with the whole group.

2. Share about a time when you have suffered. Did God feel near or distant? What truths helped sustain you through it and what did you learn by reflecting on the experience afterwards?

3. To what degree do you expect to see miraculous healings in this age? Whatever your perspective, how can you avoid unhelpful extremes in pastoral practice with people who desire healing?

4. Brainstorm the main indicators of health in each of the following aspects of our being (acknowledge when an indicator belongs in more than one list because we are integrated beings):

    a. Physical

    b. Mental

    c. Social

    d. Spiritual

5. Consider an aspect of negative or false thoughts you have experienced or seen in someone you know. How would you use the 'lights, camera, action' approach to evaluate it?

6. Would you sound any notes of caution to someone who has attended a 'mindfulness' course in work and is now raving about it?

8. MADE FOR RELATIONSHIPS

Sam closed his morning prayer with thanksgiving for Jude's decision to take the pastoral worker role. Their meeting had gone well and he was impressed at her questions about his theology of suffering – and relieved when she seemed reassured by what he said! He also thought it was very positive that she was looking for clear guidelines for pastoral care and felt it would benefit him as well as her. Another positive outcome was Jude's agreement to join an online pastoral care course. He was joyous at the prospect of having such a thoughtful and committed co-worker. Sam's next task of the morning was to finalise his sermon prep, but he had two pastoral visits in the afternoon. What would he say to Mrs Anderson, lost in grief at the suicide of her son and dutifully visiting her demented husband in the nursing home? Then what would he have to offer Richard, wrestling with feelings of guilt after his divorce and concern for his university student son who had sent a WhatsApp saying he wanted to be known as his daughter? Despite the huge differences between their stories, in previous conversations Richard and Mrs Anderson had expressed similar intense feelings of loneliness. That had resonated with Sam in a deeply personal way. Loneliness gripped his heart too.

Sam was not proud of it, but he felt ill-at-ease being the person others depended on in such complex life situations. He was committed to their growth in Christ, but he felt more comfortable speaking from a pulpit than an armchair. He could see that had always been part of his personality – more energised by being alone than talking to others – but – and this seemed to be at the core of his struggle – preferring solitude did not mean he was not lonely. In fact, he had never felt lonelier than since he became a pastor. He felt bad about that. He was deeply committed to Beth and felt she should be enough to satisfy his need for companionship, but he wished he had real friends — people who would be in touch just to see how he was without asking for something. His life had narrowed since he was ordained. He thought of his parents and decided to call them before he opened his commentaries.

The Challenge of Loneliness

Loneliness, wrote Henri Nouwen, is 'one of the most painful human wounds'.[323] It has been recognised by government ministers as, 'one of the biggest public health challenges'.[324] It is little surprise that loneliness is a risk factor for depression.[325] Perhaps less obviously, its negative impact on physical health is equivalent to smoking 15 cigarettes daily! [326] When we consider this problem, we might instinctively think of older people living alone. It is true that older people are often isolated, but more people of all ages live alone now than in the past due to various factors including longer lifespans, greater mobility, decline in marriage, and smaller family size. We should not, however, equate loneliness with living alone. People can live alone without being lonely and loneliness can affect people of all ages and life situations. In fact, during the coronavirus pandemic older people reported lower levels of loneliness than younger people.[327] Loneliness is not simply due to lack of company either. Sam's work as a pastor ensured regular contact with people, but he discovered that people can be lonely in a crowd.

Feelings of loneliness arise from two factors. The first, perhaps more obvious one, is lack of intimate, committed relationships. Individualism and

---

[323] Nouwen, 2014, p.87.

[324] Baroness Barran, UK Minister for Loneliness, quoted in Gov.uk (2019) 'New fund for frontline organisations tackling loneliness'. https://www.gov.uk/government/news/new-fund-for-frontline-organisations-tackling-loneliness

[325] Cacioppo *et al.*, 2006

[326] Holt-Lunstad *et al.*, 2015

[327] Bennett, R. (2020) 'Over-60s most active and least lonely during coronavirus lockdown', *Times.* https://www.thetimes.co.uk/article/older-people-are-coping-better-than-the-young-in-lockdown-bh9xfqn8q

competitiveness undermine the formation of deep and lasting friendships. Excessive busyness in the 'rat race' to advance ourselves (and our children) leaves us with no time to make or keep friends. People who find it difficult to trust others, perhaps due to past hurts, but who simultaneously feel a need for affirmation can struggle especially acutely. Many relationships that we may call 'friendships' are either not intimate – they are only superficial, spending time together but not sharing about heart matters – or not committed – they are more transactional, based on what we can do for the other person. Pastors like Sam can find this especially difficult, since they are often seen by others as a source of help, but do not know where to find help themselves.

The second factor feeding loneliness is lack of rootedness. French philosopher Simone Weil wrote that, 'To be rooted is perhaps the most important and least recognized need of the human soul'.[328] Rootedness means belonging in a community with a shared understanding of the past and hopes for the future. Many people in the twenty-first century West have lost such roots because of the autonomy-authenticity-actualisation project and the individualism and subjectivism that feed it. They form 'communities' around shared experiences or feelings, but commitment is seldom expected or experienced.

Communication is more instant and constant than ever before due to social media and messaging apps, but it does not bring a sense of deep connection and can, counter-intuitively, leave people feeling enslaved to the fear of missing out and being forgotten if they do not keep posting. Somewhat ironically, pastors like Sam, although they clearly belong to a church community, can lack rootedness because their responsibilities and people's expectations of them put them at a distance from the community.

---

[328] Weil, 2002, p.40.

REFLECTION

- Have you experienced loneliness? Did lack of intimate relationships, lack of rootedness, past hurts and excessive busyness contribute to this?

- Realising that many people are chronically lonely, what can you commit to doing in response as a pastoral caregiver?

Relationships in Gospel Perspective

Pastoral caregivers need to recognise that people are made for relationships and pastoral care must work towards relational well-being. We need to understand relationships in gospel perspective.

God rules – made for relationship

God made human beings to relate to him and one another. It was not good for Adam to be alone.[329] Eve was created to be his neighbour, to become his friend and, ultimately, to enter marriage with him, so beginning the first family unit. Marriage is defined in Genesis 2:24 using three verbs:[330]

- *Leaving* the biological family for a new location, identity and loyalty. Marriage is marked by exclusivity.

- *Holding* fast to one another in an intimate, lasting, exclusive, committed relationship. Marriage is marked by commitment.

- *Becoming* one flesh, united physically in sexual intimacy, psychologically in shared responsibility for one another's growth, and practically in the work God entrusts to each member. Marriage is marked by intimacy.

---

[329] Genesis 2:18.

[330] Genesis 2:24 puts the imperative in these clauses with the man, but the dynamic is undoubtedly two-way as both man and woman leave, hold and become together.

This God-given marriage relationship is the only one described in Scripture before the fall. It is the basis for family and for society, providing stability in child-raising and putting covenant commitment at the foundation of family life. Within families built on marriage we are able to learn healthy relationships in friendship, business and romance.

Not every person will be married, but two of the qualities exemplified in marriage – commitment and intimacy – are key in every healthy relationship. Without them, trust is not possible and security cannot be experienced. The third aspect of marriage – exclusivity – is unique to this relationship and should not characterise friendships. Healthy relationships have the right degree of commitment and intimacy, but, with the exception of marriage, they are not exclusive of others.

We rebelled – sin in relationships

Sin brought shame to Adam and Eve.[331] The shattering of innocence with God resulted in lost innocence before others. Sin against others takes many forms, from seeking to control and actively abusing others to open hostility, and from neglect to unhealthy dependency.[332] These ungodly ways of relating create the context for wrong actions that hurt or harm others. We were made to cooperate in honour of one another under God. Instead, we fight for our own survival, comfort and advantage. Even the relationships that should teach us about God's covenant love – parenting and marriage – have been distorted by self-love. Selfishness and pride keep us from trusting others or being trustworthy for others. We do not love others as we love ourselves, and we do not consistently seek their good.

The existence of other people clashes with the autonomy-authenticity-actualisation project of Western culture because our desires overlap and sometimes conflict with those of others. When opportunities and resources abound, bitter feelings of rivalry and envy arise but can often be contained within our hearts or expressed through gossip. When they are limited, this

---

[331] Genesis 3:7.
[332] David Augsburger (1981, p.18) brilliantly expands upon the many ways we sin against others.

173

restraint is harder and open conflict becomes almost inevitable. In human societies, envy and selfish ambition – the hallmarks of earthly, unspiritual and demonic 'wisdom' [333] - always result in inequalities of power and wealth. No human political or economic system seems to be able to overcome this heart issue.

Fallen human beings can recognise the injustices that prevail in society. The modern mantra of autonomy often appears as a reaction to abuses of power and status. Christians should agree that people deserve liberty from oppression – that is a proper consequence of our belief in the dignity of each person created in God's image – but we must also insist that independence from God is not good, and that autonomy is ultimately an illusion. The problem human beings face is not only that some powerful people have oppressed some weaker minorities, true and unjust though that is. Our root problem is that we have unjustly accused God of being an oppressor of us all and have tried to follow our own way without him. Until we return to him and recognise that his rule is good, we cannot find true security. Only God can teach us to relate appropriately to others.

God rescues – relationship restored

The Law given by God to Israel contained much instruction about relationships between people: marriage, child-parent relationships, neighbourliness, and business. It insists on justice for the poor and punishment for harm caused to others. In a limited number of cases, crimes were to be dealt with through capital punishment, but for most there was a system of restitution of harm and restoration into the community. Undergirding all these responsibilities was the command to love one's neighbours.[334]

Importantly, however, the whole law was given in the context of God's relationship with Israel, which took the form of a covenant. Obedience to the law was to flow from the nation's understanding that God had rescued them from Egypt, bringing them to himself, and through obedience they

---

[333] James 14-16
[334] Leviticus 19:9,18

would be his 'treasured possession' among the nations.[335] The ten commandments bring together the call to worship God alone with duties towards other people.[336] The order is important. Only as Israel worshipped God truly could they learn to live harmoniously together. The command to neighbour-love flows from the foundational duty to love God with all their being.[337]

The religious leaders of Jesus' day evaded the responsibility to love their neighbours in two ways. Firstly, they limited neighbourliness only to those within the covenant community of Israel, believing they had no responsibility to love Gentiles. Secondly, they excluded people within Israel who they judged to be 'sinners', refusing to associate with them on the false premise that association would contaminate them. Jesus cut across these limitations both in his actions – eating intentionally with tax collectors and 'sinners' – and in his teaching – the Parable of the Good Samaritan,[338] for example, defined one's neighbour as everyone one interacts with, including outsiders to the covenant community.

Jesus said much about restoring relationships between people, but he also made clear that this was only possible based on a restored relationship with God through him. He described harmonious relationships between people as features of God's kingdom, but he did not tell people to build the kingdom by forging good relationships together. Rather, he said that entrance into the kingdom was through childlike faith in God and new birth from the Holy Spirit.[339] Once we enter the kingdom, we can learn from the king how to love one another.

The epistles explain this truth further. We are not by nature children of God, but children of wrath.[340] The cross made peace between humankind and God, so that Jesus now introduces believers into the grace of God, where we make our home.[341] We are called into the same kind of trusting

---

[335] Exodus 19:4-5
[336] Exodus 20
[337] Deuteronomy 6:5
[338] Luke 10:25ff.
[339] Matthew 18:3; John 3:3
[340] Ephesians 2:3
[341] Romans 5:2; Colossians 1:20

relationship Jesus had with God as Father. In the security of knowing we are God's beloved children, we learn to love and to build healthy relationships with others.

We respond – forgiven and forgiving

The gospel is not simply a set of truths to be believed; it is a summons from God, the king against whom we have been in rebellion, to enter into a new kind of relationship with him through repentance and faith. This new relationship is described as a new covenant and as becoming his child. The Spirit, through the gospel, gives us new life and assures us of that relationship. Central to this process of salvation is divine forgiveness of our sins. Receiving God's forgiveness is, however, intimately related to forgiving of others. The Lord's Prayer includes the petition, 'forgive us our debts, as we also have forgiven our debtors'.[342] Without forgiveness, human relationships would collapse rapidly and irreparably. We learn to extend grace to others from our experience of God's grace to us in Christ, as Jesus illustrated in the Parable of the Unforgiving Servant.[343] Experiencing God's grace, we learn to extend grace to others. We cannot receive forgiveness from God if we will not let go of bitterness against others.

God restores – learning to love

Jesus described his command to love one another as a 'new commandment'.[344] The basic concept of love for neighbours, as we have seen, was not new – the Old Testament law commanded it. What was radically new was the standard by which love is now defined: 'just as I have loved you, you also are to love one another'.[345] Jesus presented himself as the supreme revelation of divine love and raised the standard against which we measure ourselves. Love like his is the supreme Christian virtue,[346] the

---

[342] Matthew 6:12
[343] Matthew 18:21-35
[344] John 13:34
[345] John 13:34
[346] Colossians 3:14

dominant flavour of the fruit of the Spirit,[347] the pinnacle of growth in character,[348] and the virtue that never fails.[349] We can only understand this love by reflecting on the cross of Christ,[350] and we can only learn to love by experiencing God's love for us through the Spirit.[351]

The context in which we learn love is the church community. It is the gospel answer to the need for rootedness identified at the outset of this chapter. It is a community of deep and lasting commitment with a shared narrative of past and future. Sadly, contemporary churches often lack both authentic community and genuine rootedness. Commitment to a church can be as light and fleeting as to a social media group. Churches act as if their goal is constant reinvention in response to social change rather than rootedness in the story of God. Busy church calendars, packed with programmes, give an impression of life, but intimate relationships are lacking. To recover rootedness, the Church must facilitate meaningful relationships and it needs to know its past and its future. Its past is defined by gospel grace and a rich heritage of two millennia of Christian history as well as the specific history, for good and ill, of each congregation. Its future is defined by gospel hope, an eternal eschatological perspective that should focus its mission for the immediate future.

The gospel brings restored relationship with God and others. That is why God has ordained that the gospel spreads through people who share it in relationships with others. Rather than writing the message on the sky, God entrusted it to a people and commissioned them to become the community of his grace in which the gospel is embodied. Memories of the past and hope for the future enable the Church to be the place where people who are unrooted for various reasons – bereavement, redundancy, relocation, rejection by family, divorce – can put down deep roots in a secure and loving community. The relationships within which the gospel is communicated must reflect the gospel. The apostle Paul's faith, patience, love and steadfastness were evident to the younger Timothy through his

---

[347] Galatians 5:22
[348] 2 Peter 1:7
[349] 1 Corinthians 13
[350] 1 John 3:16
[351] 1 John 4:7-21

fatherly relationship.[352] Such relationships, as Sam discovered, are not always easy, but they are the best context for gospel growth. Pastoral care is inevitably relational.

REFLECTION

- Take time to reflect on the love of God for you in Christ Jesus. Ask him to grow this quality increasingly in you and to allow it to overcome hostility and desires you may feel for revenge against others.

- Read over the Parable of the Unforgiving Servant (Matthew 18:21-35). Do you see yourself in the servant who would not forgive despite having been forgiven much? Take time to remember how much God has forgiven you – to meditate again on his grace.

Love and Relationships

Four loves and four kinds of relationship

Our understanding of what it means to love others is confused by the many different connotations of the word 'love'. The Greek language in which the New Testament was originally written had at least four words that could be translated 'love' in English. Their distinct emphases have proven fruitful for describing different kinds of love in human relationships:[353]

- *Storge* describes natural affection, such as the love between family members or for one's nation.
- *Philia* is affectionate regard for others, including co-workers and friends.

---

[352] 2 Timothy 3:10
[353] See Lewis, 1960; Helm, 2013

- *Eros* is a passionate desire for intimacy, often sexual and usually exclusive.

- *Agapē* is a committed love that is chosen and does not demand reciprocation. Christians sometimes think that *agapē* is a distinctively Christian term for love from and for God. That is not quite true. The word was occasionally used in non-Christian writings and in a few New Testament verses it denotes love for ungodly things including sin, praise from people, and the world, praise from people.[354] Still, the word's primary use in the Bible is in verses referring to a distinctive quality of love that comes from God, so it seems reasonable for us to use it that way.

Without implying a hard and fast distinction between the four words, we may think of them as ideal types of love appropriate to different kinds of relationships.

Family relationships - *storge*

The first set of relationships we normally experience, is within the biological family. The natural affection within families is best described as *storge*. It begins with biological relatives, in whom we see something of ourselves, but embraces children by adoption and additions through marriage. We can love family members without liking them or counting them as friends. In healthy families, however, *storge* will be blended with *philia*, as members will count one another as friends.

Neighbourly relations - *agapē*

As we progress through life, we interact with people outside the family. These are, in biblical terms, our 'neighbours' and our relationship with them may be called 'neighbourliness'. Within this category are relationships in business and the workplace as well as involvement in shared interest groups such as community associations or sports clubs. Such relationships may not normally be thought of as 'loving' in wider society, but Christians have a

---

[354] John 3:19; John 12:43; 2 Timothy 4:10

179

duty to love their neighbours, including those we do not naturally 'gel' with and even those who are hostile to us. Unlike *storge*, it is not natural. Nor is it the love of friendship. Rather, it is chosen and does not demand return. It is best called *agapē*, the word used in Jesus' commands to love fellow believers, neighbours, and enemies.[355] Love even of enemies is possible because *agapē* is a commitment to the other person's good independent of our emotions. Pastoral relationships are an extension of neighbourliness and must, therefore, be grounded in *agapē*.

Friendships - *philia*

A third kind of relationship, friendship, may develop between neighbours and family members. Friends share mutual affection and care. They share in trusting self-disclosure of intimate things and choose to spend time in shared activities. The love of friendship, which C.S. Lewis described as, 'the least natural of loves' is *philia*.[356] Greek philosopher, Aristotle (384-322 BC), described friendship as, 'a virtue [...] most necessary with a view to living. For without friends no one would choose to live, though he had all other goods'.[357] True friendship, what Aristotle called 'perfect friendship', is about more than just mutual benefits or pleasure. It also includes a shared vision of what it means to be good. Sadly, because many relationships are motivated by a desire for pleasure or benefit, so that people abandon others when they no longer offer these things, many people lack true friends.

Marriage - *eros*

The final kind of relationship is marriage, when two people come together in a covenant commitment as life partners to form a new family unit. Marriage, as explained when we considered relationships in gospel perspective, differs from friendships in its exclusivity. Commitment to friends is non-exclusive and non-possessive, but marriage is appropriately

---

[355] John 13:34; Luke 10:27; Matthew 5:44.
[356] Lewis, 1960, p.70
[357] Aristotle, 350 BCE

exclusive. A wife can rightly be jealous of her husband's love. Many people in the West today seek this kind of committed relationship without calling it marriage, but the public exchange of vows is essential to creating the stability within which such a relationship can flourish.

Married couples should have deep friendship (*philia*), marriage is the soil in which *storge* grows as children are included in the new family, and a Christian marriage should exhibit *agapē*. In God's design, however, the fourth kind of love – *eros* – finds its proper expression in sexual intimacy within marriage. It is the exclusive dimension of marriage that takes the relationship to the level of becoming 'one flesh'.[358] It is not that sex is the fullness of the 'one flesh' principle, but that it is the physical expression of the covenant bond that makes one new person from two. This principle explains why marriage should be life-long and interdependent.

Church relationships

Relationships within the church cannot be reduced to one of these concepts alone. Believers are brothers and sisters and the Spirit creates a natural affection between us. Within the Church we can discover deep friendships with people who share our vision of good. What sustains church relationships through challenges, though, is a deep, selfless commitment to one another's good. *Storge*, *philia* and *agapē* are all, therefore, appropriate dimensions of love within the Church. The apostle Paul blends compounds of these three words together when he writes, 'Let love [*agapē*] be genuine. [...] Love [*philostorgoi*] one another with brotherly affection [*philadelphia*]'. Notice again, however, that the one kind of love that has no place in Christian relationships outside marriage is *eros*.

The debt to love

Christian love for others is, like God's love for us, sacrificial. That quality alone does not set it apart from other loves. Dietrich Bonhoeffer describes 'a human love of one's neighbour [...] capable of prodigious

---

[358] Genesis 2:24

sacrifices' that often 'far surpasses genuine Christian love in fervent devotion and visible results'.[359] What truly sets Christian love apart, Bonhoeffer explains, is not sacrifice, but selflessness:[360]

Human love is directed to the other person for his own sake [...] it loves him not as a free person but as one whom it binds to himself. It wants to gain, to capture by every means; it uses force. It desires to be irresistible, to rule.

Bonhoeffer is saying that human love for others always has a selfish element. We want approval or reward or simply to feel good about ourselves. Christian love, by contrast, commits to the good of others for the sake of Christ, rather than for our own sake or even for the other's sake. The love the Spirit produces in us has the same desire for them as God's love has for us – to bring them into deeper trusting relationship with Christ. It therefore eschews attempts to dominate or control. This selflessness love contrasts with our culture's autonomy-authenticity-actualisation project.

Scripture describes *agapē* as a debt we owe others.[361] Normally, a debt is incurred when we do not pay for something we receive. Yet, the apostle Paul says we have a debt to love everyone, including enemies who have never shown love to us. This is not a debt created by failure to repay something we receive. There is another way to become indebted to someone – if one person gives you money and tells you to pass it on to someone else, you are now indebted to the person you are supposed to give it to. God gave his love to us and commanded us to pass it on. We owe love to people he commands us to love. God showed us the selfless nature of *agapē* by giving Jesus to die for us while we were still rebels against him.[362] Jesus demonstrated it fully by laying down his life for us.[363] We can love selflessly because we have been loved selflessly.[364]

---

[359] Bonhoeffer, 1954, p.33-34.
[360] Bonhoeffer, 1954, p.34.
[361] Romans 13:8
[362] Romans 5:8
[363] 1 John 3:16
[364] 1 John 4:19

Agapē – *perfecting love*

Agapē interpenetrates and perfects each of the other loves, keeping them from selfishness and transforming relationships.

Perfected friendships

Friendship without *agapē* easily deteriorates into possessiveness and dependence. *Agapē* enables us to build friendships with people who do not share our vision of good, even if *philia* is not there to begin with.[365] It produces in us the qualities of a good friend. Gary Inrig summarises these qualities, as revealed in Proverbs, as, 'Personal integrity, the ability to say no graciously yet firmly, the capacity to stand alone under fire and not to cave in under peer-group pressure'.[366] Proverbs warns against association with unvirtuous people who can lead us astray. Christians should be aware of this danger, but, like our Lord, we will also be compelled by *agapē* to extend friendship to people who are utterly unlike Christ so we can share him with them. As we do so, we will need other friends who share our values to encourage us and to influence us to stay true to the Lord. The friendship of king-to-be David and Saul's son Jonathan provides a biblical pattern for such virtuous friendships. It was marked by affection, shared experience, intimacy, encouragement and commitment.[367]

Perfected family relationships

Agapē also transforms family relationships. It enriches *storge*, saving it from rivalry and transforming it into a commitment to love one another unconditionally, by cooperating selflessly. *Agapē* fosters the following qualities of a healthy, stable family develops:[368]

---

[365] Both Liz Carmichael (2004, p.198) and John Swinton (2000, p.39) argue this point.

[366] Inrig, 1981, p.124,

[367] 1 Samuel 18:1-55. Inrig (1981, p.51ff.) draws out similar principles from David's friendship with Jonathan.

[368] These qualities are influenced by Balswick and Balswick (1999, p.19, 46ff.) and the work of researcher Dolores Curran cited by Gary Collins (1988, p.438).

- *Gracious truth* – the members serve each other with their varied gifts and grow in understanding of God's truth, ready to forgive and receive forgiveness when needed.

- *Shared experiences* – all members interact in all directions, including through play, humour, rituals and traditions that affirm the importance of family and each generation within it.

- *Honoured intimacy* – members know and trust one another while honouring each other's individuality, right to privacy and unique contributions to the family.

- *Clear communication* – members listen well to one another, leading to understanding, and express **feelings, opinions, wishes and desires openly and unambiguously.**

- *Responsible roles* – clarity about the role each member plays, with age-appropriate responsibilities shared across all members and mutual support (especially from parents to children) as needed.

- *Stable flexibility* – members affirm commitment and goodwill clearly and routines are set with sufficient flexibility to permit adaptation as needed to changes, needs and challenges

Perfected marriage

Without *agapē*, the intense and jealous *eros* that drives romance can become possessive and controlling. *Agapē* will also protect sexual activity from being a means to either individual's own gratification and maintain the mutuality that is commanded in Scripture.[369] When the passion goes and romance fades, it may seem like a reason to end a marriage. Marriages in which *philia* has developed – where the partners are friends – may survive when *eros* fails, but without *agapē* the temptation to unfaithfulness if *eros* develops towards another will be harder to resist.

Forgiving Others

---

[369] 1 Corinthians

Healthy relationships inevitably require forgiveness. Inability or unwillingness to forgive others is a major barrier to restored relationships. An essential aspect of forgiving is letting go of the desire for revenge, which is a common human response to being wronged. Croatian theologian Miroslav Volf writes that, 'Deep within the heart of every victim, anger swells up against the perpetrator, rage inflamed by unredeemed suffering'.[370] We may think that taking revenge will assuage these emotions, but it only compounds them. Vengeance is a selfish desire to destroy another person for our own well-being, and selfishness always breeds death. We may argue that our act of revenge would be just, but strong emotions blind us, so we cannot judge fairly and are likely to go beyond just punishment. When we do so, we spark an escalating cycle of 'tit for tat' actions. If we are to forgive, we must let go of our desire for revenge. We can do so without losing hope for justice because God says, 'Vengeance is mine, I will repay'.[371] Only God has complete knowledge and is utterly fair and he will bring justice in the final judgement. We can, therefore, leave vengeful feelings with God. Words from the psalms may help us express our lament to him.

Knowing God's justice, we trust him ultimately to put everything right. Knowing God's grace, we are moved to hope that the person who harmed us will experience God's forgiveness. We must refuse to demonise the wrongdoer. When we do so, we act as if evil is an, 'aberration that is carried out by distorted individuals who bear little if any resemblance to "us"'.[372] It is impossible to forgive someone we have demonised. Volf warns that in this case, 'Forgiveness flounders because I exclude the enemy from the community of humans even as I exclude myself from the community of sinners'.[373] *Agapē* enables us to repay a person's evil with good in the hope that we may 'heap burning coals on his head' and move him to repentance.[374] Everett Worthington describes this as the, 'magical economics of payback', when one party in a conflict, instead of punishing the other, absorbs the pain by showing love, thus breaking the destructive

---

[370] Volf, 1996, p.120
[371] Romans 12:19-21, quoting Deuteronomy 32:35
[372] Swinton, 2007, p.1153
[373] Volf, 1996, p.124
[374] Romans 12:21

cycle.[375]

Some authors argue that once we have released the desire for revenge, forgiveness is complete. They claim that only God has the right to put a condition of repentance on forgiveness.[376] We are clearly commanded to let go of bitterness and to offer forgiveness to others,[377] but a person is not forgiven simply because we offer to forgive them. A wrongdoer can only experience forgiveness when he acknowledges his sin. To say a person is forgiven when they do not accept they have done wrong is to collude in denying the sin and excusing the sinner. Excusing wrongdoers makes it harder for them to find God's forgiveness. We cannot say someone is forgiven until they admit their wrongdoing, apologise for it and accept our forgiveness.

Forgiving others, especially for deep wrongs, is normally, David Augsburger writes, 'a complex and demanding process'.[378] It begins with letting go of the desire for revenge, then honestly acknowledging the hurt and the wrong that caused it. If the wrongdoer accepts the facts, the wronged person must listen and accept the apology without making unreasonable demands that they will not fail again. It is often helpful to do this in the presence of a witness or to express acceptance of repentance in writing. The final step in forgiveness is reconciliation. A trusting relationship is rebuilt over time. Importantly, full reconciliation is not always possible or desirable. It is impossible when the wrongdoer is dead or cannot be contacted or when trust cannot be rebuilt, for example in some cases of marriage breakdown. When abuse has happened, reconciliation may be undesirable, even when repentance seems genuine, as the vulnerable person must be protected from the risk of future abuse.

If forgiveness is not received, the Christian who offered it must continue to let go of any recurrent desire for revenge and seek, where possible, to bless the other person. Christians may continue to be friendly towards non-believers who will not repent as an expression of *agapē*. Within

---

[375] Worthington, 2009, p.31ff.
[376] See, for example: Smede, 1996, p.24-25; Worthington, 2009, p.48
[377] Mark 11:25
[378] Augsburger, 1981, p.30.

the Church, however, this should not be the case, since denial of sin is a denial of the gospel. Jesus commanded us to seek reconciliation with brothers and sisters who sin against us but taught that repentance is a precondition for reconciliation. He even required exclusion from the Church of wrongdoers who refuse to acknowledge or repent from their sin.[379]

REFLECTION

- Which of the four kinds of relationships and four loves have you experienced? How can you cultivate *agapē* in each of your relationships, including as a pastoral-caregiver?

- Reflecting on your own experiences of giving and receiving forgiveness, what are the challenges with helping others to forgive wrongdoers?

CHAPTER SUMMARY

Loneliness arises from lack of intimate relationships and lack of rootedness. The Church, the community of believers created by the Spirit, provides both trusting relationships and roots in the gospel. The gospel tells us we were made for relationships, and the experience of restored relationship with God through Christ teaches us to forgive others and to love them. From God's love for us we learn a new quality of selfless love for neighbours, in our friendships and family relationships. This love also enables us to forgive those who wrong us, releasing our desire for revenge, blessing them and reconciling with them if they repent.

---

[379] See Matthew 18:15-17; Luke 17:3-4.

CHAPTER 8 - DISCUSSION QUESTIONS

1. Have you experienced loneliness? What is/was it like? How did lack of trusting relationships and lack of roots contribute to it?

2. Why is the gospel essential for healthy relationships? How does our relationship with God as Father through Christ and our experience of his love inform and transform our other relationships? Consider:
    a. Friendships

    b. Family relationships (with siblings, children and parents)

    c. Marriage

3. Share about a time when you had to forgive someone. What was easy or difficult about it? What would you do differently after reading this chapter?

SECTION 4

HOW?

GOSPEL-SHAPED HELP

9. PASTORAL LISTENING

The weekend was looming, and Sam was looking forward to informing the congregation that Jude had joined his pastoral team — if two people could be called a team! She was clearly teachable, and he sensed they could work well together and draw in other suitably gifted people. Jude's partnership was certainly part of the reason for his newfound confidence, but so was his phone conversation this morning with John, a godly retired pastor who served with a ministry that supported pastors. Sam was relieved that John had agreed to meet him monthly as a mentor. He was confident that the prayers and advice John would bring would help him develop in his ministry. Even just having a trusted person who would listen would be a blessing. He remembered his nerves before yesterday's pastoral visits. He reckoned the most significant thing he had done for Mrs Anderson and Richard was just listening. That was what had helped him in his call with John too. John was a great listener! Sam had felt like he had his full attention and John had summarised accurately everything he had shared when he prayed at the end of the call. Sam hoped to become as good a listener, perhaps with John's help.

Mrs Anderson had talked at length about memories of her son, the words flowing from her at pressure. She had asked if she had been responsible for his suicide. Sam had said very little but assured her it was not her fault and her son, who was a believer, was now with the Lord. That seemed appropriate, but he was not sure he should have added the line, 'I'm sure you were a good mother'. He had no idea if that was true. He wondered what she had left unsaid and whether he had shut her down from sharing more by his empty platitude. Richard had been quite different. Their meeting started with some small talk about the weather and politics, but when Sam asked any questions about his child's gender identity issues, Richard's answers were monosyllabic. Worse, when Sam asked if he had talked to his former wife, Richard firmly told him the divorce was 'nothing to do with' what his child was experiencing. That visit seemed like it had been a waste of time. He could see there were real issues to work through but could not work out how to get to them. That was something else to chat to John about!

The Challenge of Communication

Communication is a complex process in which messages are sent by 'senders' and received by 'receivers'. In a conversation, two or more parties take turns to be senders and receivers. When 'senders' decide to communicate in speech or in writing, and even when they communicate non-verbally either intentionally or not, they are projecting something from their inner selves for others to detect. John Savage identified four things that remain private, inside the sender, until they are expressed: *feelings, intentions, attitudes* and *thoughts*.[380] Each of these can be expressed not only in words, but also through tone of voice and body language. As the receiver interprets the communication there are four responses happening inside her: *feelings* evoked by the communication; *inferences* drawn about the sender's intended meaning; *attitudes* through which she filters the message; and *thoughts*, about what the message means and how to respond. Figure 3 displays this process visually.

Figure 3   The process of communication

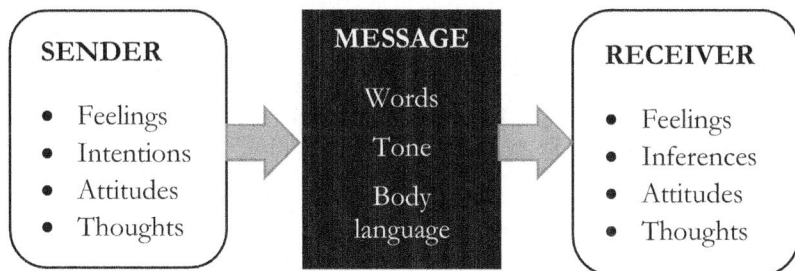

---

[380] Savage, 1996, p.16

Problems in communication can occur on either side of this equation. The message may not accurately reflect the sender's feelings, intentions, attitudes and thoughts, either because she wants to deceive the receiver or her message is unclear. The receiver, meanwhile, may misunderstand the message because she does not listen well, her attitudes distort her interpretation, or she draws wrong inferences about the intended meaning. This is made all the more difficult by factors in the context in which the communication happens. Sounds and sights can distract the sender or receiver and concerns about other people overhearing or observing the interaction can also limit the sender's openness.

The goal of pastoral listening is for the pastoral caregiver to understand the feelings, intentions, attitudes and thoughts of the care-seeker. It is vital, therefore, that pastoral caregivers develop good listening skills.

REFLECTION

- What challenges do you face in communication with others and how can you overcome them?

Effective Listening

Listening is the core skill needed in pastoral presence. Dietrich Bonhoeffer described it as the 'first service that one owes to others in the fellowship' and 'the beginning of love for the brethren'.[381] Only by listening well can we know what provision is needed, how to intercede for the other and what instruction is appropriate. To be effective pastoral listeners we need the right attitude, the right focus, and the right skills.

---

[381] Bonhoeffer, 1954, p.97

Right attitude: honouring others

If we want to listen well, we must pay attention to our own feelings and attitudes. Anne Long reminds us that listening is 'in the first place to do with attitudes rather than skills – availability, compassion, belief in people – knowing from our own experience what being heard can do for us'.[382] Bonhoeffer warns that people who do not listen to others soon cease listening to God. He recognised our proneness to 'listening with half an ear that presumes already to know what the other person has to say [...] an impatient, inattentive listening, that despises the brother and is only waiting for a chance to speak and so get rid of the other person'.[383] Pastoral listening begins with a conviction that the other person matters enough to be heard. This quality is sometimes described as 'respect', but I suggest that the correct word is 'honour'.

Respect, properly understood, means high regard for someone because of a quality we admire. It must be earned and can be lost. Honour, by contrast, is a response to the intrinsic value of the person that cannot be diminished by their behaviour or circumstances. A gospel-shaped attitude to people begins with the conviction that every person has dignity because each individual was created by God, is loved by God enough for him to send Jesus, and has potential to share eternal life with God. These three roots for human dignity mean that each person we encounter has immense value and we should honour them accordingly.

We show people honour by offering 'meaningful space and time that is uncluttered and personal, but spacious and appropriately comforting'.[384] In this space, we are ready 'to listen to the unattractive parts' of people's stories.[385] Margaret Guenther describes this as 'holy listening' in which we are 'open to anything' and says that the holy listener:[386]

is willing to hear about darkness and desolation, the times of God's seeming absence and neglect. She is not frightened by another's anger, doubt or fear; and she is

---

[382] Long, 1990, p.35
[383] Bonhoeffer, 1954, p.98
[384] Stairs, 2000, p.21
[385] Culbertson, 1999, p.273
[386] Guenther, 1993, p.150

comfortable with tears. At the same time, the holy listener knows the truth of the resurrection.

When we listen well to people, we value them as God does and they may begin to believe in their value to God too.

Building on our commitment to honour others, we will grow in effectiveness as listeners as we increase in 'three qualities for effectiveness in listening' that Peter White writes have been 'clearly identified' through extensive research: genuineness, warmth and compassion.[387] These qualities resonate with the apostle Paul's list of the fruit of the Spirit, reminding us that they will grow in us as we continue to be shaped by him into the likeness of Christ.[388] They create an environment in which others can grow to trust us and so share honestly about their needs, fears and hopes.

Another important factor in honouring others and encouraging openness in the conversation is the physical environment of the pastoral conversation. In addition to the need to ensure privacy without secrecy by having conversations where we can always be seen but not overheard (see Chapter 5), there are some other factors to consider, such as comfortable seats, minimal risk of interruption and having a box of tissues handy in case someone cries. Pierre and Reju also recommend positioning a clock strategically where you can check on time discretely without looking at a watch or mobile phone and having only books you would recommend visible in the room to avoid pointing people in unhelpful directions.[389]

Right focus: the heart

In addition to knowing *how* to listen, we must consider *what* we are listening for. Pastoral caregivers must listen for the soul's questions, feelings and needs which may be conveyed in the words or hidden behind them. Jean Stairs reminds us that, 'In most cases, people seeking pastoral care do

---

[387] White, 1998, p.111. I have replaced his 'empathy' with 'compassion' for the reasons outlined in Chapter 2.
[388] Galatians 5:22
[389] Pierre and Reju, 2015, p.52-53

not present obvious and explicit spiritual and theological issues', so we need to listen for 'the holy in the ordinary'.[390] John Patton writes that this means more than 'using one's ears and hearing words. It is a total response to the way that the caregiver is experiencing the other'.[391] We want to sense what Michael Jacobs calls, 'the base line' beneath the melody of words, the deeper feelings the care-seeker may not even be fully conscious of.[392] If we can recognise these, we can help the care-seeker disentangle mixed emotions about experiences.

One way to recognise unspoken emotions is the person's tone of voice. We should be attentive to sarcasm or irony. Breaking of the voice or relatively high-pitched speech may indicate emotional highs and lows or simply nervousness. A relatively low and monotonous voice can indicate sadness, pain or uncertainty. We must also watch body language, noting when it does not match what is said. We may miss something important if we do not notice moist eyes, broken eye contact or rapid breathing. Even silences can convey meaning, whether acceptance, processing, embarrassment or resistance.[393] Body language can help the wise listener make an informed guess about what a silence means and decide whether to invite the care-seeker to share his unspoken thoughts.

In pastoral conversations, especially as trust deepens, care-seekers will often share about feelings of guilt and shame. In such cases, we must help them distinguish false guilt from true guilt. False guilt is when we feel guilty without having sinned because we fall short of our unrealistic expectations of ourselves or those of others, especially parents or peers, or we have misunderstood God's will due to Satan's lies and false teachings. True guilt, by contrast, is a response to sin. It should not surprise us when people confess sin to us. Indeed, mutual confession is expected in Scripture.[394] Confession to a trusted person is often an important part of the journey to wholeness. As Bonhoeffer wrote, 'He who is alone with his sin is utterly

---

[390] Stairs, 2000, p.28
[391] Patton, 2005, p.29
[392] Jacobs, 1985, p.21
[393] See Long, 1990, p.50
[394] See James 5:16

alone'.[395] In the moment of confession the care-seeker is at her most vulnerable and the caregiver should beware the danger of coercion or manipulation. At the same time, it is in this moment that the opportunity for the Spirit to work is greatest. The person hearing confession should remember he is not superior to the one who confesses and avoid giving any impression that he has authority to absolve sins. Rather, the two together should accept the sin in the context of their shared confession that Jesus Christ is Lord and pray for his mercy.

Bonhoeffer described three benefits of confessing sins to others:[396]

- Firstly, as a representation of God's presence, the hearer helps the confessing person overcome the impression that no one is listening and that the person is only forgiving herself.

- Secondly, hidden sin 'gnaws away at us and poisons us'; bringing it into the open helps neutralise it.

- Thirdly, confessing sins to another is the 'the profoundest kind of humiliation',[397] and breaks the pride that is the root of all sin more effectively than anything else.

In general, such confession should be confidential, although we should not forget the limits to confidentiality outlined in Chapter 5. We also need to know how to respond, but that leads into the ministry of instruction and will be addressed in Chapter 10.

Right skills: active listening

The concept of 'active listening' developed within Carl Rogers's person-centred counselling approach and was popularised by American psychologist Thomas Gordon. It comprises four helpful skills.

First, active listeners **pay attention**. They intentionally put distracting thoughts out of their minds, ignore distractions, and focus on the other

[395] Bonhoeffer, 1954, p.110
[396] Bonhoeffer, 1985, p.62-63
[397] Bonhoeffer, 1954, p.114

person. They convey this through their own body language. The best stance for listening is described by the acronym SOLER:[398]

- Square on or at a slight angle;

- Open body posture with legs and arms uncrossed;

- Leaning forward;

- Eye contact; and

- Relaxed and non-fidgety.

Other ways to show interest are smiling, nodding occasionally and encouraging with small verbal responses such as 'yes' or 'uh huh'.

Second, active listeners **provide feedback**. This ensures they have understood. Feedback takes five forms:

- Paraphrasing – repeating in your own words what you heard (e.g., "What I'm hearing is …"; "Sounds like you are saying …"; "If I'm hearing you right, you are …"). This is particularly useful if you are struggling to understand, whether because of your own condition (e.g., tiredness or illness), the person's way of communicating (e.g., fast speech through tears, a heavy accent or lack of clear focus) or cultural factors (e.g., limited English or different reference points).

- Interpreting – compassionately assessing what is really in the person's heart and sharing it tentatively, always open to correction.

- Self-disclosure – sharing something of one's own struggles and experiences. This must be done judiciously so that the care-seeker's needs remain the priority above one's own.

- Summarising what you have heard periodically helps move longer conversations forward, ensure understanding and stimulate reflection.

- Questioning should be used judiciously to fill gaps or clarify meaning, never merely to satisfy personal curiosity. Questions can also help care-seekers recognise when they have distorted the truth by using generalising phrases like 'everyone', 'no one', 'always' or 'never'. John

---

[398] White, 1998, p.113

Savage suggests that we can expose this issue simply by using the generalising word as a single word question. For example, if someone says, 'No one listens to me!', you may respond, 'No one?' [399] Some additional helpful principles for using questions are:

- o It is best to ask questions without interrupting the speaker, if possible, since interruptions can frustrate the care-seeker and derail his train of thought.

- o The best questions are 'open', meaning they do not imply that the questioner is looking for a specific answer and do not put ideas into the person's mind.

- o Do not string multiple questions together to avoid confusion.

- o Questions may be direct ('What do you think?') or indirect ('What do people in your situation usually think?'). Which kind is best depends on the care-seeker's cultural norms and the level of trust in the pastoral relationship.

- o Including phrases the care-seeker has used in your questions can help assure them they have been heard.[400]

Third, active listeners **postpone judgement**. When listening to others, we can be tempted to judge them and interpret their meaning before we have heard the whole story. We must be aware of our prejudices and potential to misunderstand. It would be wrong to suggest that pastoral caregivers should not make judgements. We must seek to discern truth from falsehood and good from bad. We must, however, defer judgement until we have adequate understanding. This delay allows trust to build in the pastoral relationship and creates space for the caregiver to pray for insight and take advice from colleagues and overseers if needed. What we should never do is to condemn people, meaning to declare final judgement and inevitable divine judgement upon them. To do so is counter-gospel and leaves them with no hope for change.

Fourth, active listeners **plan responses**. Pastoral caregivers must decide the appropriate course of action in response to what they have heard. It is

---

[399] Savage, 1996, p.35
[400] Long, 1990, p.53

best to be open and honest with the care-seeker about intended responses. It is helpful to end each pastoral conversation with a summary of any agreed next steps or at least an assurance that you will be prayerfully considering how best to respond. Express your own opinions with humility and gentleness, never imposing them on others, and treat the other person as you would like to be treated yourself. This process of discernment and planning responses leads to the second stage of pastoral listening – evaluating needs.

REFLECTION

- Do you have the character qualities of a good listener? How can you develop them further in relationship to God through deepening your gospel understanding?

- Which active listening skills do you use effectively, and which could you improve? How will you hone them? How would you respond if someone confessed something to you that they have been feeling guilty about or ashamed of for many years but have never admitted before?

Evaluating Needs

Having listened well, we need to evaluate what we have heard. This process is often most effective during prayerful reflection after a pastoral encounter, so we must make space and time to do so. Evaluation involves determining whether the person has spoken truthfully, prioritising among his needs, and seeking wisdom to know what help he needs.

The whole truth?

Pastoral caregivers must recognise that communication is not always truthful. Using the familiar adage from the courts, our aim is to understand 'the truth, the whole truth and nothing but the truth' of the care-seeker's heart. It is helpful to recognise two qualities that make for truthful communication: sincerity and completeness: [401]

- **Sincerity** – the care-seeker means what she says. She could be sincerely mistaken, but is not intentionally misleading the caregiver.

- **Completeness** – the care-seeker is not withholding anything the caregiver needs to know to respond appropriately in pastoral provision, intercession and instruction.

The presence of absence of these two qualities results in four possibilities, which are described in Table 5 using variations on the courtroom oath.

Table 5   ***Sincerity and completeness in communication***

| | | Is the communication sincere? | |
		Yes	No
Is the communication complete?	**Yes**	**"The truth, the whole truth and nothing but the truth"** This ideal form of communication is open, direct and honest. It allows healthy relationships to be built and issues to be identified and addressed	**"Untruth, the whole untruth"** Nothing is omitted, but facts are distorted, either intentionally (lies were told) or unintentionally (the communicator is deceived or deluded)
	No	**"The truth, but not the whole truth"** Some details (often unresolved tensions, fears, shame or guilt) are omitted, whether on purpose (perhaps due to lack of trust) or not (lack of clarity or forgetfulness)	**"Untruth, but not the whole untruth"** The truth is distorted (either intentionally or unintentionally) and important details are omitted (on purpose or not). When a person communicates in this way, care will never result in gospel growth.

---

[401] For a similar scheme see Savage, 1996, p.15

The ideal is, obviously, for communication to be sincere and complete. It is important to realise, however, that even in this case the care-seeker may still be wrong because she lacks self-awareness or believes falsehoods. Our aim is, thus, threefold:

- Firstly, to understand the care-seeker accurately, including recognising falsehood in his story.

- Secondly, to help the care-seeker understand himself better.

- Thirdly, to help the care-seeker towards truth, first in his understanding of his experiences and, ultimately, in the gospel so that real change can occur.

As a care-seeker expresses openness to gospel truth, the ministry of instruction can proceed but before we can know what instruction is needed, we need to discern spiritual issues and then diagnose soul sickness.

Discernment: spiritual wisdom

As we listen to care-seekers, we also listen to God. What is the Spirit doing in this person, in this situation, at this time? It is possible that God could reveal this to you or to the care-seeker through a vision, a dream or a prophetic message, but Scripture points discernment rather than supernatural revelation as the normal means of God showing us his will.[402] His desire for us is that we grow in maturity to make godly judgements according to his wisdom. Discernment entails, 'judging whether a certain word, action, decision or conclusion is an appropriate response to God's call at a particular time in our life'.[403]

Even if we believe that God has spoken in a vision or dream or through a message that claims to be prophetic, discernment is still needed to test and weight the apparent revelation.[404] It must be tested for its truthfulness and consistency with the Scriptures in consultation with other godly people.

---

[402] See, for example, Romans 12:2; Ephesians 5:15-17; Colossians 4:5
[403] Johnson and Dreitcer, 2001, p.102
[404] 1 Corinthians 14:29; 1 Thessalonians 5:20-21

The Spirit will not lead people to disobey Scripture and the direction of his leading in a person's life will always be consistent with biblical priorities. Even if we remain convinced that this is a message from God, it should be weighed as to its appropriate application in a specific situation, and this should be done by and with the overseers of the church.

Discernment must not be thought of as a means to a 'quick fix' solution to a problem. Johnson and Dreitcer remind us that it 'has more to do with deepening our relationship with Christ than it does with making right decisions'.[405] Discernment requires wisdom, which God promises to give to those who seek it.[406] The 'heavenly' wisdom he gives differs from, worldly (earthly, unspiritual or demonic) wisdom. The difference is outlined in James: worldly wisdom justifies and expresses jealousy, selfishness, boasting and falsehood; heavenly wisdom is 'first pure, then peaceable, gentle, open to reason, full of mercy and good fruits, impartial and sincere'.[407] In the choices facing people, when there is no clear command in Scripture, we can help them see which option embodies worldly wisdom and which expresses heavenly wisdom. More often than not when a person is torn between two options, the real issue is not whether it is clear which is more aligned with God's wisdom, but whether the person is willing to submit to God's will. Sometimes when we listen to people and hear their reasons for choices and justifications for desires, we can discern that there is a deeper sickness in their soul – worship of some idol or refusal to acknowledge God's truth.

Diagnosing soul sickness

Diagnosis of soul sickness is the bridge between understanding what a person is saying and knowing how to help with the person's needs. Consider what a doctor does routinely. She hears her patient's 'history', examines the patient's body, and orders investigations if appropriate. She then brings all the evidence together to reach a diagnosis of the underlying problem and plans appropriate treatment. What the physician does for the

---

[405] Johnson and Dreitcer, 2001, p.101
[406] Proverbs 2:6; 2 Timothy 2:7; James 1:5
[407] James 3:13-18

body, pastoral caregivers can do for the care-seeker's soul.

No X-ray or blood test will expose the condition of a person's heart, but the caregiver can seek corroborating perspectives. You might ask a person who has disclosed marital friction to meet again, this time with both partners present to hear both perspectives. You could ask a single woman to ask her closest Christian friends how they perceive her problem. Or you might simply ask the care-seeker to tell you honestly what he thinks his parents, colleagues or children would say if he asked them. The primary source for pastoral diagnosis, however, will always be what you see and hear in what the person tells you and how they tell it along with insights you may gain through intercessory prayer for the person.

Diagnosing soul sickness entails disentangling what may seem like a hopelessly knotted account containing truths, half-truths and lies. In doing so, we should consider the three areas of needs described in Chapters 6 to 8: relationship with God, physical and mental/emotional well-being, and relationships with others. In each aspect, we seek to recognise where the person's beliefs and behaviours are right and wrong. There are four key questions to consider:

- What false ideas does she believe?
- What wrong actions has she taken and what bad patterns of behaviour has she developed?
- What truth does she need to trust?
- What right actions does she need to take and what good patterns of behaviour should she develop?

These four questions can be reduced to two words – repent and believe – applied to two spheres – thoughts (and feelings) and actions (and habits). We are seeking real change in beliefs and behaviours. Chapter 10 will explore how biblical truth can be applied to the needs identified through this process.

REFLECTION

- Are you a sincere and complete communicator when you are sharing gospel truth with others? Repent of any failings and commit to a faithful approach in future.

- How do you expect God's guidance to come to people? How can you be sure that it is God's idea and not your own?

CHAPTER SUMMARY

Communication is challenging because we struggle to express and understand meaning and because we deceive ourselves and others. Pastoral listeners need the right attitude – honouring people and learning to show genuineness, warmth and compassion. We need the right focus – on the heart issues that lie behind people's stories and need healing in the gospel. We need the right skills – active listening by paying attention, providing feedback, postponing judgement and planning our responses. Only then can we evaluate and prioritise people's needs and make an appropriate response. To do this, we need to evaluate what we have heard for completeness and sincerity, then exercise spiritual wisdom and discernment in diagnosing soul sicknesses.

CHAPTER 9 - DISCUSSION QUESTIONS

1. Share about an experience when communication went wrong with humorous or embarrassing consequences. What can you learn from it?

2. From your experience and what you have read in this chapter, how might you identify the truth behind communication that is incomplete and how might you help to bring it into the open?

3. In groups of three, practise listening through the following exercise:
    - One person should share their personal story of faith in 2 to 3 minutes, while another person listens without interrupting to ask questions, and the third person observes and makes notes.
    - Now rotate the roles twice so everyone has a turn to be a speaker, a listener and an observer.
    - After everyone has shared, each person should summarise in 1 minute what they remember from what they listened to in. After they have finished, the person whose story they were recounting should (gently) correct any mistakes.
    - The observer should then comment. What good listening skills did the listener use? Were the errors in understanding due to poor communication by the speaker or poor listening or both?
    - Finally, in your group of three identify what made this exercise easy or difficult. Share your insights with the whole group.

4. Review the skills for active listening outlined in this chapter. Choose one that you find especially helpful. Share with the group what you like about it and how you intend to put it into action.

5. How do we discern God's perspective on a person's needs? What means might God communicate through and how can we develop spiritual wisdom to recognise his leading?

10. PASTORAL SPEAKING

Eager to serve well in her new role, Jude had begun reading about pastoral care. She found some interesting articles online but wasn't sure what she thought about some of their ideas. One said the 'heart of all true pastoral care' is showing people their sin and pointing them to God's truth in Scripture. That was exactly what she felt incapable of doing, and she had told Sam as much. If she could not do 'the heart of pastoral care', how could she be the right person to coordinate it? Then she checked her school's pastoral care policy. It said emphatically that pastoral care is not about guiding people in a certain direction. Rather, it said, the role of pastoral caregivers is simply to provide 'a supportive environment for people to gain strength and self-confidence to work through their problems'. That sounded very different from the online article, and Jude was confused. She added this to her list of things to ask about in the online course and her meetings with Sam.

Then Jude remembered what Sam said about their respective roles. She was glad he was well qualified to provide the guidance people might need. Her mind returned to how Sam had handled her question about her mother's suffering. If she were critical, she would say he could have listened a bit more and that he had not seemed to notice the tears in her eyes. Nevertheless, his response was very helpful. He made it clear he was still learning but said a particular Bible passage helped him process his grief after his grandparents' deaths. Knowing his preaching style, she had expected three points from Romans, but instead he described Jesus' interactions with Mary and Martha after their brother's death. Sam's retelling of John 11 engaged her imagination and brought Jesus into focus. Even if she could not preach a sermon, Jude reckoned she could at least share stories like that with people in need. Maybe it was not so ridiculous after all to think that she could do more to help people find God's truth?

The Challenge of Counselling

Counselling services and psychotherapy are widely available in Western countries. Many people regard them as the obvious source of help with struggles with emotions, relationships and thoughts. Pastoral caregivers will often encounter care-seekers who have had or are currently receiving counselling. Many countries, including the UK, have no legally recognised definitions of 'counsellor' and 'counselling', so there is no standardisation in the training counsellors receive or the values underpinning their approaches.

The term 'counsellor' originally meant the same as 'adviser'. A counsellor gave counsel, which is synonymous with advice. More recently, the concept of 'person-centred counselling' has shifted the meaning of the word. Instead of wise guides, counsellors are now understood to be facilitators of their clients' work of personal growth. They are expected to adopt a non-judgemental stance and to offer unconditional affirmation to those who seek their help. Counselling is generally expected to follow a formal process that 'lays due emphasis on psychological mechanisms'.[408] This process is generally subject to a contract, often paid for and always confined to a limited number of consultations.

We might be tempted to reclaim the term 'counselling' for the aspect of pastoral care that relates biblical truth to the needs of people. After all, the word 'counsellor' has biblical resonances, being a possible translation of the Greek word *paraklētos*, used by Jesus to describe himself and the Holy Spirit who came after him.[409] Given the predominance of non-directive approaches to counselling in the wider culture and the expectations of formality, however, it may be best to distinguish pastoral care from counselling altogether and to reserve the words 'counsellor' and

---

[408] Hurding, 1992, p.63.
[409] John 14:16

'counselling' for people trained in a recognised psychological methodology and operating under supervision within a code of practice. For this reason, level 4 pastoral care in the scheme introduced in Chapter 4 has been called 'counsel' rather than 'counselling, while this book calls the ministry of guiding people in God's truth 'pastoral instruction' rather than 'pastoral counselling'.

Non-directive counselling can be helpful for many people. At the very least, it creates space for people to reflect more deeply on their issues in the affirming presence of a supportive person. It is not, however, without its risks. 'Person-centred' counsellors claim not to convey values to their clients, but they may bring their personal values into their work in subtle ways. Furthermore, the basic premise of the non-directive approach is the counter-gospel belief that care-seekers can solve their own problems. Some psychological approaches also rest on beliefs about human nature that contradict biblical truth. Pastoral caregivers should, therefore, have some awareness of schools of counselling and aim to signpost care-seekers who may benefit from formalised counselling to counsellors whose approach is most consistent with the gospel. They must also recognise the vital role pastoral instruction plays in pastoral care and how it differs from professional counselling.

REFLECTION

- What is your experience of Christian people who have received counselling? Do you think it was beneficial? Do you have any concerns, or might you have any unfair prejudices to be examined?

'Christian' counselling?

Before considering pastoral instruction, we need to think further about approaches to counselling. When confronted with a person with complex or seemingly intractable struggles with emotions, thoughts or relationships, it may be helpful to point them towards professional counselling. This should not, however, be a substitute for pastoral instruction and we should not underestimate the immense potential of pastoral instruction. Still, the more structured and formal approach of a counsellor and the use of psychological techniques may help break an impasse in a person's progress. The more formal environment can help bring issues into the light more clearly or quickly than in pastoral care.

It is, therefore, advisable that every pastoral caregiver be aware of one or more counsellors to recommend to care-seekers. Our starting point might be to look for a 'Christian counsellor', but that is too broad a category. 'Christian counselling' is a catchall term that encompasses a wide range of approaches. It could mean anything from a counsellor who happens to be a Christian but whose approach to counselling is not informed at all by the gospel to a person who has thoughtfully applied gospel truth to every aspect of counselling. Before we recommend a counsellor to a person in need, we need to know something about the values behind the counsellor's approach and how it fits with pastoral instruction.

Approaches to 'Christian counselling' can be categorised according to the relative importance they place on insights from psychology and truth revealed by God. Considering divine revelation, a second question is whether we expect to find is primarily in Scripture or directly from the Spirit through prophecies. Considering these options, we can identify five categories of 'Christian counselling', which are summarised in Table 6.[410] As with any attempt to categorise a complex field, there is overlap between these broad groups and considerable variation within them. The names used for them here may be disputed or used in more specific ways by other authors. Despite these limitations these broad categories can help us recognise important differences between approaches to counselling. The first three approaches make considerable use of psychological theories:

- *Compartmentalised* approaches regard mental and emotional issues as the domain of psychology rather than the gospel, which is said only to be relevant to spiritual needs.

---

[410] This scheme, although my own, has been influenced by Keller, 2010, McMinn *et al.*, 2010, and Winter, 2005.

- *Integration* approaches look equally to psychology and the gospel for help with mental and emotional needs and seeks to bring insights from both together to help people.

- *Christian psychology* seeks to develop a distinctively Christian approach by modifying psychological theories in light of the gospel

The remaining two options are suspicious of psychology and look directly to God for answers to mental and emotional needs. Where they differ is the way in which they expect God to reveal these answers:

- *Nouthetic counselling* looks to Scripture for insights. It is often called 'biblical counselling' by advocates, although others who use this term are less resistant to psychological ideas.

- The approach I have called *prophetic counselling* [411] seeks direct insights from the Spirit through mental impressions and visions, prophesies or words of wisdom and knowledge.

These last two approaches are favoured by conservative evangelicals and Charismatics respectively.

'Christian counselling' without a clear gospel framework may cause greater harm than counselling that makes no claim to be 'Christian' by misleading a person about God's will. We must evaluate these approaches and decide which is most gospel-shaped. 'Compartmentalised' approaches are fundamentally incompatible with gospel-shaped pastoral care. They imply that Scripture has nothing to say to mental and emotional issues, whereas the Bible speaks a great deal to such matters and claims to be sufficient to equip God's servants for every good work.[412] Our aim is an integrated life under Christ (see Chapter 7), not fragmentation into unrelated spiritual and mental dimensions.

---

[411] A number of ministry organisations and authors use the term 'Prophetic Counselling' in broadly similar ways as I have done, although sometimes with distinctive features that are not typical of all approaches the wider category. My usage does not refer to the work of any specific ministry organisation or author, but to all approaches that major on seeking direct revelations from the Spirit for the person in need.

[412] 2 Timothy 3:17

Table 6   Forms of 'Christian counselling'

Openness to psychology

Greater ← ─────────────────── → Less

Compart-mentalised	Integration	Christian psychology	Nouthetic Counselling	Prophetic Counselling
PREMISE†				
Psychology is sufficient '	Both psychology and Scripture	Scripture is primary	Scripture is sufficient	The Spirit is sufficient
DETAIL				
Psychology and theology use different methods to address different needs (mental / emotional and spiritual respectively)	Psychology and theology address the same needs using truth from 'general revelation' and 'special revelation' respectively	Theology must provide the foundation for understanding needs and answers but ideas and tools from psychology can assist people to recognise them	Psychological theories conflict with Scripture by denying the root problem of sin and need for salvation and so should be treated with extreme caution	Various approaches seeking the Holy Spirit's work, including some forms of 'prayer ministry' that expect direct revelation from the Spirit about individual needs
CRITIQUE				
Scripture and psychology both speak on many issues (e.g., guilt, shame, abuse, anger, worry, fear) and often disagree	Could default to simply using a little psychology uncritically or a little Scripture carelessly without truly integrating	May grant too much influence to counsellors with psychology training and neglect the authority of Scripture	Extremes neglect insights from psychology and emphasise cure to the neglect of care; may also neglect the Spirit's work	Extremes neglect insights from psychology; may be overly subjective and expect instant change not promised in Scripture

†Where can help for mental and emotional problems be found according to this approach?

On the other side of the spectrum, 'prophetic counselling' and 'nouthetic counselling' approaches that reject insights from psychology altogether deny the possibility of God's general revelation of truth in creation, which can be discovered by studying the world and people. To ignore all ideas from psychology when dealing with mental and emotional health could be like rejecting the benefits of science for physical health, for example by praying for miraculous healing without seeking medical help. Chapter 6 suggested that psychological tools can help us understand people's experiences. Given the prevalence of psychology in popular thought, some understanding of psychological concepts will also help pastoral caregivers connect with the frames of reference people use to understand themselves.

Considering the middle options in the spectrum of approaches to Christian counselling, 'integration' approaches give too much weight to psychology, placing it on a par with Scripture. If we are convinced of the divine authority of Scripture and the active work of the Spirit, we must keep psychological insights subject to them. 'Christian Psychology' is a valid attempt to do just that. The ideal Christian counsellors follow this approach. There is a need for Christians to engage in the field of psychology and to develop therapies that are thoroughly consistent with the gospel.

In practice, we may not have access to the ideal for those we care for. We need not dismiss counsellors who are not Christians as their approaches may not conflict with Christian faith. Methodologies like cognitive behavioural therapy, which aims to help clients understand the interconnections between thoughts, feelings and actions and how to break the cycle of negative thoughts trapping them in habitually unhelpful behaviours, can be perfectly consistent with the gospel if the positive role of faith is encouraged. The input of a therapist using this approach can work well alongside gospel-shaped pastoral care, especially if there is mutual respect between the pastoral caregiver and the counsellor and consent from the care-seeker for them to communicate with each other.

REFLECTION

- What approach to Christian counselling do you think is best? What counsellors do you know to whom you would recommend people who may benefit from professional counselling?

Principles for Pastoral Instruction

Pastoral instruction aims to speak God's truth to people in need. As the apostle Peter wrote, we are 'stewards of God's varied grace', so when we speak we should do so 'as one who speaks oracles of God'.[413] To be faithful in pastoral instruction, we must consider how we know what God's oracles are for the people care for, how we can connect God's truth with their lives and what responses we can expect and hope for.

Recognising and speaking God's truth

In Chapter 9, we considered the process of discernment that follows pastoral listening and can lead to a diagnosis of soul sickness. The next step in the process is to decide what truth from God will bring correction to the sickness. 'Nouthetic counselling' and 'prophetic counselling' can each offer helpful insights into this decision. We should appreciate the strengths of each of these ways of thinking since gospel-shaped pastoral care recognises both the Spirit's work in people's lives *and* the supreme authority of Scripture.

'Prophetic counselling' takes seriously the activity of the Holy Spirit in the lives of caregivers and care-seekers, but it will become imbalanced if experiences, including impressions about what God might be saying in this moment, are not subjected to Scripture. As argued in Chapter 9, supposed insights from the Spirit must be tested and weighed. It would also be wrong to create expectations that God will always reveal insights immediately, to suggest that certain prayer techniques can precipitate them, or that change

---

[413] 1 Peter 4:10-11

caused by the Spirit always happens suddenly.

'Nouthetic counselling' takes the authority and effectiveness of Scripture seriously, but it could neglect the reality of the Holy Spirit's work in the immediate situation. We should be firmly committed to the authority of Scripture whilst still seeking the Spirit's guidance on what scriptures to turn to and how to communicate biblical truth with relevance to specific needs. We must not bypass the mind or conscience of people seeking pastoral guidance. It is as people respond to truth revealed by God that the Spirit works change in their lives. At the same time, there is a work of the Spirit in the heart that is deeper than our consciousness [414] and that produces peace that 'surpasses all understanding'.[415]

Once we are confident that we have some truth from God to share with a person in need, we must speak it to them. We must encourage care-seekers to follow the voice of the Chief Shepherd as the Spirit leads them. We can have confidence that God will show them what they need to know in God's time. In humility, we simply seek to help them see what God is saying to them in this moment. What we say may come from a mixture of three sources: wisdom gleaned in life experience; insights from the Spirit; and the words of Scripture. These sources have differing levels of authority and we should seek to distinguish between them:

- **Wisdom from our experience** – when sharing what we have learned from reflection on our experience, we must distinguish between the timeless wisdom principle and our specific experience, since the person's situation will not be identical to ours. We should not say, 'You should do what I did', but 'Here's what I did and why I think it was wise/foolish. Now how would the principle I recognised work out for you?'

- **Insights from the Spirit** – when we share something we think is an insight from the Spirit (after testing and weighing what claims to be a prophetic message), we must have humility to recognise we may be mistaken and confidence in the fact that God can speak. We walk the line between two unhelpful approaches: emphatic statements

---

[414] Romans 8:26
[415] Philippians 4:6

about God's guidance ('God is telling me that you should …') and appearing clueless about his will when we believe he is speaking ('I wonder have you considered …'). A better approach is to say, 'I think God may be saying this, but let's keep praying and look to his Word to see if that makes sense. What do you think he is saying?'

- **Truths from Scripture** – when we share from the Bible, we must work to understand its words accurately and to apply them appropriately. We can have confidence, however, that God's word is true and authoritative. The various ways in which Scripture speaks in pastoral instruction will be explored later in this chapter.

Modes of instruction: paraklesis *and* nouthesis

Pastoral instruction works in two modes, which can be labelled with two New Testament Greek words: *paraklesis* and *nouthesis*.[416] In Scripture these words are not completely separate in meaning, but the core idea within each is distinct enough to make them useful labels for two broad approaches to instruction.

Paraklesis may be translated as 'comfort' or 'reassurance'. It reminds people of God's presence and promises and encourages them to be true to what they already believe and know. *Paraklesis* expresses the 'care' dimension of *cura animarum*, sustaining people through trials. It is beautifully expressed by the apostle Paul early on in 2 Corinthians:[417]

> *Blessed be the God and Father of our Lord Jesus Christ, the Father of mercies and God of all comfort (paraklēseōs), who comforts (parakalōn) us in all our tribulation, that we may be able to comfort (parakalein) those who are in any trouble, with the comfort (paraklēseōs) with which we ourselves are comforted (parakaloumetha) by God.*

This form of instruction is a central aspect of level 3 pastoral care (comfort). It is generally the most appropriate form of instruction in the

---

[416] I am indebted to Roger Hurding (2003, p.400) for these terms, although the comments are my own and I have not used his English names for them (pastoral and prophetic) and have excluded his third mode (priestly).

[417] 2 Corinthians 1:3-4

early stages of relationship and in the aftermath of traumatic experiences.

Nouthesis entails words of warning and challenge.[418] In the apostle Paul's letters, words related to *nouthesis* are variously translated 'warning', 'advising', 'admonishing' and 'instructing'.[419] *Nouthesis* is powerfully modelled later in 2 Corinthians, when the apostle Paul acknowledges that his words sometimes caused grief but adds that 'godly grief produces a repentance that leads to salvation without regret'.[420] Nouthesis is not content with the generalised truth that every person is a sinner. It looks for, 'the particular forms that sin takes in individual histories [...] then loves, prays, witnesses, converses, and preaches the details of grace appropriate to each human face'.[421]

Confronting sin and falsehood always risks irreparable damage to a pastoral relationship, but if we are so afraid of hurting people that we fail to speak truth to them, we cannot truly help them. Confrontation will be much easier if the person has previously experienced *paraklesis* from us and we speak, like the apostle Paul, humbly as people who know weakness.[422] In pastoral support after crises, *nouthesis* may come relatively late in the relationship, but it should be expected in communities that habitually speak truth in love to one another.[423]

We need *nouthesis* because we are sinners who are often deceived. Sword-like, God's Word cuts to the heart of our thoughts and intentions, exposing our sin.[424] Such a sharp sword can cause damage if mishandled. Roger Hurding warns that 'people in need can be badly damaged by insensitive or overzealous handling of the word of God'.[425] We should pray for insights from the Spirit to wield the Word, which is described as his sword,[426] skilfully. This includes choosing the best passages to share and deciding

---

[418] Nouthetic, as in 'Nouthetic Counselling', is the adjectival form of this noun.
[419] Romans 15:14; Colossians 1:28; 3:16; 1 Thessalonians 5:14; 2 Thessalonians 3:14; Titus 3:10
[420] 2 Corinthians 7:8-10
[421] Peterson, 1989, p.121
[422] 2 Corinthians 12
[423] Ephesians 4:15
[424] Hebrews 4:12
[425] Hurding, 1992, p155
[426] Ephesians 6:17

whether to comment upon them. Sometimes it is best to say relatively little because we know that the Spirit wields his sword more skilfully than we can. We trust that he can bring change through the words of Scripture without additional words from us.

Dietrich Bonhoeffer recognised that pastoral instruction is 'beset with infinite perils' and so must follow careful listening and be undertaken with the right attitude:[427]

If [instruction] is not accompanied by worthy listening, how can it really be the right word for the other person? If it is contradicted by one's own lack of active helpfulness, how can it be a convincing and sincere word? If it issues, not from a spirit of bearing and forbearing, but from impatience and the desire to force its acceptance, how can it be the liberating and healing word?

Despite these risks we must not shy from instruction. Bonhoeffer warns us that 'It is unchristian consciously to deprive another of the one decisive service we can render him' by declaring God's Word and will to him.[428] Correction can be an expression of love, and failure to bring a challenge may indicate the absence of love. As Bonhoeffer writes, 'Nothing can be more cruel than the tenderness that consigns another to his sin. Nothing can be more compassionate than the severe rebuke that calls a brother back from the path of sin'.[429]

Nouthesis must stick to what Scripture reveals and call people to obedience to Christ rather than to the caregiver.[430] When we demand obedience to some standard other than Scripture or person other than Christ, we are no longer acting as under-shepherds of the Good Shepherd but have become false shepherds feeding ourselves on the flock. We must also open ourselves to rebuke from those we care for, since we are committed to seeking and obeying truth along with them. As far as possible, we should remove logs from our eyes so our vision is clear to remove specks from others' eyes.[431] We must not sin by rebuking unlovingly

---

[427] Bonhoeffer, 1954, p.104
[428] Bonhoeffer, 1954, p.105
[429] Bonhoeffer, 1954, p.107
[430] Titus 2:15
[431] Matthew 7:3-5

and we must be open to the possibility that we have misjudged.

Wisdom is required to know when *paraklesis* or *nouthesis* should predominate in pastoral instruction. When a person is weak in faith or discouraged, we should major on *paraklesis*, whereas lazy people need *nouthesis*.[432] Many pastoral encounters will mix both approaches, as Scripture often does, since people often exhibit a combination of faithfulness and unfaithfulness. We should aim to allow Scripture to speak on its own terms and to reflect the character of God who, as a good Father, both encourages and corrects us.

Confronting sin directly and indirectly

A direct rebuke, as envisaged by Bonhoeffer, is not the only way to confront sin. When engaging with care-seekers who trust you and accept the authority of God's word, you can often expose their sin directly and openly. A less direct approach may be more effective with people who are suspicious of authority, who do not trust you fully, whose sin is so deeply ingrained that they cannot separate it from their sense of identity, or whose culture or personality type make them resistant to direct challenges. Some more indirect ways to confront sin include: [433]

- telling a fictional story, perhaps from your imagination or from a familiar book, film or television series, that illustrates the point as the prophet Nathan did with king David;[434]

- sharing a true story of a person's experience with the same issue, whether yourself, a Bible character, someone from history or the news;

- inviting the person to consider alternative interpretations of events (e.g., 'Do you think there's a different way to see that?');

---

[432] 1 Thessalonians 5:14
[433] For some of these ideas I am indebted to Anderson, 2005, p.204-205
[434] 2 Samuel 12

- repeating the person's false idea so he hears it in another voice, since it is often easier to recognise falsehood in the words of others than our own;

- taking their idea to the extreme to expose logical flaws ('If everyone did that all the time, what would happen?');

- presenting the alternative perspective to provoke thought.

Jesus' parables exemplify indirect confrontation of sin and false thinking. Eugene Peterson suggests that parables subversively enter the 'citadel of self' to effect change from within.[435] He also reminds us that the gospel of Jesus Christ is subversive in many details: 'illegitimate (as was supposed) conception, barnyard birth, Nazareth silence, Galilean secularity, Sabbath healings, Gethsemane prayers, criminal death, baptismal water, eucharistic bread and wine'. Peterson suggests that pastors often abandon subversion in favour of frontal assaults on sin for two unworthy reasons:

- a vain desire for significance and prestige; or

- naiveté because they underestimate the depth of sin's roots.

Recognising these two risks, Peterson suggests that humility and wisdom, may lead us to use stories and questions more often to help people towards truth.

Responses to the Word

The Word of God is powerful. Our responsibility in pastoral instruction is to communicate it to people. We cannot, however, control their response to the Word. Jesus explained the diverse responses we should expect in his Parable of the Sower.[436] He explained that this parable acts as a key to all the parables, because it illustrates what happens every time the word of God is communicated. Four kinds of response are illustrated by four kinds

---

[435] Peterson, 1989, p.33
[436] Matthew 13:1-23; Mark 4:1-20; Luke 8:4-15

of ground:

- **The path** represents people who do not understand the word. The evil one snatches away what has been sown. These people are resistant to God's truth. It cannot penetrate their hardness of heart.

- **Rocky ground** represents people who initially receive the word joyfully, but who do not allow it to penetrate deeply into their hearts. When their faith is tested through opposition or hardship, they abandon it and fall away.

- **Thorny ground** represents people who care more for the things on offer in this world, including riches, than they do for the promise of God's kingdom that comes through the word. The seed cannot grow because these other priorities choke it.

- **Good soil** represents those who hear the word and understand it. They 'hold it fast in an honest and good heart'.[437] It takes root in their lives and grows into a plant that bears fruit that lasts. These people are changed by the word.

When we engage in pastoral instruction, we should expect to see each of these four kinds of response. Some will reject what we say. Some will seem to accept it gladly and may even seem to change, but there will be no lasting effect. When it becomes tough, especially if others oppose the change, they may return to their old patterns. Some will seem to listen and understand, but they will be unwilling to give up something else in obedience to God. It can be discouraging when we see any of these responses, but we should not be surprised. We can be confident that some people will receive the word and be transformed as a result.

What makes the difference in the responses is not what is communicated – the word is the same in all cases – or how it is communicated – the sower does nothing different – but the state of the person's heart. Until people are open to the work of God, soft of heart, ready to suffer for the truth, caring more about God's kingdom than their own desires, there can be no change. This is why our pastoral instruction must always be in parallel with the ministry of intercession. We pray that

---

[437] Luke 8:15

the Spirit will soften hearts and that people will humble themselves to receive God's word.

Responding to sin

When the seed of the word penetrates a person's heart, the Holy Spirit brings assurance of God's promises and conviction of sin through it. When a person is convicted of sin, we should help them to respond to God appropriately. One of the clearest biblical descriptions of the actions we must take when we recognise sin is found in 1 John 1:5-2:2. It outlines four steps, which we can remember with 'r' words: repent, receive, repay, reduce.

1. *Repent* of sin

God is light – the standard of holiness and purity – and we are in darkness when we do not walk according to his truth (1:5-6). We tend to deny our sin and deceive ourselves about it (1:8,10). The gospel first shows us our sin, then our Saviour. Remember, even actions that do not breach God's commands are sinful if not done for God's glory and even our best thoughts fall short of God's glory. We are, therefore, more likely to underestimate our guilt than to overestimate it. Pastoral caregivers can be tempted, because of embarrassment, compassion or the awareness of our own sinfulness, to minimise or excuse confessed sin ('We all do that sometimes' or 'It's not that big a deal'). We must resist this temptation. Even if we recognise much false guilt and unnecessary shame in someone's story, we must be wary about dismissing it outright, since there will often be some sin tied up in the details. We should make it our aim to speak God's truth alone, allowing the Spirit of God to convict them by the Word of God, then leading them through these biblical principles. That way, we will not minimise the seriousness of sin or the glory of God's grace in Christ.

To receive God's forgiveness, we must step into the light and own up (1:9). God sits as Judge, and we stand in the dock. We must plead guilty. Otherwise, we continue in self-deception and cannot receive forgiveness. True repentance makes no excuses for sin. In Psalm 51, king David's expresses his repentance after he was shown his sinfulness in plotting the

221

death of his loyal soldier Uriah to cover up his adultery with Uriah's wife Bathsheba.[438] David says, 'Against you, you only, have I sinned and done what is evil in your sight, so that you may be justified in your words and blameless in your judgement'.[439] He was not denying the harm done to others, but acknowledging that his fundamental problem was his guilt before God. Repentant people confess their sin openly without excuses and accept God's judgement that they are sinners.

3. *Receive* forgiveness and cleansing

When God forgives sins, he does not compromise his standards. Forgiveness expresses his character of faithfulness and justice (1:9) because Jesus' death is the propitiation for our sin – the sacrifice that turns away God's wrath (1:7; 2:2). We do not face judgement because he did. God's justice is satisfied. Sin has not been ignored – it has been paid for. Wonderfully, God does not merely forgive us, he also cleanses 'us from all unrighteousness' (1:9). There is no stain left from past sin. We are clean. There is, therefore, no need for shame before God or others.

Some writers speak of 'self-forgiveness', by which they mean release from the damaging effects of self-condemnation after receiving God's forgiveness.[440] This concept does not fit with what Scripture teaches, since it shifts our focus from what God says (and has done) to what we decide (and our ability to do it). If my sin is against God alone, how can I forgive myself? Scripture does assure us, however, that when we have been forgiven by God we need not carry guilt or shame any longer. The objective truth of forgiveness and cleansing becomes our subjective experience as we trust God's assuring promises in Scripture and the inward testimony of the Spirit, who pours God's love into our hearts and causes us to cry out 'Abba Father'.[441] Care-seekers often need reminders of God's forgiveness and cleansing as they continue to work through residual false guilt amidst the devil's accusation. Romans 8 is a helpful chapter in such cases, from the

---

[438] 2 Samuel 11
[439] Psalm 51:4
[440] Worthington, 2013.
[441] Romans 5:5; 8:15

declaration in verse 1 that 'There is therefore now no condemnation for those who are in Christ Jesus' to the rhetorical questions of verses 31 to 39.

4. *Repay* whatever we can

Fellowship with other Christians arises from walking in the light (1:7). Experiencing God's forgiveness motivates us to seek forgiveness from others we have wronged and, as far as possible, to make restitution for losses our sins have caused. Sins that are serious criminal offences should be confessed to the proper authorities to allow justice to be done. In a church community seeking the light of God's truth, it should be normal for people to confess their sins and to celebrate forgiveness of one another. The process of restitution for sin will normally include an effort to reconcile broken relationships.

An important exception is when the sin involved abuse. If the repentant abuser pursues reconciliation, it could perpetuate the trauma of the abuse for the victim. The wrongdoer may offer to meet their victim but should never demand it, allowing their victim to set the extent and pace of any reconciliation. Not every wrong can be put right this side of glory. We must rest in God's forgiveness whilst accepting the consequences of our sin. People who are clearly repentant cannot reconcile with an injured part or whose requests for reconciliation are not granted are likely to need clear and repeated assurances of God's forgiveness and cleansing.

5. *Reduce* future sin

Our perseverance in salvation depends not on our own effort, but on Jesus (2:1). Not only has he paid for our sin; he is also our living advocate, pleading for us in God's courtroom. From him we learn to walk in righteousness. We must take action to reduce the likelihood of repeating the sin by avoiding situations of temptation and seeking accountability to others. We do not seek God's forgiveness simply so we can get back on the track to self-actualisation. Thinking of sin only in terms of our wrong actions and their consequences for us reduces the gospel to what Dallas

Willard called 'sin management'.[442] The gospel calls us to much more, a lifelong loving relationship with God of transformation into Christ's likeness. God's purpose is not merely that we avoid sin, but that we become holy and do his will. The Church community is our support in this process. In this context, we learn to obey God's command to love one another as 1 John 2 continues to say.

REFLECTION

- Do you find it easier to engage in *paraklesis* or *nouthesis* and to confront sin directly or indirectly? Why do you think that is and how can you ensure you are not imbalanced in your approach?

- Take time to read and meditate on 1 John 1:5-2:2, perhaps even memorising it. Be sure you have grasped its truths and worked through its four principles concerning your own sin.

Scripture's Functions in Pastoral Care

Through Scripture, God exercises authority over his people. Gospel-shaped pastoral caregivers hope that care-seekers will come to obey its truth. Different writers suggest varied ways in which Scripture functions in pastoral care.[443] I find it most helpful to recognise how the different genres of communication in the Bible function in different ways. All Scripture is God-breathed and profitable for us,[444] but different scriptures work in different ways. Taking this approach, we can identify four pastoral functions of Scripture. Two – performative and formative – convey truth indirectly, and two – normative and transformative – are more direct.

---

[442] Willard, 1998, p.35
[443] Stephen Pattison (2000, p.115-129) describes five of these, each of which he associates with one predominant author.
[444] 2 Timothy 3:16-17.

PERFORMATIVE – words expressing the heart

Scripture's words can become the words of people in need. 'Performative' does not mean putting on a show but using biblical words to express oneself. In doing so, we learn biblical patterns of thought. We can encourage care-seekers to pray the prayers of Scripture and express emotions from deep despair to jubilant praise using corresponding psalms. The performative function is especially important in crises when it affirms the legitimacy of lament and the validity of mixed emotions as modelled in Psalms. Performance of the words of Scripture can also unify a Christian community in collective expressions of faith and may help non-believers begin to speak to the God they do not yet know.

Performative use of Scripture can achieve both *paraklesis* and *nouthesis* indirectly. Psalms and biblical prayers affirm God's character and promises and the legitimacy of our experience and emotions (*paraklesis*). They also challenge our sin and false ideas (*nouthesis*). For example, I cannot pray with meaning, 'forgive us our trespasses as we forgive those who trespass against us', without being convicted of my sin and the hardness of my heart towards others.

FORMATIVE – stories echoing circumstances

The Old Testament historical books, the Gospels and the book of Acts contain accounts of historical events in the lives of individuals and nations. These true stories (also known as narratives) resonate with our stories. Entering into biblical narratives with imagination opens new horizons for us. We need not imagine feelings, thoughts or motivations of characters in the story that are not revealed in the text, but we can place ourselves in the story as a means to reflection. 'What would I have done in that situation and what does that say about me?' 'Which character do I identify with and why?' 'Where was God in that moment and what did he think of what happened?' 'How does that set of events make me feel and why?' This function of Scripture can be called *formative*, because these stories form the person we become as we reflect on them.

As people walk through difficult situations and relational tensions or face major decisions, we can show them how people in Scripture faced and responded to similar challenges. Times may have changed since the Bible was written, but human nature has not. People are still complex mixtures of faith and doubt, hope and dismay, pain and rejoicing. There are great resonances in the examples of Scripture with our experiences. Consider the following examples:

- Abraham stepping out in faith to follow God;[445]

- God working through Abraham's dysfunctional family riddled with parental favouritism and sibling rivalries;[446]

- Joseph refusing to give in to temptation despite the consequences;[447]

- Moses waiting for the right time to lead God's people;[448]

- Samson wasting his potential because of lust;[449]

- Hannah turning to God in her childlessness;[450]

- David and Peter experiencing restoration through repentance;[451]

- Mary and Martha struggling to comprehend God's purposes in their grief.[452]

These stories, and many more, provoke reflection and set good and bad examples for us to follow or avoid.

Narratives do not always tie up loose ends and often contain ambiguity. As a result, they can be an indirect path to *paraklesis* – stabilising faith by inspiring endurance or helping us resolve contradictions in our thinking – or *nouthesis* – destabilising sin by subverting expectations and undermining false values.[453]

---

[445] Genesis 12
[446] Much of the content of Genesis Chapters 13 to 50
[447] Genesis 39
[448] Exodus Chapters 1 to 3
[449] Judges Chapters 13 to 16
[450] 1 Samuel 1
[451] 2 Samuel 12; John 21
[452] John 11
[453] Anderson (2005, p.204-205) describes a similar dual impact of biblical narratives, using the terms *parabolic* (subversive and destabilising) and *mythic* (reaffirming and stabilising).

NORMATIVE – the gospel call

The many stories in the Bible weave together into one great story or 'metanarrative'. It would not be true to Scripture if we merely left care-seekers with a few isolated stories of Bible characters. Paul Tripp writes that, 'Being truly biblical means that my counsel reflects what the entire Bible is about […] a story of redemption [whose] chief character is Jesus Christ'.[454] From Genesis to Revelation, God reveals himself and his plan of salvation. We can present this great story to care-seekers, whether sharing the gospel for the first time with a non-believer or reminding believers of its majestic scope. This function of Scripture can be called *normative*, because it tells the true story of the gospel and calls us to embrace it as the 'norm' towards which we must be conformed.

Jesus is the centre and turning point of the biblical story and Scripture must make us 'wise for salvation through faith in Christ Jesus' before it becomes our guide in specific needs.[455] When people read about him in the Gospels, they not only reshape their understanding of their circumstances, they are also confronted with the person who does not compute, the ultimate subverter of our values, exposer of our sinfulness and restorer of our dignity. Jesus is the ultimate 'norm' – the full revelation of God and the perfect example of humanity.

The normative function of Scripture also reshapes our understanding of specific issues, as this book has sought to model. Using the five movements of the gospel, we can walk care-seekers through a gospel perspective on whatever they are struggling with:

- *God rules*: what was his original intention in this?

- *We rebel*: how is sin at play in my thoughts and feelings?

- *God rescues*: how do the person of Jesus and the truths of the law and epistles reframe this issue?

- *We respond*: where do I need to repent, trust and obey?

---

[454] Tripp, 2002, p.24-26.
[455] 2 Timothy 3:15.

- *God restores*: how will the Holy Spirit change me, directly or through the Church, now and in eternity?

Functioning normatively, Scripture challenges us directly through both *paraklesis* and *nouthesis*. The gospel first condemns us by exposing our sin (*nouthesis*), then brings us hope in Christ through faith (*paraklesis*). Its comfort comes after the profound discomfort of realising the extent of our sin.

TRANSFORMATIVE – *truth to obey*

The final function of Scripture gets into the nuts and bolts of people's thinking and lifestyles. It engages with the didactic (teaching) parts of Scripture found in the law, the teaching of Jesus, the epistles and the wisdom books. It listens to Scripture for warnings, promises, commands, and provocative wisdom sayings. This function can be called *transformative*, since it seeks to change people in specific areas of their thinking and actions.

We must be careful to ensure that a specific command or promise from Scripture applies directly to believers today before we call care-seekers to obey it. This is always or almost always true in the epistles, which were written to Christian believers and churches living in the same stage of salvation history as us, after Jesus' ascension and before his return. It is also generally true in the Gospels, although we must be careful to distinguish commands that were given to the apostles Jesus appointed but not necessarily to those who would believe in their message.[456] Old Testament passages are trickier, because some commands given to the nation of Israel are no longer binding on Christians because their purpose was fulfilled by Christ. We must follow the principles of sound biblical interpretation to avoid commanding people to be circumcised or avoid eating pork when these behaviours are not required of Christians.

2 Timothy 3:16 describes the transformative function people who have

---

[456] This caveat about commands to the apostles is especially important when we read John Chapters 14 to 16.

already been made wise for salvation (verse 15) using four words. Scripture:

- *teaches* us what is true and right, the things we should believe;

- *reproves* us, challenging our wrong behaviour;

- *corrects* our thinking where it is false; and

- *trains* us to do what is right.

These four words deal directly with both beliefs and behaviours through *nouthesis* (correcting beliefs; reproving behaviours) and *paraklesis* (teaching beliefs; training behaviour). They are cures for soul sicknesses diagnosed using the four questions suggested in Chapter 9. Functioning transformatively, Scripture calls people to repent from wrong beliefs and bad behaviour towards right beliefs and good behaviour.

REFLECTION

- How have you benefited from these functions of Scripture at different times in your life?

- How can you allow Scripture to function in each of these ways in the lives of people you care for?

CHAPTER SUMMARY

Some forms of counselling can be compatible with the gospel, but person-centred counselling must be a supplement to, rather than a replacement for, the ministry of instruction. Instruction takes two forms: *paraklesis*, or supportive, caring words, and *nouthesis*, or challenging, curing words. Both must be based on faithful use of Scripture guided by wisdom and insight from the Spirit as the Bible functions performatively (giving words to express our inner world), formatively (providing stories that resonate with experience), normatively (calling to faith in the gospel), and transformatively (showing what to believe and how to behave). The aim in this process is to help people to recognise sinful beliefs and behaviours so that they can confess them and experience God's forgiveness and cleansing and to embrace true beliefs and behaviours so they can live faithfully for God.

CHAPTER 10 - DISCUSSION QUESTIONS

1. Have you delivered or received counselling from a professional counsellor? Were the values underlying the approach compatible with growth in the gospel?

2. What would result if pastoral instruction was all *paraklesis* with no *nouthesis* or vice versa?

3. Share about times when you, or others you have observed, have benefited from Scripture functioning in each of the four ways outlined in this chapter:
   - Performative
   - Formative
   - Normative
   - Transformative

4. Share about a time when intercession and instruction clearly met in a word that was right for a person at that specific time. How did you recognise that God was guiding?

5. In pairs, role-play confessing sin to one another and working through the five steps outlined from 1 John: recognise, repent, receive, repay and reduce. This will be most effective if you share honestly about a real sin, but only do so if you are confident you can trust one another and for training it is probably best to stick to something historic for which you have already worked through the five steps.

6. What cautions would you recommend around the process of pastoral instruction? How can it be done wisely and sensitively without compromising biblical truth?

EPILOGUE: THE NEXT CHAPTER

One year after Jude commenced her pastoral care role, Sam and Beth sat down with her to review her progress. Jude and Sam had already added two others to their team. Jude had completed the online pastoral care course. To her surprise, Sam joined her on it. Her comment about the importance of presence, had helped him see the benefit of further training. The course content and discussions with people from different churches had been hugely helpful in understanding pastoral care and how best to organise it in their congregation. There had been some challenges for Jude, especially around confidentiality. She instinctively wanted to share with Sam everything she heard. Sam had been quite keen to hear it too, but when he asked his mentor John for advice, the older pastor reminded him of the importance of confidentiality for trust in pastoral relationships, assuring him that he did not need to know everything and that his desire to do so may be an unhealthy indicator of an unhealthy desire for control. So, Sam assured Jude that confidentiality was important. They were still working through how that would work with the enlarged team. Above all, they were thankful for signs of progress towards mature faith in the members of the church they prayed for.

Later that evening, as Sam and Beth prayed together by the bedside, they gave thanks for Jude. Sam confessed his struggles when he first asked her to assist him and thanked God for Beth spurring him on to do the right thing. Beth also gave thanks for John's support to Sam over the past year and the friendship Sam had renewed, on John's advice, with an old friend who lived nearby and shared his love for vintage cars. Beth prayed that the elder development programme due to start in a couple of weeks, would lead others to share pastoral oversight of the congregation with Sam. As she said 'Amen' and opened her eyes, she realised Sam had left the room during her prayer. She walked to the door. Sam was standing in the hallway looking lovingly into the bedroom of their eight-month-old daughter, Grace.

As we come towards the end of this book, I encourage you to ask what the next chapter of your journey as a pastoral caregiver may look like. Is there a new responsibility you should step in to? Are changes needed to the organisation or provision of pastoral care in your congregation or organisation? Do you need further training or perhaps, if you read the book alone, should you revisit it with a group of people so you can learn and develop your practice together? This book is intended to serve as a guide and reference in constantly improving pastoral care by shaping it increasingly around the gospel.

My prayer for you, whether you are a Sam or a Jude, is that you will increasingly be a gospel-shaped person, helping people in need through gospel-shaped care towards wholeness in Christ.

I pray that you will be motivated by the compassion of the Father, that you will follow the methods exemplified by the Son, and that you will depend on the means of the Holy Spirit. May you have wisdom to recognise the needs of people you care for and to walk with them towards wholeness in Christ. May you do this within a gospel community in which you and they are learning to love God and others. May you always work within wise boundaries accountable to godly recognised shepherds.

I pray that you will understand yourself and the needs of care-seekers in light of the gospel, knowing that we were made for God, for wholeness and for relationship. May you see people released from the idolatry of self-love into the joy of worshipping the true and living God. May you work towards wholeness in Christ, seeing lives transformed into his likeness as we await the fullness of his kingdom at his return. May you see broken relationships restored and families, friendships and churches thriving in selfless love for one another.

I pray that you will play your part in the priesthood of believers by engaging in gospel-shaped ministry according to your gifts and capacities.

May you see needs met through the mobilising of provision for people's practical needs, the presence of caregivers as re-presentations of Christ, committed intercession for others, and faithful instruction in biblical truth that leads towards Christ-likeness. May you learn to listen well to people in their words, body language and silences so that you help them to understand truth in their stories. May you and others in your team know how to speak God's truth with spiritual insight and discernment, always serving them without coercion for the glory of God.

The call to pastoral care is challenging and exacting, but the Lord has equipped us thoroughly through the gospel and the Spirit. We serve others with expectancy and hopefulness because our confidence is in the Chief Shepherd of their souls. We lean on the compassion of our Father who holds us firmly in his love so it can overflow into the lives of others through us.

APPENDIX: GOSPEL THEMES AND GROWTH

The following table outlines themes emerging from each of the five gospel movements and their relevance for five questions people may ask.

Gospel movement	Themes	Growth in faith
Question 1: Where did I come from?		
God rules The sovereign Creator and Sustainer of the universe made us to know, love and serve him	God, the eternal Creator alone is sovereign and to be worshipped The physical universe is not everything The world was originally good and remains beautiful Human beings have unique dignity as God's stewards	Realising God exists and is sovereign over all things Understanding God is involved in the world and wants us to enjoy and care for it Discovering that God is love and truth and, therefore, trustworthy Recognising my value as a unique creation of God
Question 2: Who am I?		
2. We rebelled We sinned, seeking independence from God and so deserve God's judgement, death and hell, and are subject to Satan's influence	Sin is a personal offence against God – guilt and shame for wrongdoing are real We are powerless to redeem ourselves or escape death Satan tempts us through lies on which we build false beliefs, values and actions	Recognising my sinfulness and accountability to God Understanding that death is inevitable but not final Realising the spiritual battle for our hearts Distinguishing God's purpose for me from my feelings and ideas
Question 3: What is a good life?		
3. God rescues God revealed himself in words of Scripture and worked to save us through his Son Jesus who died for our sins and rose again	Scripture is God's true and trustworthy authoritative Word God binds himself faithfully in covenant to his redeemed people Jesus is the Saviour from	Learning to accept, trust and obey God's Word in Scripture Knowing my true identity is in God and among his people Trusting in Jesus as my

	sins and Lord over all Through suffering Jesus defeated death and sin God's love and truth are perfectly revealed in Jesus' ministry	Lord and Saviour Recognising that suffering can grow faith and character

Question 4: What is the purpose of life?

4. We respond Inclusion in God's redeemed people and growth to maturity are through repentance (turning from sin) and faith (trusting in Christ)	Victory over sin and death is only possible through Christ Christian life is a journey of repentance and faith Christian identity is about being in Christ and belonging to him Being in Christ means union with his people in the Church	Experiencing forgiveness and hope through Christ. Shifting from pursuit of happiness to pursuit of godliness Daily taking up my cross, denying myself and following Jesus I need to become less so Jesus can become more I need to commit to engagement in church community

Question 5: What is my destiny (is there real hope)?

5. God restores The new creation begins now in us as the Spirit changes us to become like Christ and will be completed in a new universe where we will live with God forever	The Holy Spirit lives in us with power to transform us The goal of life is Christ-like character (the Spirit's fruit) The Spirit empowers us to serve others and make Jesus known The hope of heaven is real and certain through Christ's resurrection	I must allow the Spirit to fill me and follow his leading I must live in Christ though prayer and the Word I must serve and share the gospel with those who don't know Christ I must share hope and live hopefully in face of troubles

BIBLIOGRAPHY

ACC (2016) *Guidelines for Good Practice in Pastoral Care*, revised 20.09.16. Coventry: Association of Christian Counsellors.

Anderson, H. (2005) The Bible and Pastoral Care. In: Ballard, P., and Holmes, S.R. (eds.) *The Bible in Pastoral Practice*. Grand Rapids: Eerdmans.

Anderson, N. (2000) *Victory Over the Darkness*, new edn. London: Monarch.

Aristotle (350 BCE) *Nicomachean Ethics*, Book VIII, trans. by Ross, W.D.

Augsburger, D. (1981) Caring Enough to Not Forgive: False Forgiveness. Ventura: Regal.

Balswick, J.O. and Balswick, J.K. (2014) The Family: A Christian Perspective on the Contemporary Home, second edn. Grand Rapids: Baker Academic.

Baxter, R. (1656) *The Reformed Pastor.*

Benner, D. (2004) The Gift of Being Yourself: The Sacred Call to Self-Discovery. Trowbridge: Eagle.

Bonhoeffer, D. (1954) *Life Together: The Classic Exploration of Christian Community*, trans. by John W. Doberstein. San Francisco: HarperOne.

_____ (1985) *Spiritual Care*, trans. by J.C. Rochelle. Philadelphia: Fortress Press.

Boyd, K. (2000) Pain, sickness and suffering (1980). In: *Spiritual Dimensions of Pastoral Care*, Practical Theology in a Multidisciplinary Context. Ed. by Willows, D, and Swinton, J. London: Jessica Kingsley.

Bucer, M. (2009) *Concerning the True Care of Souls*. Trans. by P. Beale. Edinburgh: Banner of Truth

Bunting, I. (2000) Pastoral Care at the End of the Twentieth Century. In: *A History of Pastoral Care*. Ed. by G.R. Evans. London: Cassell.

Calvin, J. (1989) *Institutes of the Christian Religion*, trans. by Henry Beveridge, single volume edn. Grand Rapids: Eerdmans.

Cacioppo JT, Hughes ME, Waite LJ, Hawkley LC, Thisted RA (2006). 'Loneliness as a specific risk factor for depressive symptoms: crosssectional and longitudinal analyses'. *Psychology and Aging*, 21(1), p.140-51.

Carmichael, E.D.H. (2004) *Friendship: Interpreting Christian Love*. London: T&T Clark.

Chester, T. (2008) You Can Change: God's Transforming Power for our Sinful Behaviour and Negative Emotions. Nottingham: IVP.

Collins, G.R. (1988) *Christian Counsling: A Comprehensive Guide*, revised edn. Nashville: W Publishing.

Cornick, D. (2000) Post-Enlightenment Pastoral Care. In: *A History of Pastoral Care*. Ed. by G.R. Evans. London: Cassell.

Crossley, G. (1992) Counselling: Pastoral Care or Psychotherapy? *Foundations*, 29, p.12-24.

Culbertson, P.L (1999) Caring for God's People: Counselling and Christian Wholeness. Minneapolis: Fortress Press.

Dawn, M.J. (2000) The Call to be a Living Doxology. In: Dawn, M.J. and Peterson, E.H. (eds.) The Unnecessary Pastor: Rediscovering the Call. Grand Rapids: Eerdmans.

Doehring, C. (2006) The Practice of Pastoral Care: A Postmodern Approach. Louisville: Westminster John Knox.

Farley, E. (1996) *Divine Empathy*. Minneapolis: Augsburg Fortress.

Goodliff, P. (1998) Care in a Confused Climate: Pastoral Care and Postmodern Culture. London: Darton, Longman and Todd.

Graham, E. (2006) Pastoral Theology in an Age of Uncertainty, *HTS Teologiese Studies/Theological Studies*, 62(3), p.845-865

Gregory of Nazianzus (Undated) *Oration 2*.

Gregory the Great (Undated) Book of Pastoral Rule. In: *Nicene and Post-Nicene Fathers, Series II, Volume 12*. Ed. by P. Schaff.

Guenther, M. (1993) *Holy Listening: The Art of Spiritual Direction*. London: Darton, Longman and Todd.

Guinness, O. (2015) Fool's Talk: Recovering the Art of Christian Persuasion. Downers Grove: IVP.

Harbaugh, G.L., Brenneis, R.L., and Hutton, R.R. (1998) *Covenants and Care: Boundaries in Life, Faith, and Ministry*. Minneapolis: Fortress Press.

Harrison, G. (2013) *The Big Ego Trip: Finding True Significance in a Culture of Self-Esteem*. Nottingham: IVP.

Helm, B. (2013) Friendship. In: *The Stanford Encyclopedia of Philosophy*, Fall 2013 edn., ed. by Zalta, E.N.

Herbert, G. (1632) *A Priest to the Temple, Or, The Country Parson His Character, and Rule of Holy Life*.

Hiebert, P. (1985) *Anthropological Insights for Missionaries*. Grand Rapids: Baker Books.

Holt-Lunstad, J., Smith, T. B., Baker, M., Harris, T., and Stephenson, D. (2015). 'Loneliness and social isolation as risk factors for mortality: A meta-analytic review'. *Perspectives on Psychological Science*, 10, p.227-237.

Horsfall, T. (2010) *Working from a Place of Rest: Jesus and the Key to Sustaining Ministry*. Abingdon: BRF.

_____ (2012) *Rhythms of Grace: Finding Intimacy with God in a Busy Life*. Abingdon: BRF.

Hurding, R.F. (1992) *The Bible and Counselling*. London: Hodder and Stoughton.

_____ (2003) *Roots and Shoots: A Guide to Counselling and Psychotherapy*, updated edition. London: Hodder and Stoughton.

Inrig, G. (1981) *Quality Friendship: The Risks and Rewards*. Chicago: Moody Press.

Jacobs, M. (1985) *Swift to Hear: Facilitating Skills in Listening and Responding*, New Library of Pastoral Care. London: SPCK.

Johnson, B.C. and Dreitcer, A. (2001) *Beyond the Ordinary: Spirituality for Church Leaders*. Grand Rapids: Eerdmans.

Johnson, E.L. ed. (2010) *Psychology and Christianity: Five Views*, second edn. Downers Grove: IVP Academic.

Keller, T. (2010) Four Models of Counseling in Pastoral Ministry. *Redeemer City to City*.

_____ (2012) *The Freedom of Self-Forgetfulness*. Leyland: 10Publishing.

Kwon, D. (2017) The Limits of Empathy. *The Psychologist*, 30, pp.28-32.

Lane, T.S., and Tripp, P.D. (2006) *How People Change*. Winston-Salem: Punch.

Lewis, C.S. (1940) *The Problem of Pain*. New York: MacMillan.

_____ (1960) *The Four Loves*. London: Geoffrey Bles.

_____ (1961) *A Grief Observed*. London: Faber and Faber.

_____ (1972) *God in the Dock: Essays on Theology and Ethics*, reprint edn. Grand Rapids: Eerdmans.

_____ (2018) *How to Pray: Reflections and Essays*. London: William Collins.

Long, A. (1990) *Listening*. London: Darton, Longman and Todd.

Lyall, D. (2001) *The Integrity of Pastoral Care*. London: SPCK.

Lynch, G. (2002) *Pastoral Care and Counselling*, Ethics in Practice. London: Sage.

Mahlberg, A.F., and Nessan, C.L. (2016) *The Integrity of the Body of Christ: Boundary Keeping as Shared Responsibility*. Eugene: Cascade.

Manning, B. (1985) *The Importance of Being Foolish, How to Think Like Jesus.* New York: Harper Collins.

Marinker, M. (1975) Why make people patients? *Journal of Medical Ethics,* 1, p.81-84.

McGrath, A.E. (1992) *Suffering and God.* Grand Rapids: Zondervan.

McMinn, M.R., Staley, R.C., Webb, K.C., and Seegobin, W. (2010) Just What Is Christian Counseling Anyway? *George Fox University Faculty Publications - Grad School of Clinical Psychology,* Paper 113.

Moon, G.W., and Benner, D.G. (2000) Spiritual Direction and Christian Soul Care. In: Moon, G.W., and Benner, D.G., eds. *Spiritual Direction and the Care of Souls: A Guide to Christian Approaches.* Downers Grove: IVP.

Murray, D. (2017) *Reset: Living a Grace-Paced Life in a Burnout Culture.* Wheaton: Crossway.

Nouwen, H.J.M. (1977) *The Living Reminder: Service and Prayer in Memory of Jesus Christ.* New York: Harper Collins.

_____ (2006) *Spiritual Direction: Wisdom for the Long Walk of Faith.* New York: HarperOne

_____ (2014) *The Wounded Healer: Ministry in Contemporary Society.* London: Darton, Longman and Todd.

Oates, W.E. (1992) The Levels of Pastoral Care. In Chapman, T.W. (ed.) *A Practical Handbook for Ministry from the Writings of Wayne E. Oates.* Louisville: Westminster John Knox.

Oden, T.C. (1984) *Care of Souls in the Classic Tradition.* Augsburg: Fortress Press.

Parrott, L. (2000) *Helping the Struggling Adolescent: A Guide to Thirty-Six Common Problems for Counselors, Pastors, and Youth Workers,* updated and expanded edn. Grand Rapids: Zondervan.

Pascal, B. (1958) *Pascal's Pensées,* trans. by W.F. Trotter. New York: E.P. Dutton & Co.

Pattison, S. (1999) Are professional codes ethical? *Counselling*, 10(5), pp.374-380

_____ (2000) *A Critique of Pastoral Care*. London: SCM

Patton, J. (2005) *Pastoral Care: An Essential Guide*. Nashville: Abingdon.

Peterson, E.H. (1980) *Five Smooth Stones for Pastoral Work*. Grand Rapids: Eerdmans.

_____ (1989) *The Contemplative Pastor: Returning to the Art of Spiritual Direction*. Grand Rapids: Eerdmans.

_____ (1994) *Working the Angles*. Grand Rapids: Eerdmans.

Pierre, J., and Raju, D. (2015) *The Pastor and Counseling: The Basics of Shepherding Members in Need*. Wheaton: Crossway.

Sayers, D.L. (1949) *Creed or Chaos?* New York: Harcourt Brace.

Savage, J. (1996) *Listening and Caring Skills: A Guide for Groups and Leaders*. Nashville: Abingdon.

Shelly, J.A. (2000) *Spiritual Care: A Guide for Caregivers*. Downers Grove: IVP.

Sobrino, J. (2004) *Where is God: Earthquake, Terrorism, Barbarity, and Hope*. Maryknoll: Orbis.

Stackhouse, J.G. (2002) *Humble Apologetics: Defending the Faith Today*. New York: Oxford University Press.

Stairs, J. (2000) *Listening for the Soul: Pastoral Care and Spiritual Direction*. Minneapolis: Fortress Press

Swinton, J. (2000) *Resurrecting the Person: Friendship and the Care of People with Mental Health Difficulties*. Nashville: Abingdon Press.

_____ (2007) *Raging With Compassion: Pastoral Responses to the Problem of Evil*. Grand Rapids: Eerdmans.

Taylor, C. (1991) *The Ethics of Authenticity*. Cambridge: Harvard University Press.

TIME Magazine (2015) Bounce Back: Scientists Now Know Why Some

People Rebound So Well From Setbacks. TIME, June 1 2015, pp.36-42

Tournier, P. (1986) *Guilt and Grace,* trans. by Arthur W. Heathcote, J.J. Henry and P.J. Allcock. Crowborough: Highland Books.

Tripp, P.D. (2002) *Instruments in the Redeemer's Hands: People in Need of Change Helping People in Need of Change.* Phillipsburg: P&R.

Volf, M. (1996) *Exclusion and Embrace: A Theological Exploration of Identity, Otherness, and Reconciliation.* Nashville: Abingdon Press.

Whipp, M. (2013) *SCM Studyguide to Pastoral Theology.* London: SCM.

White, P. (1998) *The Effective Pastor: The Key Things a Minister Must Learn to Be.* Fearn: Mentor.

Willard, D. (1998) *The Divine Conspiracy: Rediscovering Our Hidden Life in God.* San Francisco: HarperSanFrancisco

Winter, R. (2005) The Search for Truth in Psychology and Counseling. *Presbyterion: Covenant Seminary Review,* 31(1), p.18-36

World Health Organisation (1946) Constitution of WHO: Principles.

Worthington, E.L. (2009) *A Just Forgiveness: Responsible Healing without Excusing Injustice.* Downers Grove: IVP.

_____ (2013) *Moving Forward: Six Steps to Forgiving Yourself and Breaking Free from the Past.* Colorado Springs: Waterbrook Press.

ABOUT THE AUTHOR

Dr Paul B. Coulter lives in Lisburn, Northern Ireland, with his wife and their two teenaged children. They are members of a nearby Baptist church.

Paul works as Head of Ministry Operations with Living Leadership, a network of experienced Christian leaders who provide training, support and resources for leaders and their spouses to help them live joyfully in Christ and serve him faithfully. He is also Executive Director of the Centre for Christianity in Society, which seeks to connect Christ with contemporary culture by explaining Christianity truthfully, engaging issues thoughtfully and equipping Christians thoroughly. Additionally, he is chair of New Horizon Ministries, and an adjunct lecturer in two theological colleges.

Paul committed his life to Christ as a child and his faith has grown with him through every stage of his journey since: as a teenager in a school in Lisburn, a student at university in Belfast, a doctor in NHS hospitals and a hospice in Northern Ireland, a cross-cultural pastor with a Chinese Church, director of youth and equipping ministries in a large suburban church, and a lecturer in practical theology in a non-denominational college. He holds degrees in medical genetics, medicine and theology and a PhD in divinity.

Paul's passion in every aspect of ministry is to see Christians and churches living consistently in faithfulness to the Word of God and to learn what it means to say "to live is Christ, to die is gain" (Philippians 1:21). For relaxation and recreation, he enjoys reading popular history and science books, watching movies, playing board games with family and friends, cycling in country lanes and walking the hills with his dog.

You can find out more about Paul, connect with him and access other resources on his personal website: www.paulcoulter.net.

Printed in Great Britain
by Amazon

23344331R00145